Hiking
Colorado Volume II

Caryn and Peter Boddie

FALCON®

HELENA, MONTANA

A **FALCON** GUIDE ®

Falcon® Publishing is continually expanding its list of recreation guidebooks. All books include detailed descriptions, accurate maps, and all the information necessary for enjoyable trips. You can order extra copies of this book and get information and prices for other Falcon® books by writing Falcon, P.O. Box 1718, Helena, MT 59624 or calling toll free 1-800-582-2665. Also, please ask for a free copy of our current catalog. Visit our website at www.FalconOutdoors.com or contact us by e-mail at Falcon@falcon.com

©1999 Falcon® Publishing, Inc., Helena, Montana
Printed in the United States

05 04 03 02 01 00 MG 99 10 9 8 7 6 5 4 3 2 1

Falcon and FalconGuide are registered trademarks of Falcon® Publishing, Inc.

All photos by author unless otherwise noted.

Library of Congress Cataloging-in-Publication Data

Boddie, Caryn.
    [Hiker's guide to Colorado]
    Hiking Colorado: formerly, The hiker's guide to Colorado / by
Caryn and Peter Boddie.
        p. cm.
    ISBN 1-56044-377-4 (pbk.)
    1. Hiking—Colorado—Guidebooks. 2. Colorado—Guidebooks.
I. Boddie, Peter. II. Title.
GV199.42.C6B64 1997
917.88—dc21   97-1392
                                                                  CIP

CAUTION

Outdoor recreational activities are by their very nature potentially hazardous. All participants in such activities must assume the responsibility for their own actions and safety. The information contained in this guidebook cannot replace sound judgment and good decision-making skills, which help reduce risk exposure, nor does the scope of this book allow for disclosure of all the potential hazards and risks involved in such activities.

Learn as much as possible about the outdoor recreational activities in which you participate, prepare for the unexpected, and be cautious. The reward will be a safer and more enjoyable experience.

♻ Text pages printed on recycled paper.

Contents

The Southern Mountains

The Western Plateaus and Canyons

The Eastern Plains and Foothills

Appendices

Dedication

To God,
with gratitude for the infinite variety of wild places that are Colorado.

Hikers explore the Great Sand Dunes.

Acknowledgments

First and foremost we would like to thank Crystal and Robin, our children—who have seen more of Colorado as children than most people see in a lifetime—for contributing to this book, often not by choice. Thanks for being good sports and for leaving your footprints next to ours.

Thank you again to Falcon Publishing, Inc., and best wishes for further success. Thank you to Ryan Starr for helping. Finally, thank you to the folks we've talked to in our travels, while hiking on the trail, or who we've heard from in the mail for information you've shared or words of encouragement you've offered.

On the way to Petroglyph Point.

Overview Map

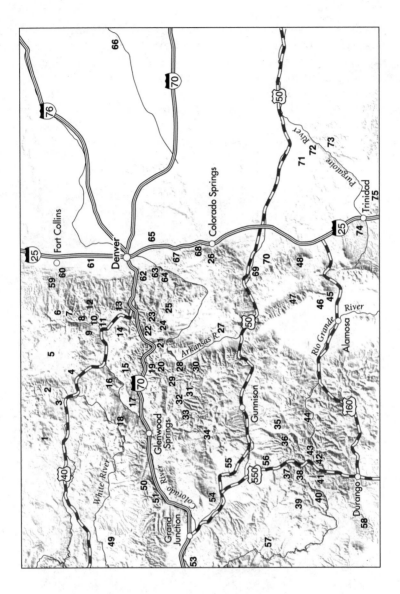

Legend

Interstate	(00)	Campground	▲
US Highway	(00)	Picnic Area	⊼
State or Other Principal Road	(00) (000)	Cabins/Buildings	▪
National Park Route	[000]	Cliffs/Mesa	
Interstate Highway	⟹	Peak	9,782 ft.
Paved Road	⟹	Hill	
Gravel Road	⟹	Elevation	9,782 ft.
Unimproved Road	======⟹		X
Trailhead	○	Gate	•—•
Main Trail(s)/Route(s)	••••••	Mine Site	⚒
Alternate/Secondary Trail(s)/Route(s)	- - - -	Overlook/Point of Interest	◙
Main Cross Country Trail(s)/Route(s)	··········	National Forest/Park Boundary	
Alternate/Secondary cross-country Trail(s)/Route(s)	·········	Map Orientation	N
Parking Area	(P)	Scale	0 0.5 1 Miles
River/Creek	∿		
Spring	⌀		
One-way Road	One Way		

Introduction

HOW TO USE THIS GUIDE

As we did with our first book, we have tried in *Hiking Colorado, Volume II* to introduce our readers to *all* of Colorado—from the plains the settlers crossed on the Santa Fe Trail and the tundra the Ute Indians traversed to the plateaus where wild horses run. We gathered the information for this book between 1995 and 1998 by personally hiking the trails described. A few hikes were traveled for us by friends.

We hiked year 'round. And, that's how you will get the most out of this guide—by using it to explore Colorado all year and in all its variety. Choose a region or terrain you've never seen, select a hike of the length and difficulty you prefer, prepare, and go. That's what's exciting about hiking Colorado—there are so many landscapes, so little time!

You can pick up this book and take a hike when you're vacationing in your favorite region of the state or while on a long weekend getaway. Then put it on the shelf until you want to take another hike or until you come back to Colorado.

Hiking Colorado, Volume II will inform you of a hike's length and difficulty, tell you just how to get there, and give you a few key words about what makes a particular hike interesting. Many of the hikes in this volume are shorter than those in volume one, but you can extend many to longer day hikes or backpacks. Likewise, many of the longer or more difficult hikes can be done as shorter, easier hikes; just hike shorter segments or attain intermediate destinations, then return to your starting points. Read the "Options" section of hike descriptions for this information.

We not only give you the basic information you need but also have described flora and fauna, geology, and history *briefly* within the hike descriptions to give you more for your hiking experience. On longer hikes we include a list of key points that you can use to follow your hike's progress or to check that you are on the right trail, headed in the correct direction.

The elevation profiles show you how steeply you will climb or descend in elevation, so you can know how difficult the hike will be for you or your companions, and judge how long it will take. For instance, if you hate climbing up very steep trails, you may not choose a certain hike. Or if one of your hiking companions has bad knees or ankles, you may not want to hike where it's necessary to descend a hill at a sharp angle for a long time. This feature of the hike descriptions should help you have adventures that are more enjoyable.

We give you clear, accurate directions to the trailheads, and a little information about what you will find once there. We have tried to make the maps clear, accurate, and user friendly. Read the description, then read the map, and go back to the description, if necessary, in order to get the most out of the maps. On longer and more difficult hikes, take along topographic maps and forest maps—and know how to use them. We have found errors in some maps as we have hiked the state, so take several different maps and check them against each other.

The section "Special Considerations" gives you information on any permits, fees, hiking restrictions, safety concerns, or other information you must know *before* you reach the trailhead.

We must all practice Leave No Trace hiking and backpacking so that Colorado will remain beautiful for future generations. We've worked with land agencies in selecting trails for this book, not wanting to publicize those that are overused or to adversely affect delicate areas or wildlife. Still, no trail can sustain careless use. Information herein will help you touch the land lightly while enjoying it immensely.

You will also find information to help you organize trips and make them safe. Our resource section will direct you to hiking and conservation organizations and to the agencies that care for our trails and wild lands so you can help protect them.

We hope that *Hiking Colorado, Volume II* will lead you to and through many rewarding adventures. May it help you discover Colorado for the first time, or may it help you discover *more* of this incredible state.

About the maps: The maps that accompany each of the hikes have been prepared from U.S. Geological Survey (USGS) topographic maps and land agency maps. With each one is a small map of Colorado indicating the general location of the hike in the state as well as a north-south directional indicator and a scale. A general legend for all the maps is on page ix.

Although these maps are up-to-date, take along USGS topographic map(s) on more difficult hikes, or the Trails Illustrated maps, which are based on the USGS maps. National forest maps and some of the topographic atlases, such as those produced by DeLorme, are also helpful, offering an excellent overview of an entire national forest or section of the state. The appropriate maps for each hike are listed in the introductory information prior to each hike description. (See Appendix VII, Finding Maps for more about maps.)

If you are not used to reading maps, particularly topo maps, set out on one of the easier hikes with a national forest map, topo map, the book map, and compass, and learn how to use all of them. Then, when you *really* need a map, you'll know how to use it. (Also, consult the appropriate land management agency before your hike if you must drive to the trailhead on a low-grade road. Also, call to check on snow closures or to check on road conditions after bad weather. You just want to make sure you can get to the trailhead!)

Trail Finder Table

	EASY	MODERATE	DIFFICULT
For a day hike	4 Rabbit Ears Peak	1 Black Mountain	6 Signal Mountain
	8 Tombstone Ridge	2 Three Island Lake	12 Chasm Lake
	9 Bowen Gulch Old-Growth Forest	3 Mad Creek	20 Notch Mountain
		5 Owl Ridge	25 Ben Tyler Gulch
	10 Adams and East Inlet Falls	7 Bridal Veil Falls	32 American Lake
		13 Rogers Pass Lake	33 Buckskin Pass
	11 Colorado River Walk	14 Byers Peak	34 Oh-Be-Joyful Pass
		15 Elliott Peak	37 Sneffels Highline Loop
	19 Cross Creek	16 Rock Creek	
	26 The Crags	17 Picture Lake	39 Lone Cone
	27 Little Cottonwood Creek	18 Wall Lake	42 Highland Mary Lakes
		21 Crystal Lakes	46 Lower Medano Creek and the Great Star Dune
	29 Lyle Lake	22 Porcupine Gulch	
	31 Ashcroft	23 Square Top Lakes	
	38 East Fork Bear Creek	24 Gibson Lake	47 Sand Creek Lakes
		28 Native Lake	51 East Fork Parachute Creek
	49 East Fourmile Draw	30 Graham Gulch	
		35 Powderhorn Lakes	70 Grape Creek
	50 Rifle Arch	36 Alpine Gulch	73 Picket Wire Canyons
	53 McDonald Canyon	40 Calico Trail	
	55 Exclamation Point	41 Engineer Mountain Overlook	
	56 Dallas Creek at Ridgway State Park	43 Continental Divide at Stony Pass	
	58 Petroglyph Point	44 Bristol Head	
	61 Rabbit Mountain	45 Zapata Falls and South Zapata Creek	
	62 The Brother and Three Sisters	48 Greenhorn Mountain	
	65 Castlewood Canyon	52 Hanging Lake	
	66 Beecher Island	54 Adobe Badlands	
	71 Santa Fe Trail	57 Dry Creek Anticline	
	72 Vogel Canyon	59 Kreutzer Trail, Mount McConnel	
	74 Levsa Canyon	60 Horsetooth Rock	
		63 Deer Creek Canyon Park	
		64 Pine Valley Ranch	
		67 Devil's Head	
		69 Horsetail Gulch	
		75 Fishers Peak Mesa	

	EASY	MODERATE	DIFFICULT
For a backpack	10 Adams and East Inlet Falls 19 Cross Creek 29 Lyle Lake	1 Black Mountain 2 Three Island Lake 7 Bridal Veil Falls 13 Rogers Pass Lake 17 Picture Lake 18 Wall Lake 21 Crystal Lakes 23 Square Top Lakes 28 Native Lake 36 Alpine Gulch 40 Calico Trail 45 Zapata Falls and South Zapata Creek 57 Dry Creek Anticline	12 Chasm Lake 25 Ben Tyler Gulch 32 American Lake 33 Buckskin Pass 34 Oh-Be-Joyful Pass 37 Sneffels Highline Loop 42 Highland Mary Lakes 47 Sand Creek Lakes 70 Grape Creek
That are handicap accessible	31 Ashcroft 65 Castlewood Canyon 66 Beecher Island 68 New Santa Fe Trail 72 Vogel Canyon		
For a family	4 Rabbit Ears Peak 8 Tombstone Ridge 9 Bowen Gulch Old-Growth Forest 10 Adams and East Inlet Falls 11 Colorado River Walk 19 Cross Creek 26 The Crags 29 Lyle Lake 31 Ashcroft 38 East Fork Bear Creek 49 East Fourmile Draw 50 Rifle Arch 53 McDonald Canyon 55 Exclamation Point 56 Dallas Creek at Ridgway State Park 58 Petroglyph Point	1 Black Mountain 2 Three Island Lake 3 Mad Creek 5 Owl Ridge 14 Byers Peak 15 Elliott Ridge 16 Rock Creek 23 Square Top Lakes 35 Powderhorn Lakes 36 Alpine Gulch 40 Calico Trail 41 Engineer Mountain Overlook 44 Bristol Head 48 Greenhorn Mountain 52 Hanging Lake 59 Kreutzer Trail, Mount McConnel 60 Horsetooth Rock 63 Deer Creek Canyon Park 64 Pine Valley Ranch	46 Lower Medano Creek and the Great Star Dune

EASY	MODERATE	DIFFICULT
61 Rabbit Mountain 62 The Brother and Three Sisters 65 Castlewood Canyon 66 Beecher Island 68 New Santa Fe Trail 71 Santa Fe Trail 72 Vogel Canyon 74 Levsa Canyon	67 Devil's Head 69 Horsetail Gulch	

	EASY	MODERATE	DIFFICULT
To see a lake	10 Adams and East Inlet Falls 11 Colorado River Walk 29 Lyle Lake 56 Dallas Creek Ridgway State Park 74 Levsa Canyon	2 Three Island Lake 13 Rogers Pass Lake 17 Picture Lake 18 Wall Lake 21 Crystal Lakes 23 Square Top Lakes 24 Gibson Lake 28 Native Lake 35 Powderhorn Lakes 41 Engineer Mountain Overlook 45 Zapata Falls and South Zapata Creek 52 Hanging Lake 75 Fishers Peak Mesa	12 Chasm Lake 32 American Lake 33 Buckskin Pass 42 Highland Mary Lakes 47 Sand Creek Lakes
To see a stream	10 Adams and East Inlet Falls 11 Colorado River Walk 19 Cross Creek 26 The Crags 27 Little Cottonwood Creek 29 Lyle Lake 31 Ashcroft 38 East Fork Bear Creek 56 Dallas Creek at Ridgway State Park 65 Castlewood Canyon 66 Beecher Island	2 Three Island Lake 3 Mad Creek 5 Owl Ridge 7 Bridal Veil Falls 13 Rogers Pass Lake 16 Rock Creek 17 Picture Lake 18 Wall Lake 21 Crystal Lakes 22 Porcupine Gulch 23 Square Top Lakes 24 Gibson Lake 28 Native Lake 30 Graham Gulch 36 Alpine Gulch 40 Calico Trail 41 Engineer Mountain Overlook	6 Signal Mountain 12 Chasm Lake 25 Ben Tyler Gulch 32 American Lake 33 Buckskin Pass 34 Oh-Be-Joyful Pass 37 Sneffels Highline Loop 46 Lower Medano Creek and the Great Star Dune 47 Sand Creek Lakes 51 East Fork Parachute Creek 70 Grape Creek 73 Picket Wire Canyon

	EASY	MODERATE	DIFFICULT
		45 Zapata Falls and South Zapata Creek	
		52 Hanging Lake	
		59 Kreutzer Trail, Mount McConnel	
		60 Horsetooth Rock	
		69 Horsetail Gulch	
		75 Fishers Peak Mesa	
To see a waterfall	10 Adams and East Inlet Falls	2 Three Island Lake	12 Chasm Lake
	19 Cross Creek	7 Bridal Veil Falls	33 Buckskin Pass
	38 East Fork Bear Creek	13 Rogers Pass Lake	34 Oh-Be-Joyful Pass
		24 Gibson Lake	37 Sneffels Highline Loop
		36 Alpine Gulch	42 Highland Mary Lakes
		45 Zapata Falls and South Zapata Creek	51 East Fork Parachute Creek
		52 Hanging Lake	
		69 Horsetail Gulch	
To see a canyon	27 Little Cottonwood Creek	3 Mad Creek	51 East Fork Parachute Creek
	49 East Fourmile Draw	16 Rock Creek	70 Grape Creek
	53 McDonald Canyon	44 Bristol Head	73 Picket Wire Canyon
	55 Exclamation Point	52 Hanging Lake	
	58 Petroglyph Point	54 Adobe Badlands	
	65 Castlewood Canyon	57 Dry Creek Anticline	
	66 Beecher Island	59 Kreutzer Trail, Mount McConnel	
	72 Vogel Canyon	63 Deer Creek Canyon Park	
		64 Pine Valley Ranch	
		69 Horsetail Gulch	
		75 Fishers Peak Mesa	
To see wildflowers	4 Rabbit Ears Peak	2 Three Island Lake	12 Chasm Lake
	8 Tombstone Ridge	3 Mad Creek	20 Notch Mountain
	10 Adams and East Inlet Falls	7 Bridal Veil Falls	25 Ben Tyler Gulch
	11 Colorado River Walk	13 Rogers Pass Lake	32 American Lake
	19 Cross Creek	14 Byers Peak	33 Buckskin Pass
	29 Lyle Lake	15 Elliott Ridge	34 Oh-Be-Joyful Pass
	31 Ashcroft	17 Picture Lake	37 Sneffels Highline Loop
		18 Wall Lake	39 Lone Cone
		21 Crystal Lakes	

EASY	MODERATE	DIFFICULT
38 East Fork Bear Creek 49 East Fourmile Draw 61 Rabbit Mountain 62 The Brother and Three Sisters 65 Castlewood Canyon 66 Beecher Island 74 Levsa Canyon	22 Porcupine Gulch 23 Square Top Lakes 24 Gibson Lake 28 Native Lake 30 Graham Gulch 35 Powderhorn Lakes 36 Alpine Gulch 40 Calico Trail 41 Engineer Mountain Overlook 43 Continental Divide at Stony Pass 45 Zapata Falls and South Zapata Creek 48 Greenhorn Mountain 60 Horsetooth Rock 63 Deer Creek Canyon Park 64 Pine Valley Ranch 69 Horsetail Gulch 75 Fishers Peak Mesa	47 Sand Creek Lakes 51 East Fork Parachute Creek 73 Picket Wire Canyon
For alpine tundra	8 Tombstone Ridge 29 Lyle Lake	13 Rogers Pass Lake 14 Byers Peak 15 Elliott Ridge 21 Crystal Lakes 22 Porcupine Gulch 23 Square Top Lakes 24 Gibson Lake 28 Native Lake 30 Graham Gulch 35 Powderhorn Lakes 40 Calico Trail 41 Engineer Mountain Overlook 43 Continental Divide at Stony Pass 44 Bristol Head 45 Zapata Falls and South Zapata Creek 48 Greenhorn Mountain	6 Signal Mountain 12 Chasm Lake 20 Notch Mountain 25 Ben Tyler Gulch 33 Buckskin Pass 34 Oh-Be-Joyful Pass 37 Sneffels Highline Loop 39 Lone Cone 42 Highland Mary Lakes 47 Sand Creek Lakes

	EASY	MODERATE	DIFFICULT
To see aspens	10 Adams and East Inlet Falls 19 Cross Creek 26 The Crags 27 Little Cottonwood Creek 31 Ashcroft 38 East Fork Bear Creek 62 The Brother and Three Sisters	2 Three Island Lake 3 Mad Creek 7 Bridal Veil Falls 17 Picture Lake 36 Alpine Gulch 40 Calico Trail 75 Fishers Peak Mesa	25 Ben Tyler Gulch 32 American Lake 33 Buckskin Pass 37 Sneffels Highline Loop 42 Highland Mary Lakes 51 East Fork Parachute Creek
To view wildlife	8 Tombstone Ridge 9 Bowen Gulch Old-Growth Forest 10 Adams and East Inlet Falls 11 Colorado River Walk 27 Little Cottonwood Creek 29 Lyle Lake 49 East Fourmile Draw 50 Rifle Arch 53 McDonald Canyon 55 Exclamation Point 56 Dallas Creek at Ridgway State Park 58 Petroglyph Point 61 Rabbit Mountain 62 The Brother and Three Sisters 68 New Santa Fe Trail 72 Vogel Canyon 74 Levsa Canyon	2 Three Island Lake 3 Mad Creek 5 Owl Ridge 7 Bridal Veil Falls 14 Byers Peak 15 Elliott Ridge 16 Rock Creek 17 Picture Lake 18 Wall Lake 28 Native Lake 35 Powderhorn Lakes 40 Calico Trail 44 Bristol Head 57 Dry Creek Anticline 59 Kreutzer Trail, Mount McConnel 63 Deer Creek Canyon Park 64 Pine Valley Ranch 69 Horsetail Gulch 75 Fishers Peak Mesa	6 Signal Mountain 12 Chasm Lake 25 Ben Tyler Gulch 37 Sneffels Highline Loop 42 Highland Mary Lakes 47 Sand Creek Lakes 51 East Fork Parachute Creek 73 Picket Wire Canyon
For scenic views	4 Rabbit Ears Peak 8 Tombstone Ridge 10 Adams and East Inlet Falls 19 Cross Creek 26 The Crags 38 East Fork Bear Creek 49 East Fourmile Draw 50 Rifle Arch	1 Black Mountain 2 Three Island Lake 3 Mad Creek 7 Bridal Veil Falls 13 Rogers Pass Lake 14 Byers Peak 15 Elliott Ridge 17 Picture Lake 18 Wall Lake 21 Crystal Lakes	6 Signal Mountain 12 Chasm Lake 20 Notch Mountain 25 Ben Tyler Gulch 32 American Lake 33 Buckskin Pass 34 Oh-Be-Joyful Pass 37 Sneffels Highline Loop 39 Lone Cone

EASY	MODERATE	DIFFICULT
55 Exclamation Point	23 Square Top Lakes	42 Highland Mary Lakes
58 Petroglyph Point	24 Gibson Lake	46 Lower Medano Creek
61 Rabbit Mountain	28 Native Lake	and the Great Star
62 The Brother and	30 Graham Gulch	Dune
Three Sisters	35 Powderhorn Lakes	47 Sand Creek Lakes
65 Castlewood	36 Alpine Gulch	51 East Fork Parachute
Canyon	40 Calico Trail	Creek
66 Beecher Island	41 Engineer Mountain	
68 New Santa Fe Trail	Overlook	
71 Santa Fe Trail	43 Continental Divide	
72 Vogel Canyon	at Stony Pass	
	44 Bristol Head	
	45 Zapata Falls and	
	South Zapata	
	Creek	
	48 Greenhorn	
	Mountain	
	52 Hanging Lake	
	54 Adobe Badlands	
	57 Dry Creek	
	Anticline	
	59 Kreutzer Trail,	
	Mount McConnel	
	60 Horsetooth Rock	
	64 Pine Valley Ranch	
	67 Devil's Head	
	75 Fishers Peak	
	Mesa	
To view interesting geology	4 Rabbit Ears Peak	1 Black Mountain	12 Chasm Lake
	8 Tombstone Ridge	2 Three Island Lake	20 Notch Mountain
	10 Adams and East	3 Mad Creek	32 American Lake
	Inlet Falls	13 Rogers Pass Lake	33 Buckskin Pass
	19 Cross Creek	15 Elliott Ridge	34 Oh-Be-Joyful Pass
	29 Lyle Lake	17 Picture Lake	37 Sneffels Highline
	49 East Fourmile	18 Wall Lake	Loop
	Draw	23 Square Top Lakes	46 Lower Medano Creek
	50 Rifle Arch	28 Native Lake	and the Great Star
	53 McDonald Canyon	44 Bristol Head	Dune
	55 Exclamation Point	45 Zapata Falls and	47 Sand Creek Lakes
	58 Petroglyph Point	South Zapata	51 East Fork Parachute
	61 Rabbit Mountain	Creek	Creek
	72 Vogel Canyon	52 Hanging Lake	70 Grape Creek
		54 Adobe Badlands	73 Picket Wire Canyon
		57 Dry Creek	
		Anticline	

EASY	MODERATE	DIFFICULT
	59 Kreutzer Trail, Mount McConnel 60 Horsetooth Rock 67 Devil's Head 75 Fishers Peak Mesa	
To learn about history and archaeology	4 Rabbit Ears Peak 8 Tombstone Ridge 31 Ashcroft 38 East Fork Bear Creek 49 East Fourmile Draw 53 McDonald Canyon 56 Dallas Creek at Ridgway State Park 58 Petroglyph Point 61 Rabbit Mountain 65 Castlewood Canyon 66 Beecher Island 68 New Santa Fe Trail 71 Santa Fe Trail 72 Vogel Canyon	3 Mad Creek 7 Bridal Veil Falls 13 Rogers Pass Lake 21 Crystal Lakes 35 Powderhorn Lakes 40 Calico Trail 59 Kreutzer Trail, Mount McConnel 60 Horsetooth Rock 67 Devil's Head	12 Chasm Lake 20 Notch Mountain 25 Ben Tyler Gulch 34 Oh-Be-Joyful Pass 37 Sneffels Highline Loop 42 Highland Mary Lakes 73 Picket Wire Canyon
If you want a long hike (over 10 miles)			6 Signal Mountain 20 Notch Mountain 25 Ben Tyler Gulch 34 Oh-Be-Joyful Pass 37 Sneffels Highline Loop 46 Lower Medano Creek and the Great Star Dune 47 Sand Creek Lakes 73 Picket Wire Canyon

BEING PREPARED: BACKCOUNTRY SAFETY AND HAZARDS

Safety: The history books—and today's media—detail many a tragic story of men, women, and children who ventured into the wilds of Colorado unprepared and overconfident only to meet with a sad end or to be rescued by others.

Be safe:

- Travel with the proper equipment for any climate, elevation, and weather you might encounter.

- Dress in layers that you can put on and take off with changes in the weather.

- Carry a first-aid kit, topo map, compass, waterproof matches, a space blanket, and high-energy snacks.

- Take plenty of water with you.

Be smart:

- Don't underestimate the power of nature. Hike early in the day to summits or ridges and watch for signs of an electrical storm's approach: clouds and electricity in the air (hair on the arms or head may stand on end). Don't get caught in a gully after a rainstorm when there might be a flash flood. "Hug a tree" if you get lost or in case of a whiteout from an unexpected snowstorm, and make yourself visible in some way, maybe with a scarf of hunter orange or a bright piece of a candy wrapper hung on a branch.

- Know how to react if you should encounter wildlife on the trail. Keep children from running ahead down the trail.

- Know how to react in emergency situations. Take a first-aid course.

- Listen to your body. Learn the symptoms of problems such as hypothermia or altitude sickness and guard against fatigue.

Be cautious:

- In general, don't take unnecessary risks by glissading down steep snowfields with cliffs or boulders below, climbing rock faces without ropes, exploring abandoned mines, jumping ravines or canyons, or wading across swift mountain streams.

- Always file a "flight" plan with someone before you leave, stating where you're going and when you'll return.

- Do not drink the water unless you are positive it is safe to do so. Boil it or treat it chemically. Become familiar with *Giardia lamblia* and the illness it causes, giardiasis (see "Water: To Drink or Not to Drink?").

- Don't hike alone.

- When hiking in a group, gear your pace to the slowest member and don't push on to a destination if a group member is really not up to it. Avoid splitting up.

- Follow your topo map from the beginning of the hike.

- If you become lost, don't panic. Sit down and relax. Consult your map and compass. Thousands of hikers have spent unplanned nights in the wilderness. If you left a flight plan, someone will be searching for you. Find shelter—but make yourself visible with something bright—and stay put. Do not wander. If you have a whistle, blow it every now and again: three short blasts mean distress. During the day reflect the sun with a small mirror to signal for help. At night use a flashlight: three quick flashes signal distress.

Hypothermia and other hazards: Be aware of the dangers of hypothermia, a below normal body temperature. Lowering of internal temperature leads to mental and physical collapse. Hypothermia is caused by exposure to cold and is aggravated by wetness, wind, and exhaustion. It is the number one killer of outdoor recreationists.

The first stage is exposure and exhaustion. The moment you start to lose heat faster than your body produces it, you undergo exposure. When this occurs, your body makes involuntary adjustments to preserve normal temperature in the vital organs. Exercising to stay warm only makes matters worse as both responses drain your energy reserves. The only way to stop the drain is to reduce the degree of exposure.

The second stage is hypothermia. If exposure continues until your energy reserves are exhausted, cold reaches the brain, depriving you of judgment and reasoning power. You will not be aware that this is happening, and you will lose control of your hands. This is hypothermia. Your internal temperature slides downward, and without treatment this slide leads to stupor, collapse, and death.

To defend against hypothermia, stay dry. When clothes get wet, they lose about 90 percent of their insulating value. Choose raingear that covers the head, neck, body, and legs, and provides good protection against wind-driven rain. Also, understand cold. Most hypothermia cases develop in air temperature between 30 and 50 degrees F. If your party is exposed to wind, cold, and wet, think hypothermia.

Watch yourself and others for these symptoms: uncontrollable fits of shivering; vague, slow, slurred speech; memory lapses; incoherence; immobile, fumbling hands; frequent stumbling; lurching gait; drowsiness (to sleep is to die); apparent exhaustion; and inability to get up after a rest.

When a member of your party has hypothermia, he/she may deny any problem. Believe the symptoms, not the victim—even mild symptoms demand treatment.

Get the victim out of the wind and rain, and strip off all wet clothes. If the victim is only mildly impaired, give warm drinks. Get the person into warm clothes and a warm sleeping bag. Well-wrapped, warm (not hot) rocks or canteens will help. If the victim is badly impaired, attempt to keep him/her awake. Put the victim in a sleeping bag with another person—both stripped. If you have a double bag, put the victim between two warm people. Build a fire to warm the camp.—*Courtesy of USDA Forest Service*

Water: To drink or not to drink? There are few backpacking pleasures that can top a cool drink from a high country lake or stream. Whether on a day hike or hiking miles into the backcountry, the refreshing sip along the trail is a tradition. Unfortunately, that cool sip of water from a mountain stream may be hazardous to your health.

The most common problem is a waterborne parasite called *Giardia lamblia*, an invisible protozoan that when ingested can have results far from inconsequential. The illness (called giardiasis, "beaver fever," or "backpacker's diarrhea") is caused by the ingestion of the dormant cyst form of the protozoan. These cysts can survive in cold (40 degrees F) streams for up to three months and can be spread by the droppings of animals and people.

The cysts are activated in the small intestine of the host, changing into the reproductive trophozoite stage, which attaches to the wall of the intestine. Symptoms may appear from within several days to three weeks after ingestion of the cysts and are characterized by severe diarrhea, weight loss, "rotten egg" belches, fatigue, and cramps. Apparently some people are "carriers" of giardiasis and may have only very mild symptoms of the disease.

If you suspect you have the disease, see a doctor immediately. Giardiasis must be professionally treated. Quinacrine and metronidazole (Flagyl) are the medicines most often used in treatment. Both have unpleasant side effects.

The only thing worse than coming down with giardiasis after a trip into the backcountry is coming down with it during a trip to the backcountry. There is little you can do except to try to get to a physician. You probably won't feel like eating anything, but you should avoid dairy products, which will only worsen the symptoms. It is important to drink plenty of fluids to lessen the dehydrating effects of the illness. Also, stomach-coating medicines such as Pepto-Bismol and Milk of Magnesia may calm (but not cure) the intestinal cramps and allow you to hike out to civilization.

How can you prevent the spread of this nasty protozoan? By practicing good sanitary habits in the wilderness. Studies done in Colorado indicate that backpackers may be the most common cause of the spread of *Giardia* because of improper human waste disposal. Bury feces at least 200 feet away from any waterway and cover with 6 inches of organic soil to aid in decomposition. If you travel with dogs or horses, keep them out of streams and lakes as much as possible.

The difficulty of controlling the organism stems partly from its extremely small size and its resistance to chemical treatments, and partly from the cold mountain waters. Because of the cold water temperatures, chlorine, halazone, and iodine treatments may be required in greater concentration or for longer treatment times than is either safe or convenient. Any chemical treatment kit should include thorough instructions for use in varying temperatures and water chemistry, and state its effectiveness against *Giardia*.

Even the time-honored method of boiling water is not always 100 percent effective. This is due to Colorado's high elevations. As you go up in elevation, the decreasing air pressure causes water to boil at a lower temperature, and the one-minute boiling time that is effective against *Giardia* and other organisms at sea level might barely phase the critters at your timberline campsite. To be safe, boil water for a minimum of five minutes anywhere in Colorado and increase that time for very high elevations or whenever the water is cloudy or muddy. Extreme conditions may require boiling for up to 30 minutes.

Fortunately, there is an easier solution. Mechanical filters are available that will remove *Giardia* and other microscopic organisms. There is even a drinking water bottle with a filter that you can fill directly from a stream and carry in your pack. A caution is in order, however: No filter device is effective unless properly used and maintained. Be sure to follow instructions.

Before purchasing any filter for backcountry use, be sure that it has a 5-micron or smaller pore size (smaller than a *Giardia* cyst), or that it specifically states that it's effective against *Giardia*. Before you buy the filter, make sure that you understand how to take care of it. Proper treatment of water in the backcountry will keep you from being infected with *Giardia*, and proper sanitary practices in the backcountry will help keep others from being infected.

Altitude or mountain sickness: It takes two to three days to acclimate to Colorado's high elevations, particularly if you are coming from sea level. You may experience what is called altitude or mountain sickness while hiking if you do not allow time for acclimation. This condition is caused by a lack of oxygen at high elevation, resulting in a general "sick-all-over" feeling. If you have the symptoms of altitude sickness—nausea, dizziness, headache, and loss of appetite—stop and rest, go slower, and drink plenty of water (making sure you are also getting plenty of sodium either in food or in tablets). Eat high-energy foods. If these treatments don't help, go to a lower elevation where there is more oxygen.

SEASONS AND WEATHER

If you've listened to some old-timers—and a few recently transplanted TV news anchors—you may have heard the oft-repeated phrase, "In Colorado, if you don't like the weather, just wait five minutes." If you have sunbathed in mid-January or been caught in a June snowstorm, you can certainly attest to the variability of Colorado weather. However, because you will hear this truism nearly everywhere you go in the United States, its reliability as an all-defining characterization of Colorado weather—or weather anywhere else, for that matter—is suspect. Instead we offer this very limited primer on Colorado weather, based on a knowledge of weather records, and our own experience, with an emphasis on hiking safely. But nothing is a substitute for obtaining a good local forecast before you go hiking, or for being sensitive to weather changes and using common sense when out on the trail.

Colorado's weather is about the interplay between climate and topography. Two factors are dominant in this climatic-topographic relationship: elevation and the orientation to mountain barriers. Elevation of the land surface in Colorado varies by more than 2 miles—from about 3,500 feet on the state's eastern boundary to more than 14,000 feet at the summits of several dozen mountain peaks. The effects on temperature of this altitudinal range are similar to those associated with traveling a distance from southern Colorado north to the Arctic Circle. Temperature decreases with increasing elevation.

The relationship between precipitation and elevation is just the opposite: Precipitation increases with elevation. The orientation of the mountains affects this pattern by creating a rain shadow on the leeward side. Because storm systems move predominantly from west to east across Colorado, the western slopes of the mountains generally receive greater precipitation than the eastern sides—a pattern that holds true for the length of the Continental Divide. And south-facing slopes are drier than those facing north, simply because they receive more exposure to the sun.

General weather regions in Colorado: In addition to the changes in precipitation and temperature with elevation, the state can be divided into a few large-scale geographic regions. First, there are often differences in weather patterns east and west of the Continental Divide—these general regions are referred to as the East Slope and West Slope. The eastern plains often have very different weather from any of the mountain areas, as do some of the large western valleys. Within the mountains there are differences north to south, west to east, and seasonally. Because of their proximity to moisture from the southwest, the San Juan Mountains often have weather conditions significantly different from other ranges.

Winter weather: Many trails at lower elevations can be hiked year-round, including during the middle of winter, because of milder temperatures and lack of snowpack. In general, there is a more consistent snowpack west of the Continental Divide, but trails below 7,000 feet will have little or no snow (except for short periods immediately after storms) throughout most winters. The one exception is the Yampa Valley in northwestern Colorado, which usually has a winter snowpack, even at the lowest elevations. Snow-free conditions can range as high as 9,000 feet east of the Continental Divide, and in mild winters or on south-facing slopes. This accessibility, when combined with some of those classic sunny Colorado days, can provide for some surprisingly enjoyable winter hikes. It is not unusual to have temperatures in the 50s or 60s F at lower elevations for a few days in midwinter.

In addition to the usual advice of "be prepared" and "dress in layers," we have a couple notes of caution for winter hiking. With the shorter days and dry climate, even the warmest of winter days quickly turns cold immediately after the sun goes down. This is especially true when skies are clear. Because warm air holds more moisture, some of the largest winter storms are preceded by a warming trend.

Spring weather: On the first really warm spring day, many people's thoughts turn not to love, but to hiking. Springtime can be one of the most enjoyable times to hike, particularly at lower elevations—the one time when some of these areas are truly green. However, remember that when it comes to weather, spring is the most volatile time of year. This may be the one period of the year when the cliché "just wait five minutes" actually rings true. What makes spring weather so changeable is the clash between lingering winter and oncoming summer weather patterns, and the presence of abundant moisture from either the Pacific Ocean or the Gulf of Mexico. In many areas of the mountains, the snowpack is still building from spring storms through March, April, and often into May. East of the Continental Divide, including out on the plains, the greatest snowfall typically occurs in the spring, often in quick-moving storms that can pile up deep snow in a short time. Conditions can change from sunny and warm to wind-driven wet snow in a matter of hours when a cold front moves through. The combination of wind and wet snow, followed by plunging temperatures, can bring on hypothermia as quickly as in any winter conditions. So, when the weather report predicts a front or snow, take it seriously when planning a hike, even if you have just been out basking in the sun.

On the bright side, spring brings on longer days, warmer temperatures, and melting snowpack, all of which encourage hiking and progressively open up trails at the higher elevations. In a typical year the snowpack disappears below 8,000 feet in April, below 9,000 feet in May, below 10,000 feet by early June, and below 11,000 feet by mid to late June. By July 4, most trails in the high country are passable, although there may be stretches of snow in the trees. Above timberline, many of the higher basins still have snowpack well into July, and some snowfields remain all year. These snow conditions can vary by as much as a month either way from year to year, and also vary from north to south through the state, between north- and south-facing slopes, and between various regions and mountain ranges.

Summer weather: Summer is the time when the high country opens up and is in full bloom, and when we head for the hills to avoid the heat at lower elevations. High temperatures can vary from the 90's and even 100's on the eastern plains and western valleys, to only the 60's and 70's in the higher mountains. Because cool air is heavier and sinks, nighttime cooling can result in frost in selected high mountain valleys at any time, even in midsummer. This principle of air density and temperature—in this case the tendency for warm air to rise and become unstable—also causes the most frequent weather condition associated with summer: thunderstorms.

Summer thunderstorms are common in all parts of Colorado, although they are generally more frequent in the higher mountains and for certain periods of summer in various regions. A few patterns seem to repeat to varying degrees almost every summer. In general, there are two periods during which the most severe thunderstorms are likely to occur (including some that produce tornadoes on the eastern plains). One period occurs in late May and/or early June; another period arrives during the summer "monsoon" season in late July or early August, lasting for about one to three weeks. Plan hiking, camping, and backpacking trips, particularly during the monsoon season, with the expectation of wet weather and thunderstorms. These two periods are often separated by hot, dry weather in June or July, which gradually changes to a pattern of clear mornings with regular afternoon or evening thunderstorms.

However, you never know if the pattern will hold, so it is prudent to always obtain a local weather forecast before hiking, and to be familiar with some of the indicators of thunderstorms. One of these is to watch how the clouds build early in the day. One general rule we follow when in the mountains is to take note of the clouds at about ten o'clock in the morning. If there are no clouds or the clouds are still scattered, there is a good chance that no thunderstorms will occur, or that you at least have a few hours of hiking time before getting down from a high point or exposed area. However, if larger, white cumulus clouds are already forming, there is a very good chance of afternoon thunderstorms, probably within a few hours, and you may need to alter your route or shorten your hike accordingly. And if, as often occurs during the monsoon season, it has already rained once or more during the night or early morning, and dark clouds are forming again by midmorning, you are likely in for repeated, and sometimes severe, thunderstorms throughout the day.

The most obvious danger associated with thunderstorms is lightning, and the best way to avoid lightning is to take heed of the thunderstorm indicators and avoid exposed areas. If you find yourself in an exposed area when a storm approaches, it is best to make your way down from any high point to a lower elevation (but away from water) into a group of trees. Avoid standing beneath very tall trees in a group, or solitary trees— these can attract lightning. If you hear buzzing or your hair is standing on end, a lightning strike is imminent and you must act immediately. If you are caught in an exposed area and can't reach shelter, place any metal objects such as framepacks away from you and make yourself as low as possible by crouching with only your feet touching the ground. Don't lie down, however, as you want to minimize the surface area of your body that is in contact with the ground.

Two other hazards associated with thunderstorms are hail and flash floods. Hail is most common in the high mountains, although it is most severe on the eastern plains. Hail can make footing hazardous and drastically lower the air temperature, subjecting you to hypothermia. Flash flooding is most likely in steep canyons in the foothills and western plateaus, and can result from a thunderstorm that may be out of sight or has occurred earlier at a point miles upstream. So be careful when hiking narrow canyon sections if there is thunderstorm activity. And never camp in the bottom of any narrow canyon, wash, or gully.

Fall weather: Fall can be one of the most delightful seasons to hike because of the changing colors, the usually dry weather, and mild temperatures. Colorado's autumn finery is more subtle than what you'll find on the East Coast, but, the crimsons, browns, tans, and golds are there in the hay meadows, the forest understories, and the tundra. Of course, the clear days seem to magnify the blue of the sky, and you can easily find the white bark and yellow leaves of aspen trees set against a backdrop of high peaks dusted

The Sleeping Sexton to the south of Buckskin Pass. B. H. BRYANT PHOTO. COURTESY USGS.

with early snow. Usually aspen color in the mountains is at its peak about the third week of September and can disappear quickly with a fall wind or snowstorm. The color change progresses to the lower elevations through late October for the cottonwoods on the plains and western valleys. The timing can change by a week or two from year to year.

In terms of weather patterns, there are often hot or warm clear days through September and sometimes into October. Serious snowstorms can arrive at any time beginning in September, but the snow usually melts within days. Many high-elevation hikes can still be made throughout September and into October, but sometime between mid-October and mid-November the first snows that remain for winter can arrive in the high country. You can hike the lower elevations through the winter.

BACKCOUNTRY ESSENTIALS

Nothing ruins a hiking or backpacking trip faster than improper clothing and equipment. What follows are some time-tested ideas on proper clothing and equipment for backcountry travel.

The most important thing to keep in mind is to dress in layers. At least three layers of clothing will allow you to adapt to weather conditions as they change. The first layer, next to your skin, should provide some ventilation; the next—of wool or down—should insulate; the third should be wind- and waterproof. How much money you spend on dressing for the outdoors is really up to you. You can buy the most expensive gear from your local sports store, or make do with military surplus. Just make sure the clothes you take with you will keep you comfortable, warm, and dry in any kind of weather.

Another essential item of clothing is a wool hat, if you'll be hiking in the high country. It is well known that a large percentage of body heat is lost during cold weather when a hat isn't worn, so take one with you. It's good protection against hypothermia. (Mittens or gloves are a good idea, too.)

Probably your most important items of equipment are your boots; pick them carefully. Be prepared to spend a few extra dollars; the adage that you get what you pay for definitely applies. Spending extra time picking out your boots will pay off in the long run. Shop in a reputable store and take the time to ask the salesperson some questions. Make sure your boots won't be causing pressure points on your feet. Look for quality boots made in one piece, with only one side or back seam and with a firm heel counter, box toe, and arch for good support and protection. And make sure you'll have the proper ankle support for the type of hiking you'll be doing. Finally, consider whether the boots are too heavy or too light for the type of hiking you plan to be doing, and wear them around a bit. Many lightweight boots have evolved from running shoes. They are moderately priced and feature new materials that keep feet dry but still let them breathe. Make sure the fit is right. After you've chosen your boots, take good care of them. Ask your salesperson how to do this.

What else do you need? If you're day hiking, you don't need too much: a day pack, a water bottle and water, sunglasses, sunscreen, a map and a compass, and your emergency gear (see "Being Prepared and Backcountry Safety and Hazards"). If you are backpacking, you'll need a good sleeping bag. Again, take care to select the bag that best fits your needs. Most backpackers prefer a bag that will take them through three seasons—all but winter—with high loft and a shell of ripstop nylon, which is durable and also breathes well. Check the stitching on the sleeping bag you plan to buy; stitches should be even and there should not be fewer than 10 of them to an inch.

Next, you'll need a lightweight tent. There are so many new shapes and sizes of tents on the market these days that it shouldn't be hard for you to find one to suit your needs. Just decide whether you'll be using it in humid or arid environments. If it's humid, you'll need room to store gear when it rains; if it's arid, you'll need less room. In any case, you'll always want good ventilation, mosquito netting, and a tent that will withstand occasional downpours and heavy winds.

Backpackers will want to take the time to find a framepack that fits well and suits their anticipated needs. There are many types on the market today with internal or external frames and a variety of pockets, straps, and other features. Get a good salesperson to help you find the perfect pack for you. Then, wear it around for a while with some weight in it, and make sure it's what you need.

One of the best ways to find the equipment that you like is to rent it for an outing or two. You may save quite a bit of money by not buying before you really know what you want. Beyond the clothing and equipment listed above, what you take on your hiking and backpacking outings is up to you.

Trail to The Crags.

Just keep in mind your own comfort and safety in the wilderness and consult the checklist in Appendix VI before you go to make sure you have everything you need and want to take.

LEAVE NO TRACE

More people than ever are hiking, backpacking, mountain biking, and riding horses on trails in Colorado. Colorado's backcountry has the capacity to handle the increase in use, but only if users abandon outdated ethics of past generations of hikers and horsemen who left fire rings, dug trenches around tents, and set up camp near lakes and streams. We must follow a new code based on one phrase: Leave No Trace. The basic guidelines for Leave No Trace travel in *all backcountry* are:

- Travel in small groups.
- Stay on trails or roads. Cutting switchbacks and walking alongside trails causes erosion. Walk with care on the fragile tundra and desert, in particular. They take a long time to recover from scars and trampling of vegetation.
- Leave "souvenirs" where you find them, whether they are wildflowers or Indian artifacts. Other visitors will want to see them.
- Carry out all garbage.
- Watch wildlife from a distance.
- If hiking with a dog, keep it under control at all times.
- Make no loud noises that disturb wildlife and other visitors.

Further rules for traveling in *wilderness* include:
- Limit group size to 10 people.
- Keep dogs on leashes at all times.
- Camp at least 200 feet from all lakes, streams, and trails or in designated sites.
- Bicycles or motorized vehicles are not allowed.
- Build campfires at least 100 feet away from all lakes, streams, and trails.
- Read bulletin boards at trailheads thoroughly. Regulations can vary from area to area.

While camping: Choose a site well away from trails and lakes (at least 200 feet). This practice will protect the water quality of highcountry lakes and streams, and give you and others seclusion, increasing everyone's enjoyment of the area.

Try to camp below timberline. Alpine areas are delicate and require special care. Often, it's only a short hike to a good campsite below timberline. Also, do not build any structures at your campsite.

If possible use a gas stove for cooking. If you do build a fire, keep it small. Try to use existing fire rings. Or dig out native vegetation and topsoil and set it aside, then make your fire. Don't use rocks. When breaking camp, douse the fire thoroughly, scattering or burying the cold ashes. Replace the native soil and vegetation.

Be careful with all waste. Bury human waste at least 6 inches deep, 200 feet from water. Pack out all trash.

Wastewater from boiling foods should be poured around the perimeter of the fire. This keeps the fire from spreading and protects the natural vegetation as well. Wash dishes and clothing well away from streams and lakes, and carefully discard dishwater, perhaps in a sump hole to be covered with soil later. If you use soap, carry water at least 200 feet from a water source and wash there. Strictly follow the pack-in, pack-out rule, and leave your campsites and the backcountry as you found them. You will be doing your part to protect wilderness for those who follow if you are conscientious in using these techniques.

Trail etiquette: Hikers, mountain bikers, and horsemen share many trails. All users must make an effort to get along with one another. Remember these rules:

- Hikers and mountain bikers should yield the right-of-way on trails to horses and their riders. Stop, stand quietly downhill of the animals, and be still.

- Mountain bikers are required to yield the right-of-way to hikers.

- A person traveling uphill has the right of way over a person going downhill. (This is originally a four-wheeling rule. Remember it on your way to trailheads.)

- Be courteous and friendly when you meet fellow travelers, and offer them help if they need it

NATURAL HISTORY

From the eastern plains to the mountain ranges of central Colorado and on to the plateau and canyon country, the intricate workings of natural forces have combined to paint a landscape nearly infinite in its variety. Across the landforms of Colorado live an equally varied array of plant and animal species. Ecosystems in the state range from the desert to the arctic, often over the space of only a few miles. Ecosystems depend mostly on climatic factors, which are governed largely by topography. Biologists and ecologists have categorized the plant and animal life of Colorado into several life zones. You may want to take time to visit the Walter C. Meade Ecological Hall at the Denver Museum of Natural History for a real education on the ecology of Colorado. Or pick up the first volume of *Hiking Colorado*—or books specifically on Colorado ecology—at a library or bookstore near you.

GEOLOGY

Colorado occupies portions of three major physiographic provinces: the Great Plains, the southern Rocky Mountains, and the Colorado Plateaus.

Colorado's state flower: columbine.

The landforms included in these large-scale divisions not only govern the topography of Colorado but also have largely determined the patterns of weather, plant and animal life, and human settlement in the state.

The Great Plains occupies approximately the eastern two-fifths of Colorado, rising gently from about 3,500 feet at the eastern border of the state to about 5,000 feet at the foothills. The Rocky Mountains, for which Colorado is most well known, occupy the central and west-central portions of the state. This lofty backbone—featuring numerous peaks reaching to more than 14,000 feet in elevation—is the source of four major rivers: the Colorado, Rio Grande, Arkansas, and Platte. The Colorado Plateaus are in the western portion of Colorado and are characterized by a series of uplifted plateaus and moderately dipping anticlines, synclines, and monoclines, which are dissected by many canyons and broad valleys formed by tributaries of the Colorado River.

ARCHAEOLOGY

Colorado is rich in human as well as natural history. The earliest people to arrive on the eastern plains and intermountain valleys came some 12,000 years ago. Agriculture and a more settled habitation began as much as 2,000 years ago and culminated with the Anasazi who inhabited the Mesa Verde region until about A.D. 1,300. The Utes and several plains Indian tribes followed, occupying various portions of Colorado at different times until the Spanish, the trappers, and finally the miners and settlers of varied ethnic backgrounds and races displaced them in most areas.

While hiking, think of yourself as a partner with those who are protecting archaeological sites in Colorado. First of all, be careful and respectful around sites along hikes. Second, if you discover any prehistoric or historic sites, report them to professional land managers such as the USDA Forest Service or the Bureau of Land Management.

For more information read "Our Archaeological Resources" in *Hiking Colorado, Volume I* and *The Archaeology of Colorado* by E. Steve Cassells. You may want to visit the Denver Museum of Natural History and the University of Colorado Museum in Boulder. In southwestern Colorado you'll find many educational opportunities—Mesa Verde National Park, the Anasazi Heritage Center, Crow Canyon Archaeological Center, Hovenweep National Monument, and Ute Mountain Tribal Park. On the eastern plains check out Bent's Fort, and stop in at the museums in many of Colorado's small towns as you travel to and from hikes.

HIKING WITH CHILDREN

Hiking as a family is especially challenging—and rewarding! The challenges include buying and carrying gear for people with differing needs; motivating children; lowering expectations to match the abilities of the slowest or youngest person in your family; and handling crises. The rewards include: fun; family togetherness away from everyday distractions; sharing adventures, accomplishments, and discoveries; and creating memories that will last a lifetime.

Cub Scouts and moms check the map.

Additionally, you can give a bit of sanity to your children by introducing them to the wilderness through hiking. And you have the opportunity when hiking with children to see the natural world through a child's eyes again.

Preparation: Prepare well for your family hikes and you will have the freedom to be flexible, to laugh at the mishaps you encounter, and to be spontaneous. You'll be able to enjoy the serendipitous discoveries, pleasures, and adventures that appear on your paths.

Begin by involving all members of the family in the preparations. Choose your hikes together, with the youngest, slowest, or least able-bodied person in mind, and be realistic about what every member of your family can do. You may want to take several walks around your neighborhood as a family to get an idea of how fast or how slow everyone will go. Gather information on the hike and buy the maps you'll need together. Talk about how long it will take to get to your destination, how far the hike will be, and what children expect to see and do.

How far can kids go? The key principle, which bears repeating, is to set the pace and the distance you plan to hike by the abilities of the slowest member of your family. Children should set the pace for the adults, not the other way around.

Veteran hikers often take small babies on long hikes because they can be carried and sleep most of the way. Toddlers can be carried some of the way, but need variation in activities and easy footing. They really can walk only a mile or so. Young children from five to seven years old can go 3 or 4 miles, but with young children it's a good idea to stay within a reasonable distance of civilization in case medical care is needed, particularly if you're back-packing. Older children from eight to nine can go about 6 or 7 miles with an easy pace and tend to push themselves. Preadolescents may have growth spurts when their endurance and balance may be shaky; you may want to plan easy hikes during these times. Adolescents can work up to 12 miles by the time they're 18.

Gear: Comfortable and functional are the operative words when it comes to hiking gear for children. Each member of your crew should take along layers of clothing, appropriate footwear, protection from sun, rain, and cold, and—if you're backpacking—a well-fitted pack and good sleeping gear.

For layering, a child might wear a T-shirt, wool sweater, and rain jacket on a mild day, or long johns, a pile jacket, and rain jacket and rain pants on a cold day. The layers can be taken off and put back on according to how warm or cold it is. Oh, and let your child wear clothes that can get dirty— happy hikers are meant to get dirty.

Tennis shoes are all right for first hikes, but as children hike farther, you'll want to invest in boots. The new lightweight boots that have evolved from running shoes are especially good for children and are moderately priced.

A wide-brimmed hat works better for young children than sunglasses for sun protection, but when hiking at high elevation everyone really should have sunglasses. Many good sunscreens are safe for children and babies. Use them liberally.

Raingear is also widely available for young people. If you are going to high elevations or hiking in cold weather, take along a warm cap so that the child can conserve heat and guard against hypothermia. A lightweight pair of gloves might be a good thing to stick in the pack for comfort.

Children used to carrying a pack to school can carry raingear, snacks, a small water bottle, and a sleeping bag without a framepack. For more than that they need a framepack. When fitting one to your child, fasten the waistbelt just above the hips and check to make sure that the anchor points of the shoulder straps are an inch or two below the shoulder. The pack must be comfortable or the child will be miserable.

Invest in good sleeping bags and pads for the kids if you'll be doing a lot of backpacking. Everyone will be so much happier if you do (you may be able to rent this equipment for your first few trips).

Some additional tips: Always take along meat tenderizer to put on insect bites or stings (one-quarter teaspoon meat tenderizer to one teaspoon water), and children's acetaminophen. Take along some wet wipes. It has been reported that blue clothing attracts some insects. Buy mosquito netting and attach it to your baby or toddler's hat, then drape it over the child's face for protection.

Carrying the little ones: It's great to get the toddlers and babies out with you on hikes, because the outdoors becomes part of their lives early on. "Outdoor-ese" is like a second language to them, and loving wilderness comes naturally.

Front pack carriers are excellent for babies up to about 6 months. After babies can hold their heads up, they will be more comfortable with a frame carrier, as will you. Rent a carrier or two so you can try before you buy. Keep in mind that the carrier is an investment for everyday use. Look for a frame carrier that faces the child forward so he or she can see and so that the load will be closer to your center of gravity. The child can also snooze with her head on your shoulder this way. Make sure the carrier has a safety belt. A "kick stand" is handy for stops along the trail, but never leave the child alone in the carrier. Many carriers have handy pockets for carrying child-related snacks and gear.

Food: Plan your meals and snacks together, if that works for you, then everyone will have something to eat that they enjoy. Older children can take responsibility for preparing a meal or two; younger children can help put snacks in individual bags. When planning food for the trail, take along extra snacks for children. Always take high-energy foods such as candy bars or trail mix, oranges, or fruit leathers. Kids use a lot of energy hiking. Don't give them hard candies while they're hiking, though. Choking is a real possibility.

Be sure to take along lots of water and possibly some sports drinks, which are good rechargers.

Packing up: After choosing your hikes, make checklists; possibly one main one as well as individual checklists for each family member. (See our sample checklist in Appendix VI.)

Help your children pack "an exploring kit," a treasure bag with a hand magnifier, bandanna, baby food jars or unbreakable plastic containers with holes poked in the tops, empty cardboard rolls from paper towels or toilet tissue, a small net, and tweezers. For a long trip, take a good book to read aloud. Perhaps your kids might want to take a small art notebook and some crayons.

Safety tips: In Colorado in the 1980s and 1990s, a few children were killed by freak weather and other natural events, and by wildlife. Accidents will happen, whether we're out hiking or going to the grocery store, and we know that no loving parent or guardian of children would ever want to have a child hurt or killed. These tips may help you to keep children safe:

- Spend some time teaching your children how to get found if they become lost. Provide each child with a whistle and a space blanket to put in their backpacks for emergency use. A flashlight is good, too. Instruct them to "hug a tree" and stay in one place if they get lost. Teach them to take shelter against the weather, but to leave something bright tied to a tree or shrub to keep them visible to searchers. Show teenagers how to use a map and compass.

- Show children how to behave if they come upon a wild animal. If they come upon a rattlesnake, they should back away quietly and quickly. When coming upon a mountain lion or a bear, they should make themselves appear as big as possible by putting their arms or a big stick up above their heads and standing tall. Then they should look down at their feet and back away from the animal. They should *not* look in the animal's eyes, smile, show teeth, or run. Running triggers the instinct to chase. If a moose or bull elk were to chase them, they could get behind a tree and use it as a shield.

- You, as the adult, should be aware of the surroundings, look for signs of wildlife on the trail and keep your senses up for danger, just as other adult animals do. Ideally, do not let children go down the trail ahead of you. You should hike as a group within sight of each other. If you think there are bears nearby, sing and make lots of noise, so a bear can get out of your way. If you suspect a cliff is coming up, hold on to your children. Don't let them go near rivers or lakes alone. Be aware that rocks pushed down from above have killed children, and that a climbing child who falls head first onto rock may sustain a serious head injury.

You don't have to be frightened about going outdoors with your children, even your babies, but you do have to use awareness and common sense in order to keep them safe. See the section "Being Prepared" for more information.

Hiking: You can catch more flies with honey than with vinegar, and you can motivate more young hikers with rewards, encouragement, excitement, and fun than with all the lecturing, belittling, and prodding you can muster. Make hiking fun and be flexible. Let your children and nature lead the way, and be ready to forgo the summit ascent or the botany lesson. It isn't until children are eight or nine that they can really be destination-oriented and push themselves toward a goal. If you can lower your expectations appropriately, you and your entire family will have more fun.

Positive reinforcement is a parent's greatest tool to get children to hike, and to help them enjoy hiking. Promise a snack at the next rest stop or at the destination, surprise kids with a treat at the end of the trail. Sometimes we have visited a toy store on the way home from a hike—even a "looking only" stop at the toy store feels like a reward. At the end of a day's hike on a backpack, let the kids help make camp, build the fire, and cook, and let them make choices as you do the work. Tell your children how proud of them you are when they do a good job.

Here are some games you can play with your children to keep going on the trail with less whining, and to help them experience the outdoors.

- Follow the Leader: Take turns leading the hike and doing goofy things on the trail.

- Trust Me: Family members take turns being blindfolded and led along the trail by other members.

- What's This?: The leader takes a blindfolded hiker to something—a tree, a flower, a rock—and the hiker has to tell what it is and details about it.

- Sames and Differents: Give your child a "starting object." Have him or her find things like the object and things that are different.

- Shape Search: Children search for shapes in nature.

- Add-on Stories: Families create stories as they hike. One person starts a story and everyone else takes turns adding to it. Repeat until the story is finished.

- Identify Flora and Fauna: Who can identify the most flowers, trees, animals, and birds?

When hiking with children be ready for fun and laughter, along with mishaps and arguments, then make some space for quiet time along the trail. If you prepare well for your hikes, go at a pace and to a distance determined by the slowest in your group, and make hiking fun and exciting, your trips should be memorable for the good things along the way.

Use the "Trail Finder" in this book to select hikes that are especially good for families.

The Northern Mountains

The Northern Mountains

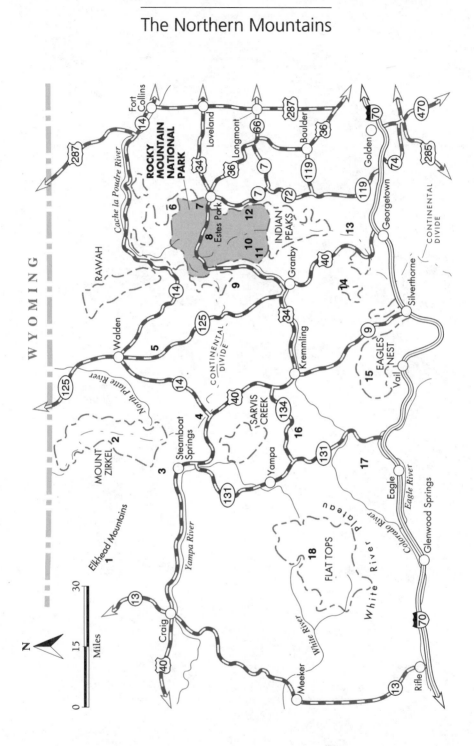

East summit of Black Mountain.

1 Black Mountain

Highlights:	Good views of the Elkhead Mountains, Yampa Valley, and north into Wyoming.
Location:	Northeast of Craig in the Elkhead Mountains.
Type of hike:	Out-and-back day hike.
Total distance:	5.4 miles.
Difficulty:	Moderate.
Elevation gain:	900 feet.
Best months:	June–September.
Maps:	USGS Buck Point quad; Routt National Forest Map.

Special considerations: Take water. Keep in mind that some maps do not show roads or trail correctly.

Finding the trailhead: Take Colorado Highway 13 north from U.S. Highway 40 in Craig about 13 miles to the Black Mountain Forest access road (County Road 27). Turn right (east) and follow this gravel road as it climbs from the sage-covered foothills to the forested slopes of Black Mountain, the unimposing flat-topped mountain to the northeast. You will enter the Routt National Forest. Continue on Forest Road 110 past numerous smaller timber sale roads, always staying on the main road, until at 14.4 miles (from the highway) you reach a small, open saddle with a small parking area on the right. This is the Black Mountain Trailhead. The trail begins on the north side of the road across from the parking area.

Black Mountain

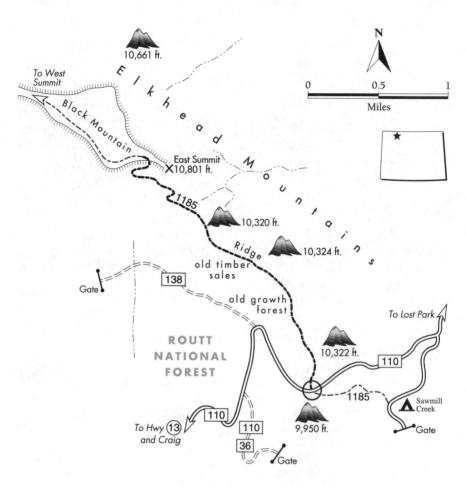

Parking and trailhead facilities: Parking area provided; no facilities.

Keypoints:
- 0.6 Old-growth forest
- 1.1 Back into old timber sale areas
- 2.0 Ridgetop views and start of climb to summit
- 2.7 Plateau top near east summit of Black Mountain

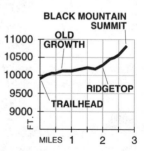

The hike: This hike takes you to the flat top of Black Mountain, a high point of the Elkhead Mountains with views of much of northwestern Colorado and parts of Wyoming. If you hike this trail in late summer, as we did, you may have the added treat of a mountaintop covered with blueberries. Just keep an eye out for bears with the same treat in mind.

Begin your hike on the north side of the road from the trailhead parking area. You will make a short climb through a meadow and then enter the forest on the west side of a long ridge that leads to Black Mountain. Once in this dark spruce-fir forest, for which Black Mountain derives its name, the trail stays nearly level for over 1.5 miles, gaining only about 200 feet in elevation. As you hike this stretch, notice the changes in the forest. You'll hike through a section of old-growth forest and then a section that was logged many years ago. The old-growth area is characterized by a variety of tree ages and sizes, including some very large spruces, along with standing dead and fallen trees in various states of decay. This is an example of the climax forest for this area and elevation—a mix of Engelmann spruce and subalpine fir. Notice the differences when you enter an area that was logged. There are no large older trees, and most of the middle-aged trees are similar in size. The real clues to logging, of course, are the stumps. If you have children along, this is a good opportunity for examining the ages of trees and the patterns of growth as represented by tree rings. On one large stump we counted more than 275 rings.

Toward the end of the forested section of trail, you get glimpses of the east promontory of Black Mountain, along with some views to the east and west as you gain the ridge at the base of the mountain. From this base the trail follows two long switchbacks to the rim.

The top of Black Mountain is nearly level and was formed by a cap of basalt that was laid down as a lava flow millions of years ago. The cliff-top viewpoint of the east summit is only 0.1 mile to the east from where the trail tops the plateau. The view includes the other peaks of the Elkhead Mountains and many smaller mountains to the north into Wyoming and to the east as far as the Park Range and Mount Zirkel Wilderness. To the south are the Yampa Valley and beyond, the Flat Tops. After enjoying the views, and maybe a few blueberries, return as you came.

Options: For a longer day hike, you could take the Black Mountain Trail another 1.5 miles west to the west summit and return. This additional round trip of 3 miles is actually very easy because it traverses the nearly level top of Black Mountain. We hiked this portion of the trail 0.5 mile to reach some views to the southwest before turning back. From the west summit, the trail drops down about another 2 miles to the southwest where it meets the Bears Ears Trail (Trail 1144). You could make a long loop back on this trail to its trailhead along FR 110, which you passed on the way to the Black Mountain Trailhead.

Camping and services: There is no camping at the trailhead. The flat top of Black Mountain offers a number of camping possibilities, none with water. Please camp away from the trail and east summit.

For more information: Routt National Forest, Bears Ears Ranger District.

2   Three Island Lake

Highlights:	Interesting view of the 1997 blowdown area; views; meadows; lake.
Location:	Northwest of Steamboat in the Mount Zirkel Wilderness.
Type of hike:	Day hike.
Total distance:	6.4 miles.
Difficulty:	Moderate.
Elevation gain:	1,450 feet.
Best months:	July–September.
Maps:	USGS Mount Zirkel quad; Trails Illustrated Map 117; Routt National Forest Map.

Special considerations: No camping at the lake.

Finding the trailhead: Go west from Steamboat Springs on Colorado Highway 40 for 2 miles. Look for the signs for Steamboat Lake and the airport and turn right on Elk River Road (County Road 129). Go north for 17.3 miles, passing the Glen Eden Ranch, and turn right (east) on CR 64, which becomes Forest Road 400. Take this road for 9.3 miles to North Lake Road (FR 443). Along the way you will pass the Hinman Road and other smaller forest roads, and the Seedhouse Campground. Turn right (south) on North Lake Road and follow it as it switches back up and over a ridge into the South Fork Elk River drainage. You will reach the trailhead in 3 miles.

Three Island Lake.

Parking and trailhead facilities: There is parking on both sides of the road, but no facilities.

Key points:
- 0.2   Intersection with trail from Seedhouse Campground
- 1.3   Blowdown area
- 2.1   Switchbacks
- 2.9   Meadow formed from old lake
- 3.2   Three Island Lake

The hike: Begin your hike on the north side of the road on Trail 1163A, a short spur that connects with the main Three Island Lake Trail (Trail 1163) after a short climb of 0.2 mile. At the trail junction, go right (east). The trail to the left drops down the north side of the ridge and crosses the road you drove up on. This provides a connection to the Seedhouse Campground and a through route for those hiking the Continental Divide Trail, which coincides with the Three Island Lake Trail for this hike.

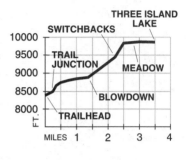

After the junction, you will climb at a fairly easy pace through alternating small meadows and aspen, lodgepole pine, and spruce-fir forest. There are a couple of small stream crossings and some good views of the areas of timber blowdown on the surrounding mountains and valleys and of the main drainage of the South Fork Elk River to the south. The impressive peak at the head of this valley is called the Dome.

At 1.3 miles cross through a portion of the blowdown, which occurred during a storm in October 1997. Winds estimated at more than 120 mph swept down from the Continental Divide and blew down thousands of acres of timber along the west side of the Park Range between Wyoming and Buffalo Pass. After the first blowdown area, the trail drops down and follows Three Island Creek, then begins to climb more steeply. At 2.1 miles the trail again leaves the creek and begins a steep climb via a series of switchbacks; you will enter the Mount Zirkel Wilderness along this stretch of the trail. Toward the top of the climb, wind back close to the creek and some spectacular cascades. After a last steep stretch, you will reach the upper valley containing Three Island Lake, and the trail levels out. There are some quiet meandering sections of the creek, which look inviting to fish, and a large wet meadow that was once a shallow lake that filled in with sediment. At 0.2 mile past the meadow is Three Island Lake.

To prevent overuse, no camping is allowed within a quarter mile of the lake. If you choose, you could circle the lake in 0.8 mile, but please do not use a route too close to the shoreline to allow some of the old fishing trails and campsites to recover. Return as you came after you enjoy your visit to the wilderness.

Three Island Lake

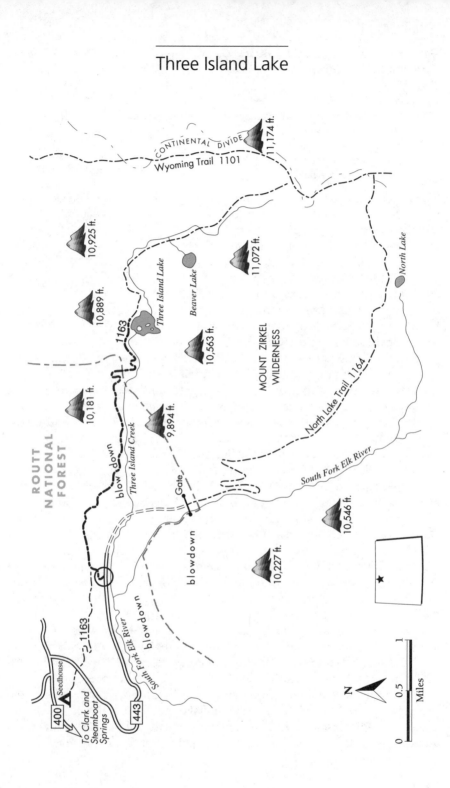

Options: Make a loop out of this hike by continuing on Three Island Lake Trail to the Continental Divide and the junction with the Wyoming Trail (Trail 1101), then go right (south) for about 1 mile to the junction with the North Lake Trail (Trail 1164). Go right (west) back to the North Lake Road and your car. If you arrange a car shuttle before your hike or have someone drop you off at the trailhead on North Lake Road, you could hike to the Wyoming Trail and backpack south along the Continental Divide all the way to Summit Lake Campground at Buffalo Pass on the southern tip of the wilderness.

Camping and services: There are limited camping opportunities along the trail below Three Island Lake, and no camping is allowed near the lake. The best camping possibilities begin 0.5 mile past the lake.

For more information: Routt National Forest, Hahns Peak/Bears Ears Ranger District.

3 Mad Creek

Highlights:	Foothills canyon and glacial valley; rushing creek; wildflowers; meadows.
Location:	Northwest of Steamboat Springs along Elk River Road.
Type of hike:	Day hike.
Total distance:	5.7 miles.
Difficulty:	Moderate.
Elevation gain:	850 feet.
Best months:	May–October.
Maps:	USGS Mad Creek and Rocky Peak quads; Trails Illustrated Map 117; Routt National Forest Map.

Finding the trailhead: Go west from Steamboat Springs on Colorado Highway 40. Look for the signs for Steamboat Lake and the airport and turn right on Elk River Road (County Road 129.) Drive north 5.3 miles. The trailhead is located on the right just after you cross Mad Creek, and is well marked. The Red Dirt Trailhead, which is part of this loop, is located 1 mile farther along Elk Creek Road. You might choose to park and begin the loop here, or shuttle another car.

Parking and trailhead facilities: There's a large parking lot at Mad Creek and a smaller parking area at the Red Dirt Trailhead; no facilities.

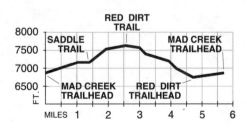

Hiking back from the meadows.

Key points:
- 1.0   Glacial moraine deposits near top of Mad Creek Canyon
- 1.3   Saddle Trail and options to explore meadows and Mad Creek
- 2.6   Top of saddle and junction with Red Dirt Trail
- 3.7   Views of the Big Creek drainage
- 4.7   Red Dirt Trailhead and highway
- 5.7   Return to Mad Creek Trailhead

The hike: This lower-elevation hike near Steamboat Springs offers many hiking opportunities in terms of length and season. The main attractions are the lower canyon and broad glaciated valley of Mad Creek, a large mountain stream that begins in the high country of the Mount Zirkel Wilderness. A return loop via the Saddle and Red Dirt Trails includes a surprising variety of forest, meadow, and foothills shrub habitats.

Begin your hike at the northeast corner of the Mad Creek Trailhead. Immediately climb a dry, south-facing slope and then turn northeast into the canyon of Mad Creek. The trails keeps high along the canyon wall, with views of the angry creek below. At 1 mile, the canyon opens up with views of a wider valley ahead. Look for the first large boulders along the trail, which indicate the moraine deposits from a valley glacier that ended near this point. The narrow canyon below was carved by flowing water, but the broad valley ahead was sculpted by glaciers that descended from the higher mountains to the east.

After crossing through a gate and entering into the meadows of the upper valley, you will reach the junction with the Saddle Trail at 1.3 miles. To complete the loop via the Red Dirt Trail, turn left at this point.

Take the Saddle Trail up through alternating aspen, shrubs, and meadows to a saddle with views along the way of the meadows and surrounding valley. After crossing the saddle you meet up with the Red Dirt Trail at 2.6 miles. Go left (west) and follow this trail through a combination of cool, moist forest and open meadows with oakbrush.

At about 3.8 miles the trail bends back south and descends to the Red Dirt Trailhead and the highway, with views of the Elk River Valley. From there it is about a 1-mile hike along the road back to the Mad Creek Trailhead.

Options: The meadows and creek in the Mad Creek valley are worth exploring, either as a side trip or as the destination for a shorter out-and-back trip via only the Mad Creek Trail. The shortest route to the creek is down and along a more primitive trail that takes off back near the gate, near the Saddle Trail junction. The huge boulders in this reach of Mad Creek were carried here by a glacier, and the creek has been unable to move them. You can make about a 2-mile loop around the end of the meadows via two of the three trails that come together at the junction with the Saddle Trail. If you stay straight on the main trail at the sign for Swamp Park, you will go through another gate and stay high through the meadows past the Mad Creek Guard Station. If you take the trail that goes right you will follow a lower route through the meadow and closer to the creek. Both of these trails meet up near the east end of the meadows where Mad Creek emerges from the

Mad Creek

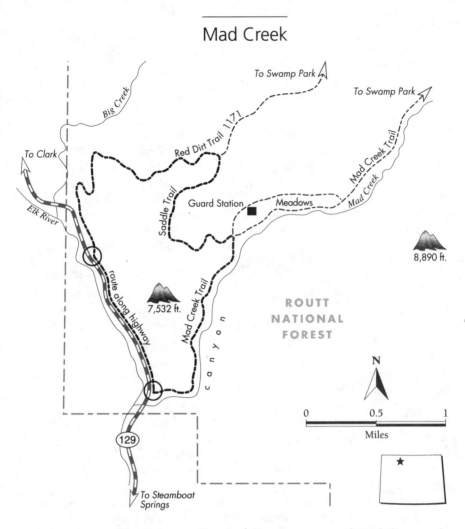

upper canyon. Please leave all gates closed or as you found them and respect the privacy of the backcountry rangers staying at the guard station.

For a much longer loop, follow Mad Creek past the meadows and along the upper canyon to where it meets the Red Dirt Trail and return via that route. These trails meet within the Mount Zirkel Wilderness at a point just over halfway to Swamp Park. Use either trail as an access point for longer backpack trips to Swamp Park and other destinations within the wilderness area. For any of these options, take along topographic maps and inquire about trail conditions.

Camping and services: Because of heavy use and cattle grazing, this trail is not appropriate for camping unless you are making a backpack trip into the wilderness area.

For more information: Routt National Forest, Hahns Peak/Bears Ears Ranger District.

4 Rabbit Ears Peak

Highlights: Fun geological formation; meadows and wildflowers; views.

Location: Northeast of Steamboat Springs near Rabbit Ears Pass in the Park Range.

Type of hike: Day hike.

Total distance: About 6 miles.

Difficulty: Easy.

Elevation gain (or loss): 1,050 feet.

Best months: July–September.

Maps: USGS Rabbit Ears quad; Trails Illustrated Map 118, Routt National Forest Map.

Finding the trailhead: Go southeast from Steamboat Springs about 20 miles on U.S. Highway 40 up Rabbit Ears Pass or northwest from Muddy Pass for 4.7 miles. Go north on Dumont Lake Road (Forest Road 315) at the sign for Dumont Lake. Take the paved road (the old pass road that was built in 1919) for 1.5 miles past Dumont Lake Campground and turn left (north) on the dirt road. Go 0.1 mile and park.

Parking and trailhead facilities: Parking available; no facilities.

Key points:
- 1.0   Meadows
- 2.0   Trail curves right (east)
- 2.7   Steep climb
- 3.0   Rabbit Ears

The hike: Follow Grizzly Creek Road to Rabbit Ears Peak (Forest Road 291). You will come to a junction with Base Camp Road (FR 311), which is the route of the Continental Divide Trail as it heads west and then north through the Park Range.

Take the right fork and keep on the main track past that junction, heading toward the Rabbit Ears through beautiful rolling meadows interspersed with evergreens. At 2 miles, the trail curves right and climbs, then levels off. A very steep climb takes you to a more moderate grade and the woods at the base of the western "ear."

We don't recommend climbing the rocks, which are about 100 feet high, but take a rest and enjoy the views, then return as you came.

Options: Make a loop out of this hike with some bushwhacking by following the ridge northwest from the Rabbit Ears to the Continental Divide, going west along the divide about 1 mile, then dropping down to the south to meet Base Camp Road. Return to the trailhead along this jeep road, which is also part of the Continental Divide Trail.

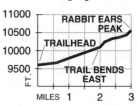

41

Rabbit Ears Peak

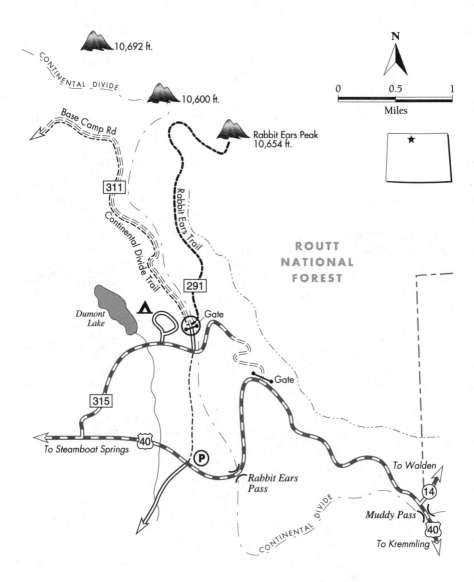

10,692 ft.

CONTINENTAL DIVIDE

10,600 ft.

Base Camp Rd

Rabbit Ears Peak
10,654 ft.

311

Rabbit Ears Trail

Continental Divide Trail

ROUTT
NATIONAL
FOREST

291

Dumont
Lake

Gate

Gate

315

40

To Steamboat Springs

P

Rabbit Ears
Pass

To Walden

14

CONTINENTAL DIVIDE

Muddy Pass

40

To Kremmling

N

0   0.5   1
Miles

★

Camping and services: Camping is available at the nearby Dumont Lake Campground.

For more information: Routt National Forest, Hahns Peak/Rabbit Ears Ranger District.

---

5 Owl Ridge

Highlights:	Views of North Park; high prairie grasslands and sage; wet meadows; wildlife.
Location:	South of Walden at the Arapaho National Wildlife Refuge.
Type of hike:	Loop day hike.
Total distance:	6.5 miles.
Difficulty:	Moderate.
Elevation gain:	740 feet.
Best months:	May and September.
Maps:	USGS MacFarlane Reservoir and Owl Ridge quads; Trails Illustrated Map 114; Arapaho National Wildlife Refuge Map.

Special considerations: Some bushwhacking. Check on seasonal restrictions. Mosquitoes in June.

Finding the trailhead: From the junction of Colorado Highways 14 and 125 southwest of Walden, drive south on CO 125 about 6.5 miles. Turn left (east) on County Road 32 at the sign for the Arapaho National Wildlife Refuge headquarters. Go east 1 mile across the Illinois River and bear left to the refuge headquarters. Park there.

Parking and trailhead facilities: Parking and limited facilities are available. The park headquarters and visitor center burned, but may be rebuilt in the future.

Key points:
- 0.9 Refuge boundary fence; enter BLM lands
- 2.0 First high point on Owl Ridge
- 2.8 Second high point; ridge bends east
- 3.0 Top of Owl Ridge
- 3.2 Backtrack to second high point, then drop into basin (no trail)
- 4.0 Southeast corner of refuge and lower jeep road
- 6.5 Return to refuge headquarters

The hike: This trail is a loop that follows Owl Ridge to a high point and then returns by way of a jeep road along the Illinois River.

Begin your hike by walking south 0.2 mile to the fork where CR 32 goes east. Hike up the county road 0.1 mile and onto a jeep road, which takes off

Owl Ridge

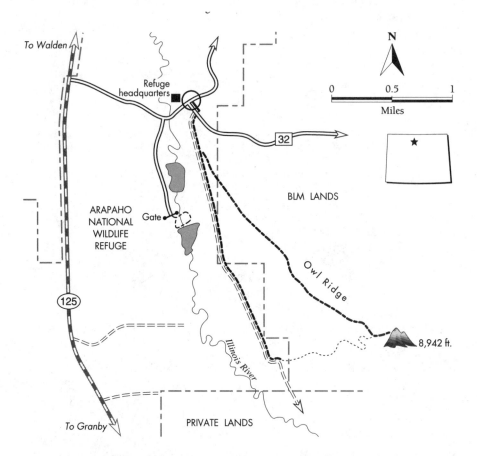

to the south (right). Follow the jeep road up the gently sloping ridge 0.3 mile to another fork and go left on another jeep road. From this point follow along the grass-and-sagebrush-covered Owl Ridge. At 0.9 mile from the trailhead is a fenceline that marks the east boundary of the refuge. This gate is usually locked and you will have to climb over or through. You are now on Bureau of Land Management (BLM) public land. At about 2 miles is the first real high point along the ridge, a good turnaround if you want a shorter hike. Notice the differences in vegetation between the ridgetop and the slopes on either side. The nearly constant winds and drifting snows in winter have a great effect on vegetation here. These same winds make Owl Ridge a favorite for hawks and eagles, where they can hover and survey the surrounding prairie, sagebrush, and wetland habitats for food.

The ridge continues to the southeast and then, at another high point at about 2.8 miles, it turns eastward to your destination—the highest point on Owl Ridge in this area at 8,942 feet. From this vantage point, you have a

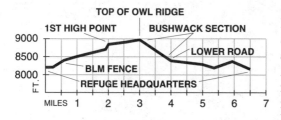

360-degree view of North Park. To the north is the Snowy Range in Wyoming and the north end of the Medicine Bow Range in Colorado. At the base of this range, in the northeast section of North Park, you can see two sets of sand dunes of which few people are aware. To the east is the Medicine Bow Range with the Colorado State Forest on the west side and the Rawah Wilderness on the east. To the southeast are the Never Summer Mountains, and straight south is the Rabbit Ears Range with the distinct peak of Parkview Mountain as its high point. Southwest is Rabbit Ears Peak near Rabbit Ears Pass, and to the west and northwest is the Park Range and the Mount Zirkel Wilderness. Finally, to the north-northwest is Independence Mountain, which marks the north end of North Park.

From the Owl Ridge high point, return as you came or make a loop by dropping down into the Illinois River valley and the refuge. To do this, backtrack along the ridge to the last high point, then drop down the slope into a basin, which falls off to the southwest. There is no trail here and you must bushwhack down the slope and through some thick sagebrush. But if you aim for a hill in the middle of the basin, you will eventually encounter a cattle trail, which follows a ridge southwest from this hill and connects with another jeep road near the southeast corner of the refuge. Please note that the land to the south of this point is private.

This lower road will bring you back to the jeep road junction where you began to climb Owl Ridge, and then to the refuge headquarters in about 2.5 miles. The road parallels the west edge of the wet meadow and willow wetlands of the Illinois River. There are two large ponds along the lower half of this road section. Keep an eye open for moose in the willows along the river and stop to enjoy the many birds of the refuge. In order to protect the wildlife from disturbance, please stay on the road unless you've gotten specific permission from the staff at refuge headquarters to explore further.

Options: Make this a shorter hike by doing only portions of either the Owl Ridge or lower refuge road routes. There is also a short nature hike on the west side of the Illinois River. For this hike, go back across the river (west) from the refuge headquarters and take the road to your left (south) about 1 mile to its end. There is a parking area, wheelchair-accessible bathrooms, and an easy trail with some boardwalk sections through the wetlands. Although a little rough in places, this trail appeared to be wheelchair accessible.

Camping and services: None. You may camp on BLM lands, but not within the refuge.

For more information: Arapaho National Wildlife Refuge.

Hikers at the rock pinnacle along the trail to Signal Mountain.

6 Signal Mountain

Highlights:	Pristine mountain creek; views of northern Colorado.
Location:	West of Fort Collins in the Comanche Peak Wilderness near Pingree Park.
Type of hike:	Long, out-and-back day hike.
Total distance:	11.6 miles.
Difficulty:	Strenuous.
Elevation gain (or loss):	2,750 feet (200 feet).
Best months:	June–September.
Maps:	USGS Pingree Park quad; Trails Illustrated Map 112; Roosevelt National Forest Map.

Finding the trailhead: From Fort Collins take U.S. Highway 287 northwest to Ted's Place and turn west onto Colorado Highway 14 into Poudre Canyon. Follow this highway about 26.5 miles to Pingree Park Road (County Road 63E). Turn left (south) and go approximately 13 miles to the Signal Mountain Trailhead, staying on the main road to Pingree Park at all junctions.

Parking and trailhead facilities: Limited roadside parking; no facilities.

Special considerations: No fishing allowed.

Key points:
- 0.6   Cross Pennock Creek; old stream gauge
- 1.7   Wilderness area boundary
- 2.2   Beaver ponds; short hike option
- 3.1   Cross two small creeks
- 4.5   Rock pinnacle
- 4.8   Saddle
- 5.8   Signal Mountain summit

The hike: This hike takes you along the beautiful canyon of pristine Pennock Creek, then climbs to the summit of Signal Mountain, a rounded peak just above timberline in the Comanche Peak Wilderness. This can be done as either a strenuous hike to the top of the peak or as an easier hike of the lower portion along Pennock Creek.

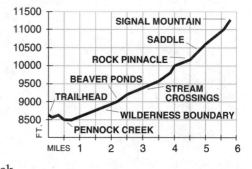

Before you start, note the regulations posted at the trailhead, and that the posted distances are optimistic. Then, begin your hike by dropping down and crossing a small tributary of Pennock Creek. The trail then traverses around the north end of a ridge and drops into the Pennock Creek drainage.

Signal Mountain

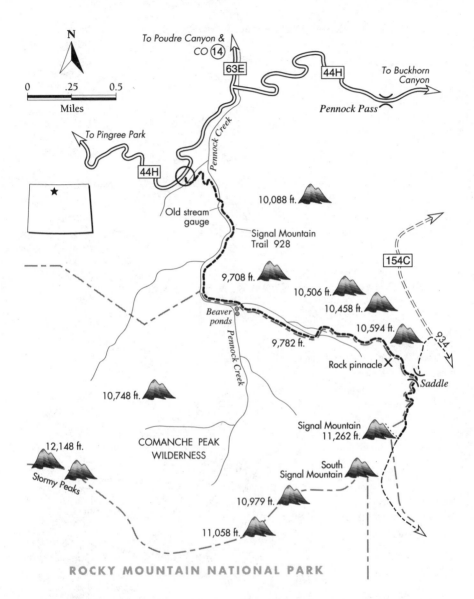

N

0 — .25 — 0.5
Miles

To Poudre Canyon &
CO 14

63E

44H
To Buckhorn
Canyon

Pennock Pass

To Pingree Park

Pennock Creek

44H

★

Old stream
gauge

10,088 ft.

Signal Mountain
Trail 928

154C

9,708 ft.

10,506 ft.

10,458 ft.

Beaver
ponds

10,594 ft.

934

Pennock Creek

9,782 ft.

Rock pinnacle ✕

Saddle

10,748 ft.

COMANCHE PEAK
WILDERNESS

Signal Mountain
11,262 ft.

12,148 ft.

South
Signal Mountain

Stormy Peaks

10,979 ft.

11,058 ft.

ROCKY MOUNTAIN NATIONAL PARK

For a short distance follow an old jeep trail, then cross Pennock Creek at 0.6 mile. Just before you enter a canyon there is an old measuring flume and stream gauging station. (Pennock Creek is a nearly pristine watershed where fishing is prohibited to protect the greenback cutthroat trout. The creek has been studied by researchers at the nearby Pingree Park campus of Colorado State University.)

The trail then follows along the west side of Pennock Creek. At 1.7 miles is the wilderness boundary, after which the valley and trail bend to the east and you gain some views of the surrounding mountains. At 2.2 miles there are some beaver ponds, and a good spot to stop and enjoy the creek or to turn around if you want a shorter hike.

A short distance past the beaver ponds, the trail crosses a tributary of Pennock Creek and begins the climb toward Signal Mountain. The trail climbs fairly steadily through spruce-fir forest for about 2 miles, crossing two small creeks a little less than halfway. At 4.5 miles you'll come to a spectacular rock pinnacle from which you can see the top of Signal Mountain. From the pinnacle the trail steepens as it climbs to a saddle separating the Pennock Creek and Miller Creek drainages. At the saddle there is an intersection with an old logging road to the left, which is Trail 934. Please note that the trail route to the saddle and the trail intersection at the saddle are incorrectly marked on some maps. Look for the trail continuing right (south) toward Signal Mountain. From the saddle the trail climbs fairly steeply and, in 0.5 mile comes to timberline. Once above timberline, the trail climbs along the east side of Signal Mountain. The last bit to the summit is a short off-trail climb.

From the top of Signal Mountain you have spectacular views of the entire Poudre River drainage to the north. To the northwest is Crown Point. To the west you can see Comanche Peak and the Stormy Peaks at the north end of Rocky Mountain National Park. To the southeast is much of the drainage of the Big Thompson River and Longs Peak to the south of Estes Park.

Enjoy the views and hike back as you came.

Options: Continue on the Signal Mountain Trail southeast to the trailhead near Glen Haven.

Camping and services: None.

For more information: Roosevelt National Forest, Estes-Poudre Ranger District.

Bridal Veil Falls.

7 Bridal Veil Falls

Highlights:	Gorgeous views; a variety of landscapes; pretty waterfall.
Location:	North of Estes Park in the Mummy Range in a lesser-known part of Rocky Mountain National Park.
Type of hike:	Day hike with shuttle between trailheads.
Total Distance:	About 9 miles.
Difficulty:	Moderate.
Elevation gain (or loss):	1,000 feet (600 feet).
Best months:	June–September.
Maps:	USGS Estes Park and Glen Haven quads; Trails Illustrated Map 200; Rocky Mountain National Park Map; Roosevelt National Forest Map.

Finding the trailhead: Begin by leaving a car at the Twin Owls Trailhead. From the junction of U.S. Highways 34 and 36 at the first stoplight west of Lake Estes take Fall River Road (US 34) north past the Stanley Hotel for 0.4 mile, then turn right on MacGregor Avenue. In 0.8 mile you'll come to the MacGregor Ranch at a sharp curve in the road. Drive into the ranch on the dirt road and follow the signs to the Twin Owls Trailhead. Park there.

In another vehicle, drive back to MacGregor Avenue and go left (east). The road now becomes Devil's Gulch Road (County Road 43). Drive east for 3 miles, and look carefully to the north (left) for McGraw Ranch Road. Go left (northwest). At this writing the road was heavily decorated with private "No Trespassing" signs and USDA Forest Service signs warning that you travel this road at your own risk. In 2.3 miles you will come to the Cow Creek Trailhead just before the McGraw Ranch. Turn around and park on the road on the south side of Cow Creek.

Parking and trailhead facilities: There is parking only along the road at Cow Creek; at Twin Owls there is a parking lot. There are bulletin boards at both sites, but no facilities.

Special considerations: No pets are allowed on this hike. You must have a backcountry permit from Rocky Mountain National Park in order to camp overnight or backpack. Permits are available at the visitor center. Note: You cannot leave a car overnight at Cow Creek (see "Options").

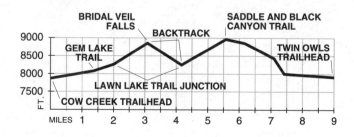

Bridal Veil Falls

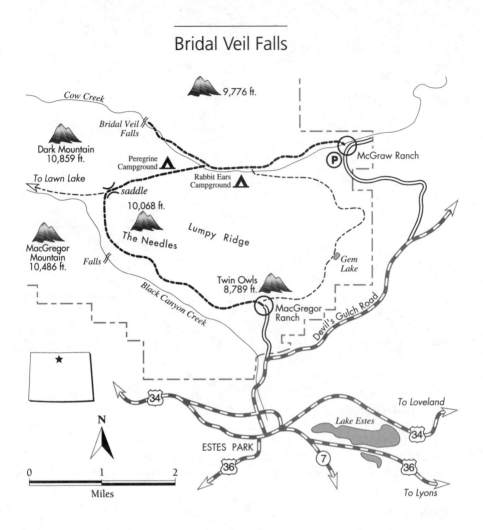

Key points:

The hike: This hike takes you on an adventure between old-time ranches, through a variety of landscapes, and to a lovely falls.

Start at the McGraw Ranch, which was settled in 1874 (Later, it became a dude ranch, which was popular for years.) There is a sign that tells you a little of the history near the ranch buildings along the trail.

Begin by walking north from your car and then west, following the signs. After passing the ranch buildings, you will hike through beautiful meadows where ponderosa, blue spruce, Douglas-fir, and aspen mix with some juniper and tall grasses. Enjoy wildflowers such as black-eyed Susan, mountain asters, bluebells, wild geranium, and more.

Hike along a meadow with a couple of streams to cross and then climb up a small hill to the junction with the Gem Lake Trail, about 1.3 miles along. Shortly beyond this junction is the Rabbit Ears Campground, which is signed. Hike a little farther and then look down valley to see the Rabbit Ears sticking up beyond the creek. The jeep road narrows to a single track and connects with the trail going to Lawn Lake. The falls is another 1.1 miles from this point. Take note of it because you will return to it after you visit the falls.

Climb out of the meadow and into the forest, then cross Cow Creek at a two-log crossing. Gain elevation as you climb into aspen and then to rocks and rocks and more rocks. After another two-log crossing of the creek you'll hike up through lush aspen groves along its laughing waters. Look closely for the trail as it heads up over the rough and steep last pitch after you pass a triangular hitching rail for horses. The falls does indeed look like a straight veil down the back of a bride with ebony skin. Enjoy a rest and snack or lunch at the falls, then return to where the Cow Creek Trail and the trail to Lawn Lake meet.

Go right (west) on the trail to Lawn Lake. You should pass the Peregrine Campground shortly after the junction. Now hike to the saddle in about 1.4 miles and the junction with the Black Canyon Trail going south. Go left so that you are hiking around to the south of The Needles (10,068 feet) and then to the south of Lumpy Ridge, following Black Canyon Creek. It's fairly easy walking downhill through the forest here. You will begin to walk away from the creek and through pretty open meadows as you head eastward to the Twin Owls Trailhead.

The meadows are dotted with ponderosa pine and reward you with great views of Longs Peak to the south. Watch for raptors above Lumpy Ridge to the north. Originally, Lumpy Ridge was an ancient plain, which was uplifted and weathered, leaving rounded lumps of solid rock. As you hike the final mile or so through meadows to the trailhead, you can really imagine what it would have been like to own and live on this other special ranch—the MacGregor—which was also settled in the 1800s. You might want to take time to stop by the museum if it is open before driving to get your other car at Cow Creek.

Options: To make this into a loop day hike or backpack, from Twin Owls Trailhead continue on the trail to Gem Lake, which begins at the east end of the parking lot and goes for 1.9 miles to the northeast. Keep going north at all forks. When you meet the Cow Creek Trail, hike east to the trailhead and back to your vehicle. If you want to backpack, you'll have to begin and end at the Twin Owls Trailhead because of the parking situation at Cow Creek. You can just skip the portion of the trail from the junction of the trail to

Gem Lake and the Cow Creek Trail east to McGraw Ranch. You could also hike this as an out-and-back day hike to Bridal Veil Falls from Cow Creek Trailhead, which is 6.2 miles.

Camping and services: The Rabbit Ears and Peregrine Campgrounds are available on the north side of Lumpy Ridge along the Cow Creek Trail.

For more information: Rocky Mountain National Park.

8 Tombstone Ridge

Highlights:	Hiking the tundra; great views; wildflowers; historic trail.
Location:	On Trail Ridge Road in Rocky Mountain National Park.
Type of hike:	Out-and-back day hike.
Total distance:	2.3 miles one way, 4.6 miles round trip.
Difficulty:	Easy.
Elevation gain (or loss):	Minimal.
Best months:	July–September.
Maps:	Trails Illustrated Map 200; Rocky Mountain National Park Map.

Finding the trailhead: From the Beaver Meadow visitor center at Rocky Mountain National Park on U.S. Highway 36, go west into the park

Hiking the tundra along Tombstone Ridge.

Tombstone Ridge

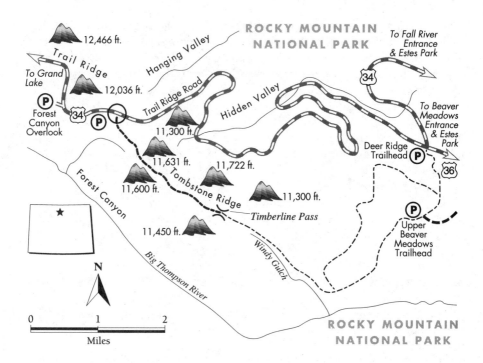

4.2 miles to the Deer Ridge junction with US 34. Continue west on Trail Ridge Road (US 34) 10.1 miles to the trailhead on the south side of the highway. If the parking lot is full, continue 1 mile to the Forest Canyon Overlook and park or turn around and park in one of the turnouts on the south side of the road. Walk back east along the road to the trailhead for the Ute Trail.

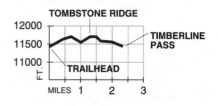

From Granby drive over Trail Ridge Road to the Forest Canyon Overlook and continue 1 mile to the trailhead.

Parking and trailhead facilities: Minimal parking; no facilities. Take care and keep children close.

Key points:
  1.3   Tombstone Ridge
  2.3   Timberline Pass

The hike: This is a very special trail, an easy introduction to the alpine tundra, and one that lets you retrace the steps of travelers who passed this way for hundreds of years and who gazed upon the same beautiful views you will enjoy.

The sign at the trailhead informs hikers, "The Rocky Mountains in Colorado presented early travelers with a difficult choice: either go around this seemingly impenetrable barrier or find a way through. The Ute and Arapaho Indians did the latter as they journeyed between their summer and winter hunting grounds. The early routes within the park crossed the Continental Divide via Big Meadows and Flattop Mountain, up Fall River and over Fall River Pass, and here along Trail Ridge. Later on, as frontier settlements flourished along both sides of the Divide, travel over the Ute Trail became fairly regular. The route first used by Indians soon became an established trail as seen today, crossed and re-crossed by the modern Trail Ridge Road."

Enjoy walking this easy trail to Timberline Pass with its rolling green hills, gusts of wind and cold, and views, views, views. Here you can see Fern Lake to the south, Longs Peak to the southeast, and Forest Canyon—the big drainage that parallels Trail Ridge Road—to the southwest.

This hike starts with a short climb gaining about 250 feet in elevation in the first 0.3 mile and then stays nearly level across the tundra. At about 1.3 miles is another minor high point. Above you on the ridge are large blocks that look like tombstones: this is Tombstone Ridge. The trail then drops down to Timberline Pass, which is marked by a large rock block. This is a good spot to turn around, because the trail drops steeply into Windy Gulch from here.

As you return to your vehicle, notice the low-growing plants. If you have a book on Colorado wildflowers, take it along and see how many species you can identify on this bit of tundra; alpine sunflowers and moss campion are two of this area's species. Also, watch for elk. Always keep an eye on the skies for thunderclouds: You are completely exposed to lightning strikes on this hike.

Options: Extend this hike by continuing on the Ute Trail past Timberline Pass and down Windy Gulch to the Upper Beaver Meadows Trailhead or to the Deer Ridge Trailhead. You have to shuttle a vehicle for this option.

Camping and services: None.

For more information: Rocky Mountain National Park.

9 Bowen Gulch Old-Growth Forest

Highlights:	Rich natural history; a wonderful family hike.
Total Distance:	1 mile.
Location:	North of Granby near the west boundary of Rocky Mountain National Park.
Type of hike:	Loop nature walk with interpretive signs.
Difficulty:	Easy.
Elevation gain (loss):	Minimal.
Best months:	July–September.
Maps:	Interpretive trail guide from the Arapaho National Forest, Sulphur Ranger District; Trails Illustrated Map 503; Rocky Mountain National Park Map.

Special considerations: Apply insect repellent before hiking.

Finding the trailhead: From the intersection of U.S. Highways 40 and 34 at Granby go northeast 39.8 miles. Turn left (west) onto County Road 4 at the northern tip of Lake Granby. (From Grand Lake at the intersection of US 34 and the road into Grand Lake, go south about 4 miles and turn right [west] onto CR 4.) Go about 4 miles to the junction with Forest Road 120 (Kawuneeche Road) at the signed fork. Turn right (north) and continue on this road for about 6 miles. Turn right (north) on FR 120.5. It is about 2.3 miles to the parking area. The hike begins 0.25 mile down the road past the gate prohibiting motor vehicles.

Parking and trailhead facilities: Small designated parking area; no facilities.

Key points: See hike description for key points.

The hike: This hike will lead you through an ecosystem rare in Colorado: old-growth forest of spruce-fir. This is one of the state's largest patches. It is a terrific hike for a family on vacation in the Grand Lake area or visiting for the day. It's not too long but very interesting. It's also easy walking, particularly for little ones and seniors, though it is not suitable for wheelchair travel.

This trail was constructed in 1993 with interpretive signs which were unfortunately vandalized shortly thereafter. A brochure was created by the USDA Forest Service to correspond with the signs and is available from the Sulphur Ranger District in Granby. When we hiked the trail in July 1998, the signs had been replaced. However, this description will paraphrase the signs in case they have been destroyed by the time you get there, and in case you don't have time to get a brochure from the ranger district.

Walk the quarter mile down the jeep road from the parking area to the start of the Bowen Gulch Interpretive Trail, which is marked by logs and by Sign 1. Begin by going uphill to your left.

Old-growth forest.

Sign 1. Bowen Gulch is a very special old-growth forest. From 1980 to 1991 there was a timber sale here, which was stopped by public outcry. The area was then declared protected from new road construction, logging, and mining.

Sign 2. Characteristics: Old-growth forests are unique ecosystems that are important for their biological diversity. As you walk the trail, look for

- large, live trees
- large, standing dead trees, which are home to insects and birds
- large, decaying trees lying on the ground
- the mix of young, medium-aged, and old trees that form canopies at various heights
- minimal evidence of disturbance from logging or fire
- trees with broken tops or large cavities, which provide nesting sites for birds and small mammals

Sign 3. Tree mortality: Tree death is an important part of the dynamics of an old-growth forest. After a tree dies, it has served only one-third of its usefulness to the forest. Standing trees provide homes for insects, birds, and mammals. Fallen trees provide nutrients to the forest floor by their decaying bark and wood. As you walk on the path, notice how spongy or springy the ground feels under your feet. When the big trees fall, they allow sunlight and space into the forest. But if you're not here, do they make a sound? Are you kidding—trees that big?

Sign 4. Wildlife: The combination of wet (riparian) areas and old-growth forests is very beneficial for wildlife. Pine martens, boreal owls, goshawks, three-toed woodpeckers, and red-backed voles are among the species that depend on old-growth forest. Other denizens of this area include moose, elk, mule deer, coyote, red fox, red squirrel, osprey, mountain lion, black bear, and mountain chickadees.

Sign 5. Rock outcropping: Here is an old talus slope exposed at the bottom of a forested hill. Lichens and mosses grow on and between the rocks. Openings among the rocks provide cover for small mammals including mice, voles, and pikas.

Sign 6. Logging: Hope of finding gold brought many people to Colorado. Others found "gold" in logging. Logging camps flourished here with the coming of the railroad. Timber continues to be a valuable commodity. In 1891 the Forest Reserves, predecessor of the USDA Forest Service, were created to manage federal lands and to supply timber to the country. The Forest Service attempts to balance the need for timber with the health of forest ecosystems.

Sign 7. Timber markings: You are in one of the cutting units of the former Bowen Gulch Timber Cuts. The trees with orange bands were scheduled to be cut. Trees with blue paint marked the boundaries of cutting units.

Sign 8. Riparian zone: Water is a major ingredient in an old-growth spruce-fir forest. Water from springs, snowmelt, and rain seeps into the soils, into the dead and decaying material on the ground, and into dozens of small creeks. The creeks have little soil in the water (sedimentation) because the large mass of tree roots holds the soil in place. Animals thrive in riparian areas because of the variety of plant species and the abundant water supply.

Sign 9. Meadow: Notice the small trees growing to the edge of the meadow. It is too wet in the meadow for them to grow there. If the meadow were to dry out, trees would replace the grass.

Sign 10. Understory growth: Trees of different ages growing in a forest create canopies of different heights—characteristic of an old-growth forest. The older trees form a high canopy that protects and shades the younger trees and plants from the hot and frying effects of the sun.

Sign 11. Fire: In subalpine areas like Bowen Gulch, wildfire occurs every 500 to 1,200 years. Because fire is infrequent, and because north-facing slopes and wet soils are found here, trees in this area grow to be very old. The older spruce trees are more than 400 years and the older fir trees are more than 300 years old.

Sign 12. Decomposition: Sometimes a fallen, decaying tree can become a nurse tree. It provides nutrients for a seedling to grow from its trunk. An important link between plants and animals is fungus, many species of which thrive on fallen trees. Small mammals called red-backed voles feed on fungi and distribute the spores in droppings. These spores envelop the roots of trees, share nutrients with trees, and produce antibiotics that protect the trees' roots.

Sign 13. Reseeding work: Before the logging sales ceased, roads were built here. Revegetation of these roads is now being accomplished.

Sign 14. Planning for the future: Threats to old-growth forest—besides logging—include fire, forest succession, and wind. The USDA Forest Service faces these challenges in protecting this area.

Sign 15. Dateline: Many trees in the Bowen Gulch old-growth area were alive during the following events:

- 1543 Copernicus publishes his work on the solar system
- 1609 Galileo builds telescope
- 1865 Civil War ends
- 1918 World War I ends
- 1969 First human lands on the moon

Camping: None.

For more information: Arapaho National Forest, Sulphur Ranger District.

10 Adams and East Inlet Falls

Highlights:	Pretty falls; good first destination hike.
Location:	At Grand Lake in Rocky Mountain National Park.
Type of hike:	Out-and-back day hike.
Total distance:	0.6 mile for Adams Falls; 5.8 miles for East Inlet Falls.
Difficulty:	Easy (Adams); moderate (East Inlet).
Elevation gain:	800 feet.
Best months:	July–September.
Maps:	USGS Shadow Mountain quad; Trails Illustrated Map 200; Rocky Mountain National Park Map.

Special considerations: No pets are allowed. Permits for overnight parking and backpacking are available at the National Park visitor center near Grand Lake.

Finding the trailhead: Drive into and through the town of Grand Lake to the east inlet of the lake, following the signs. On the east side of town go straight on Hancock. Turn left at the sign for Adams Falls and North Inlet, then turn right at the top of the road and onto County Road 667. Drive down toward the dirt parking lot. The trailhead is on the left.

Parking and trailhead facilities: Parking and facilities are provided at the trailhead.

Adams Falls.

Adams and East Inlet Falls

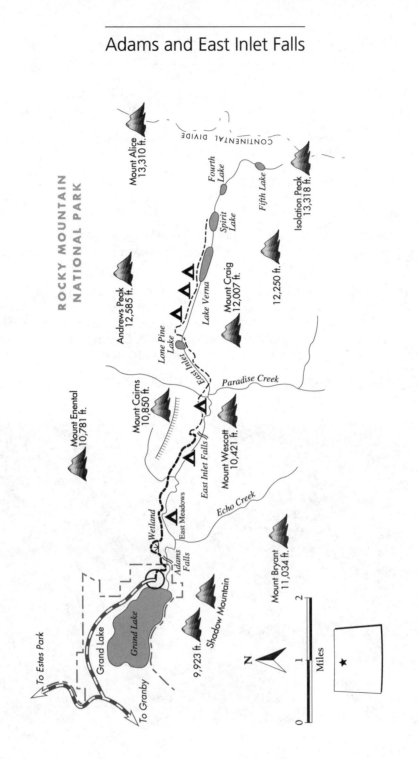

Key points:
- 0.3 Adams Falls
- 0.5 First meadow
- 1.2 East Meadows
- 2.9 East Inlet Falls

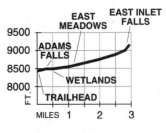

The hike: This hike gives you two options—the destinations of both are falls. The hike to Adams Falls is a good beginning hike for a family and a nice first destination hike for young children. The moderate climb to East Inlet Falls rewards you with spectacular views down the valley and of the surrounding mountains. There are some beautiful meadows halfway between that you may enjoy as well.

You will be hiking the East Inlet Trail and enter Rocky Mountain National Park right away from the trailhead. Begin at the sign, walking through stands of lodgepole pine and aspen (notice the wild roses along the way). Soon you will climb up a little pitch to reach Adams Falls. The rocks are worn smooth around the falls and can be slippery: Be sure to hang on to your children.

Take some time for a snack or just a good look at the falls before returning as you came. Or you can head up and around the falls to the northeast for more of an adventure.

After you climb up to the left (north) and east of the falls, the trail levels out through lodgepole pine forest and then circles around the north side of a meadow. It then reenters forest. At about 1.2 miles the trail emerges in East Meadows, a good place to stop and enjoy the creek, fish, and watch for beaver activity. It also makes a good intermediate destination and a short backpack.

From the end of the meadows the trail stays in forest and slowly climbs into some aspen and then rock outcrops at the base of Mount Cairns. You can hear the East Inlet Falls along this reach. The trail climbs a last steep stretch through open rock to a rock ledge, which was polished by the glacier that sculpted the entire East Inlet Valley and gouged out Grand Lake, the largest and deepest natural lake in Colorado. Here you'll overlook the falls, the valley below and Grand Lake, and the cliff face of Mount Craig to the east. After enjoying the views and the falls, return as you came.

Options: Extend this hike into a backpack by hiking up to one of the lakes, camping there, then returning as you came. Lone Pine Lake is 5.5 miles from the trailhead; Lake Verna is 6.9 miles; Spirit Lake is 7.5 miles.

Camping and services: Campgrounds are indicated at several places along the East Inlet Trail, the first at East Meadows.

For more information: Rocky Mountain National Park.

11 Colorado River Walk

Highlights:	Nice family hike. Osprey; riparian habitat and ponderosa forest; Shadow Mountain Lake and views beyond.
Location:	South of Grand Lake.
Type of hike:	Loop day hike.
Total distance:	2.8 miles.
Difficulty:	Easy.
Elevation gain (or loss):	Minimal.
Best months:	June–October.
Maps:	USGS Shadow Mountain quad; Trails Illustrated Map 200; Rocky Mountain National Park Map.

Special considerations: No pets. Watch children along the Colorado River.

Finding the trailhead: From the fork in U.S. Highway 34 where it goes north to Trail Ridge Road and another road heads east into Grand Lake, take US 34 South west for 2.8 miles. Turn left (east) at the sign for the Green Ridge Complex. Follow County Road 66 around to the right (south) past a picnic area and boat launch. Go right at the sign for fishing and through a gate with a sign for a viewing platform. Park at the area provided before the gate at mile 4.2.

Parking and trailhead facilities: Parking is provided; facilities are available in the nearby campground.

Shadow Mountain Lake.

Key points:
- 0.4   Bridge
- 0.9   Top of dam
- 1.1   East Shore Trail
- 1.8   Continental Divide Trail
- 2.0   Junction with jeep road
- 2.4   Bridge
- 2.8   Trailhead

The hike: Families should have fun with this easy adventure, which offers chances to see osprey, to walk through the riparian habitat along the Colorado River near its headwaters, and to experience the drier ponderosa pine forest. Plus, you'll get to see a dam—which kids should like—possibly some kokanee salmon, and Shadow Mountain Lake, with views of mountains beyond.

Begin your adventure by taking a moment to look for osprey from the viewing platform provided at the east end of the parking area. One of the two telescopes set up here is trained on an osprey nest.

According to *The Field Guide to Western Birds* by Roger Tory Peterson, the osprey is a large fish-eating hawk, which resembles a small eagle and is the only hawk in the West that dives into the water. You can distinguish it from an eagle by the way it flies with a crook in its wings and by the black patches on its cheeks. It also has a white underside with black markings on its "wrists." Eagles are dark on their underside. In winter, bald eagles make the area their home, because there is usually some open water that does not freeze over. Ospreys make it their summer home, diving feet first to catch trout and kokanee salmon. (We saw an osprey atop a pole with a live fish dangling from its talons.)

After looking for osprey, go through the gate and walk on the jeep road toward Mount Bryant (straight ahead). Shadow Mountain is on your left. Stay left, and notice the deep purple lupine, lodgepole pine, and willows. Cross the bridge over the Colorado River, entering Rocky Mountain National Park. Go left (north) along the river immediately after you cross the bridge (you'll be taking a fishermen's trail for the next part of your hike).

Walk past lodgepole along the river, through willows, and over logs. The trail becomes a bit faint, but look closely, you'll find it again. As you come into the open, notice the Indian paintbrush, penstemon, and the sound of hummingbirds whirring through the air.

The dam for Shadow Mountain Reservoir is to your left. Hug the river by going left of a little pond where red-winged blackbirds may scold you. Just keep going, being careful through the swampy stuff. Then take the trail to the right of the willows near the river again, and left through the willows over rocks, at the pond by a little building. Walk up to the top of the dam: You are at Shadow Mountain Lake. Walk over to the east end of the dam and find the East Shore Trail. You can walk north along the east shore on this trail as far as you like, or sit down for a snack along the water. The high mountains you see to the northeast are Little Matterhorn and Notch Top to your right (east) and Sprague Mountain to your left (west).

Colorado River Walk

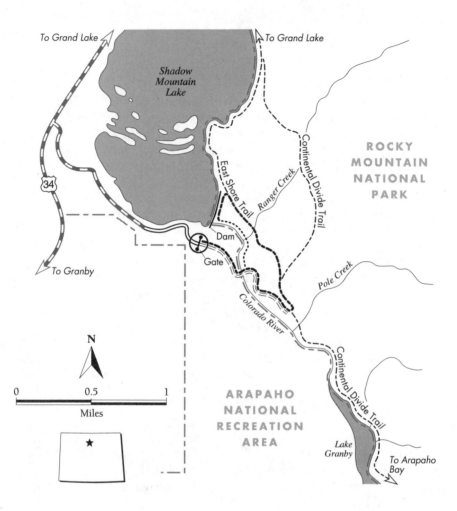

Follow the Continental Divide Trail south from the trailhead on the dam, skirting a meadow on the east. Notice the change in the ecosystem, which has much less moisture and includes sagebrush and ponderosa pine.

At all forks go right. You'll connect with the earlier jeep road, which goes back to the bridge over the Colorado River. From there retrace your steps back to your car.

Options: To make a longer loop hike the East Shore Trail north for 1.3 miles to the junction with the Continental Divide Trail, then go right (east) and south to join the loop back to the bridge and your car.

You can also begin your hike at the Arapaho Bay Campground, some 10 miles to the south and hike all the way to Grand Lake, if you shuttle cars or arrange for drop-off and pick-up. This is a nice backpack with little elevation gain.

Camping and services: Camping is available at the trailhead.

For more information: Rocky Mountain National Park.

12 Chasm Lake

Highlights:	Great views of the East Face of Longs Peak; Columbine Falls; wildflowers.
Location:	Rocky Mountain National Park.
Type of hike:	Out-and-back day hike.
Total distance:	8.4 miles.
Difficulty:	Strenuous.
Elevation gain:	2,400 feet.
Best months:	July–September.
Maps:	USGS Longs Peak quad; Trails Illustrated Map 200; Rocky Mountain National Park Map.

Special considerations: Backcountry permits and permits for overnight parking are available from the national park visitor centers. The closest visitor center to the Longs Peak Trailhead is the Lily Lake Visitor Center, which is north from the trailhead along Colorado Highway 7.

Finding the trailhead: Go south from Estes Park on CO 7 for about 8.5 miles. Turn right at the sign for Longs Peak Campground. Follow the dirt road, which becomes paved as you enter Rocky Mountain National Park. Following the signs for Longs Peak Trail, go left to the parking lot and the trailhead.

Parking and trailhead facilities: Large parking lot and restrooms are provided.

Key points:
    0.4   Junction with trail to Eugenia mine
    1.3   Cross Larkspur Creek
    2.5   Switchback near Jim's Grove
    3.2   Trail fork to Chasm Lake
    3.7   Creek above Columbine Falls
    4.2   Chasm Lake

The hike: This trail takes you to a spectacular setting at the base of the famous East Face of Longs Peak, that towering landmark of Colorado's northern mountains and Rocky Mountain National Park.

Chasm Lake

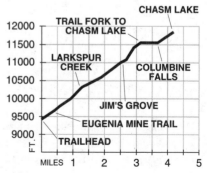

To Bierstadt Lake Trailhead

To several trailheads

Estes Cone 11,006 ft.

To Estes Park

To Glacier George Trailhead

Longs Peak Trail

ROCKY MOUNTAIN NATIONAL PARK

Eugenia mine

Inn Brook

7

Battle Mountain

Larkspur Creek

Granite Pass

Jim's Grove

Alpine Brook

Storm Peak 13,326 ft.

Mount Lady Washington

Longs Peak Trail

Mills Moraine

N

13,281 ft.

Columbine Falls

Roaring Fork

Peacock Pool

0   1   2

Miles

Chasm Lake

Mills Glacier

Longs Peak 14,255 ft.

11,417 ft.

★

Mount Meeker 13,911 ft.

Begin on the trail south of the ranger station, hiking past stands of lodgepole and aspen and going left at the junction with the trail to Eugenia mine. Hike south toward Alpine Brook, then switchback and hike west, gaining elevation as you follow the south-facing slope of Pine Ridge. The trail crosses Larkspur Creek and Alpine Brook where they merge near the Goblins Forest (look for some limber pine in the forest). Switchback and cross a bridge over Alpine Brook.

At the north end of the next switchback, just at timberline and back across Larkspur Creek, is Jim's Grove, the place where the notorious mountain man, Rocky Mountain Jim, and the Victorian lady, Isabella Bird, made camp before their climb to the summit of Longs Peak in 1874. You can read about their adventure in *A Lady's Life in the Rocky Mountains*.

CHASM LAKE

TRAIL FORK TO CHASM LAKE

LARKSPUR CREEK

COLUMBINE FALLS

JIM'S GROVE

EUGENIA MINE TRAIL

TRAILHEAD

12000
11500
11000
10500
10000
9500
9000
FT.

MILES 1   2   3   4   5

Stay on the main trail and hike south and then southwest, following cairns along the Mills Moraine, which is named for Enos Mills, a well-known naturalist and mountaineer (there is also a glacier named for him at the head of the valley, above Chasm Lake). You may want to stop by the Estes Park museum to learn more about him—and others. Longs Peak is a mountain rich with the history of many who have climbed it and some who have failed.

At about 3.2 miles, you'll arrive at the base of Mount Lady Washington (13,281 feet) and come to a fork in the trail. Rest a moment and take in the view: The little lake at the head of the Roaring Fork drainage is Peacock Pool, so named because it looks like the "eye" in a peacock's tail. Above it cascades Columbine Falls with abundant columbine growing around it. You can see a bit of the plains and Estes Cone as you look eastward. Go straight (southwest) and downhill next to a canyon wall. Be careful if there is snow along the next stretch. Hike the slope above the falls, then follow the path up behind the stone patrol hut that belongs to the national park, and hike up the gully. Go left over tundra and rock, then right up the last stretch to the lake. Before you looms the East Face of Longs Peak, a famous and popular rock-climbing venue rising nearly 2,500 feet above Chasm Lake. If you have binoculars, you might be able to spot climbers on the face. Enjoy this spectacular setting, then return as you came.

Options: Take a side trip from the junction with the spur to Chasm Lake by going right (north), following the northeastern slope of Mount Lady Washington to Granite Pass, then walk back to the junction and head down to your car. If you do some planning and shuttle a car or arrange for someone to drop you off and pick you up, you could hike northwest on the North Longs Peak Trail from the junction at Granite Pass for 2.9 miles to the junction with the trail that follows Boulder Brook north to the Bierstadt Lake trailhead in 2.3 miles. Or you could pass the trail up Boulder Brook and continue northwest to the Glacier Gorge trailhead, which is about 3 miles from the junction at Boulder Brook.

Camping and services: A campsite for individuals is at the Goblins Forest. Groups can camp at the Battle Mountain site, which is near Alpine Brook as you start up the Mills Moraine. There is also a campground at the trailhead.

For more information: Rocky Mountain National Park.

13 Rogers Pass Lake

Highlights: Scenic stretch along the creek; vistas at timberline and lakes.

Location: Southwest of Nederland and Boulder in the proposed James Peak Wilderness Area.

Type of hike: Out-and-back day hike.

Total distance: 7.6 miles.

Difficulty: Moderate.

Elevation gain: 2,000 feet.

Best months: July–September.

Maps: USGS East Portal and Empire quads; Trails Illustrated Map 103; Roosevelt National Forest Map.

Finding the trailhead: From Golden drive north on Colorado Highway 93 to the junction with CO 72. From Boulder drive south to that junction. Go west on CO 72 until it meets CO 119 south to Rollinsville. Turn right (west) on Rollins Pass Road (Forest Road 149 and County Road 16) at Rollinsville and drive west 7.7 miles, following the signs to the Moffat railroad tunnel (east portal). Keep going west until you reach the trailhead.

Parking and trailhead facilities: Parking available; no facilities.

Key points:
- 1.0 Junction with Forest Lakes Trail
- 1.7 Junction with Crater Lakes Trail
- 2.4 Tributary from unnamed lake
- 2.8 Fork in trail going to Heart Lake and Rogers Pass Lake
- 3.8 Rogers Pass Lake

The hike: This hike begins at the East Portal of the Moffat Tunnel, where much human drama took place in the early years of the twentieth century when the tunnel was bored under James Peak. You will be hiking the South Boulder Creek Trail (Trail 900), which leads you along the pretty South Boulder Creek to Rogers Pass Lake.

Begin at the signs that mark the South Boulder Creek Trail, and hike along the north side of the creek by the same name. In 0.5 mile cross a tributary to South Boulder Creek, which tumbles down from Forest Lakes and Arapaho Lakes to the north. Another 0.5 mile brings you to a junction with the Forest Lakes Trail (Trail 809). Keep traveling west at this fork, cross another tributary, which comes down from Crater Lakes, and in 0.7 mile continue left at the junction with the trail to these lakes. Continue along South Boulder Creek as it

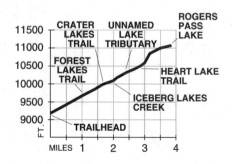

Rogers Pass Lake

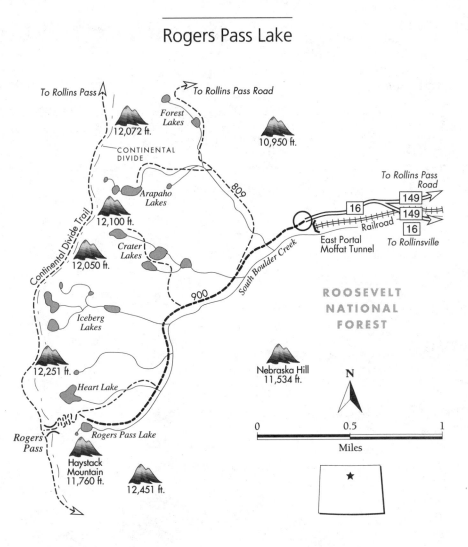

bends southwest, you will cross a tributary coming down from Iceberg Lakes to the west, and another tributary, the headwaters of which are a small, unnamed lake.

The climb will become quite steep and rocky, then moderate. At about 2.8 miles the trail forks just before you cross the last tributary you'll encounter. The right forks follows this tributary to Heart Lake. Stay left (south) and follow South Boulder Creek all the way to its headwaters and, in 1 mile, to Rogers Pass Lake.

From the lake are good views of the Indian Peaks to the north. Rogers Pass is to the west, you can see the trail winding up to the Continental Divide. Enjoy the setting of Rogers Pass Lake, make a side trip to the pass or to Heart Lake, then return as you came.

Options: Climb to the top of Rogers Pass with an additional round-trip hike of about 2 miles, gaining another 800 feet in elevation. From the pass are views of Winter Park Ski Area and northwest into Middle Park. You can also make a short climb of 0.5 mile northwest to Heart Lake, and return to the South Boulder Creek Trail by way of the Heart Lake Trail.

Camping and services: If you backpack, please camp at least 200 feet from any of the lakes and streams. Some of the best sites are in the trees a short distance from either Rogers Pass Lake or Heart Lake.

For more information: Roosevelt National Forest, Boulder Ranger District.

—Ryan Starr and Cecilia Murret

14 Byers Peak

Highlights:	Summit reached fairly easily; spectacular views.
Location:	Southwest of Fraser in the Byers Peak Wilderness.
Type of hike:	Up-and-down day hike.
Total distance:	5 miles.
Difficulty:	Moderate.
Elevation gain (or loss):	2,200 feet.
Best months:	July–September.
Maps:	USGS Byers Peak quad; Trails Illustrated Map 103; Arapaho National Forest Map.

Byers Peak.

Byers Peak

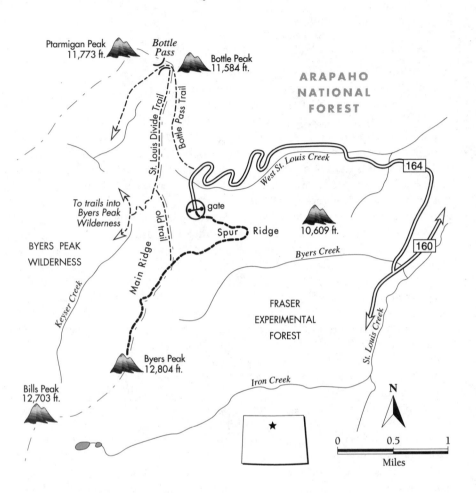

Finding the trailhead: At the light in the town of Fraser, go south on Church Park Road (County Road 50). After passing a railroad tunnel, go right on Fraser Parkway. Follow it to St. Louis Creek Road (County Road 73/ Forest Road 160), then go left (southwest) toward St. Louis Creek Campground. Byers Peak is on the left. Stay on the main road and follow signing. Go right on FR 164 at 7.2 miles past a water diversion structure. The road gets rough at 8 miles or so where you will come to a gate. Continue past this and switchback to the trailhead and turnaround at about 12 miles. Note: You'll pass the trail up West St. Louis Creek and the trail to Bottle Pass on your way to the Byers Peak Trailhead. You'll know you're at the Byers Peak Trailhead when you come to the end of the road.

Parking and trailhead facilities: Some parking; no facilities.

Key points:

- 0.6 Reach spur ridge and switchback to southwest
- 1.1 Steep climb to timberline
- 1.4 Junction with old Byers Peak Trail
- 2.5 Summit of Byers Peak at 12,804 feet

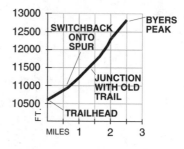

The hike: This day hike takes you to the summit of a local landmark named for the Denver newspaper publisher and mountaineer, William Byers. At 12,804 feet, Byers Peak is the high point of the Vasquez Mountains, standing out alone on a spur of this little-known range. It is visible from much of Middle Park. This is a good first summit for a family—not too long and not too steep, although you do gain 2,200 feet in elevation. You will be rewarded with spectacular views of Middle Park and the surrounding mountains, and that "tundra experience." We hiked the trail in July and there was still a lot of snow, so wear good hiking boots.

The first part of this hike from the trailhead to timberline is a fairly uneventful walk through spruce-fir and lodgepole pine forest up a spur ridge to timberline; only the very last part of the climb to timberline is steep. When the trail levels out at timberline, you will encounter the old Byers Peak Trail on your right, which connects along the ridge north to Bottle Peak. On some maps, this is still the trail shown for climbing Byers Peak.

From timberline follow the main ridge of the mountain southwest to the summit. Although the trail is fairly steep in a few places, the steady progress you make and the spectacular views keep these steep sections less noticeable. Keep an eye out for ptarmigan. We saw some in the same dress the upper mountain wore that day in early July: brown and white.

From the top, you can see as far as the Gore Range to the southwest and the mountains around Loveland Pass (Mounts Sniktau, Grays, and Torreys; McLellan Mountain, and others) to the southeast. Directly below you to the west and southwest is the Byers Peak Wilderness. There are also views of most of Middle Park, with Parkview Mountain marking the north end, and the imposing barrier of the Continental Divide forming the east side from Rocky Mountain National Park south to Winter Park. Enjoy the summit, then go down the way you came.

Options: Extend this day hike with a return loop via Bottle Peak by following the old Byers Peak Trail north to the St. Louis Divide Trail and Bottle Peak, and then down the Bottle Pass Trail to the road at a point 0.5 mile north of the Byers Peak Trailhead.

Camping and services: Because this is a popular trail, camping is not recommended either along the trail or at the trailhead. More secluded sites are available along the old Byers Peak Trail to the north, and there are a number of backpacking opportunities in the Byers Peak Wilderness to the west.

For more information: Arapaho National Forest, Sulphur Ranger District.

15 Elliott Ridge

Highlights:	Beautiful views; long stroll across tundra; chance to see wildlife and part of the Eagles Nest Wilderness.
Location:	In the Eagles Nest Wilderness near Green Mountain Reservoir between Kremmling and Silverthorne.
Type of hike:	Out-and-back day hike.
Total distance:	6.1 miles one way; 12.2 miles round trip.
Difficulty:	Moderate.
Best months:	July–September.
Elevation gain (or loss):	1,270 feet (250 feet).
Maps:	USGS Mount Powell and Ute Peak quads; Trails Illustrated Map 107.

Special considerations: Eagles Nest Wilderness may institute a permit system. Check with the Dillon Ranger District about this, and regarding road and snow conditions.

Finding the trailhead: Take Colorado Highway 9 north from Silverthorne or south from Kremmling to Spring Creek Road (County Road 10), located about 2.5 miles north of Green Mountain Reservoir between mile markers 128 and 129. Take Spring Creek Road west, then turn right for forest access at the gate to the subdivision. Go straight at the Bureau of Land Management sign (6.3 miles) and continue toward the national forest. At 7.4 miles take the right fork, which is signed for Sheephorn Drive and Mahan Lake. You'll pass lots of little timber roads, but stay on the main track. At 10.4 miles is another fork; stay left and follow the sign for Mahan Lake. In

Elliott Ridge.

Elliott Ridge

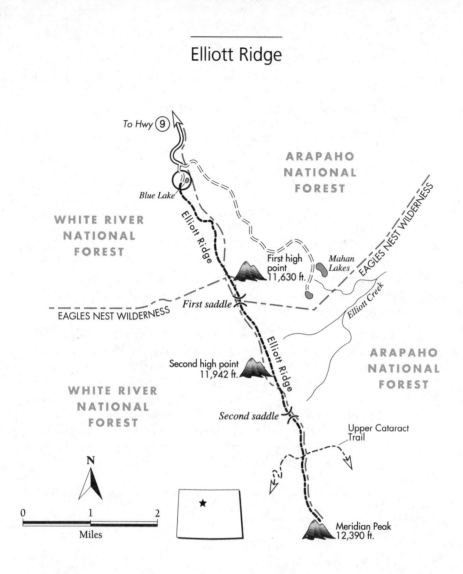

To Hwy ⑨

ARAPAHO
NATIONAL
FOREST

Blue Lake

WHITE RIVER
NATIONAL
FOREST

Elliott Ridge

First high
point
11,630 ft.

*Mahan
Lakes*

EAGLES NEST WILDERNESS

First saddle

Elliott Creek

EAGLES NEST WILDERNESS

Second high point
11,942 ft.

ARAPAHO
NATIONAL
FOREST

Elliott Ridge

WHITE RIVER
NATIONAL
FOREST

Second saddle

Upper Cataract
Trail

N

0   1   2
Miles

★

Meridian Peak
12,390 ft.

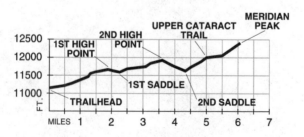

MERIDIAN
PEAK

UPPER CATARACT
TRAIL

2ND HIGH
POINT

1ST HIGH
POINT

12500
12000
11500
11000

1ST SADDLE

FT.

TRAILHEAD

2ND SADDLE

MILES 1   2   3   4   5   6   7

1.6 miles bear right at the fork. In another mile park at the fork, or bear right and continue another 0.2 mile to park at the trailhead near a small pond.

Parking and trailhead facilities: Park off the jeep road; no facilities.

Key points:
    1.9   First high point; good destination for a short hike
    3.7   Second high point
    4.9   Upper Cataract Trail
    6.1   Meridian Peak (12,390 feet)

The hike: Elliott Ridge provides a beautiful introduction to hiking above timberline, minus the long uphill hike normally required to get there. On this hike you'll have expansive views and a chance to spot mountain goats.

Note: Avoid hiking this trail too early in the year in order to prevent erosion in muddy trail sections. Also, you may want to plan to hike early in the day because you will be exposed to lightning and wind on this high ridge. If skies look threatening at any point, descend from the ridge and wait out the storm before returning to the ridge to resume your hike.

Begin your hike by the USDA Forest Service sign. Take note of the wilderness area regulations. Dogs must be leashed.

For about the first mile, follow a jeep road along the west side of Elliott Ridge as you climb slowly to timberline. Below you to the west is the basin of Sheephorn Creek, bounded on the southwest by Piney Ridge. Beyond this to the west and northwest are the high mesas of the White River Plateau and the Flat Tops Wilderness. Far to the south, beyond the drainages of the Piney and Eagle Rivers, is Mount of the Holy Cross and Mount Jackson, which mark the north end of the Sawatch Range. More distant to the southwest are the peaks of the Elk Mountains, including Mount Sopris at the northeast end of that range.

At 0.9 mile the trail bends east and crosses a wet meadow where it becomes faint in places and is marked by posts. Beyond the meadow, you will slowly climb along the west ridge through the alpine tundra. Near the beginning of this verdant stretch of tundra, and later along the ridge, we spotted a herd of mountain goats. Keep your eyes peeled and your dogs leashed, and get your telephoto prepared. Keep your distance, however, because these creatures are sensitive to human intrusion.

After climbing steadily for about 1.9 miles, you finally crest the ridge at the first high point. For a shorter hike, or if the weather is threatening, this is a good turnaround point. From this vantage point you can see many of the mountains of northern Colorado. Far to the north and northeast are the Rabbit Ears Range and some of the peaks of the northern Front Range, including Longs Peak. To the southeast are the spectacular cliffs of Eagles Nest (13,091 feet) and beyond it to the south is Mount Powell, which at 13,534 feet is the highest point in the Gore Range.

Although Elliott Ridge is an unimposing landmark compared with these many surrounding mountains, its long ridge has served as a perfect snow fence to the prevailing westerly winds, which deposit snow on the leeward (east) side of the ridge. As a result, during the last ice age, the land below you to the east was highly glaciated, forming Mahan Lake and many other glacial landforms. Even now, the long snowfields that form on this east side will remain through the summer, outlasting many of the snow patches on the higher peaks.

From this first high point, hike along as far as you wish toward Meridian Peak, enjoying the beauty of the tundra and the great views, then return as you came.

At 3.7 miles is another high point that descends to a saddle. Beyond the saddle, the Upper Cataract Trail is reached at 4.9 miles. From here the Elliott Ridge Trail continues to the summit of Meridian Peak at 6.1 miles (12,390 feet). Hiking beyond this peak is not recommended because the ridge narrows in places to a knife-edged crest forming the headwaters of Cataract Creek.

Options: You can get a taste of walking on the tundra by walking just a short way and then returning as you came.

Camping: Camping is not recommended on Elliott Ridge because of exposure, but you can drop down into the trees on either side of the ridge at some of the less steep locations.

For more information: Arapaho National Forest, Dillon Ranger District.

16 Rock Creek

Highlights:	Wetlands; beautiful stream; canyon.
Location:	Southwest of Kremmling near Gore Pass in the Gore Range.
Type of hike:	Out-and-back day hike.
Total distance:	4.8 miles.
Difficulty:	Moderate.
Elevation gain:	Minimal.
Best months:	June–September.
Maps:	USGS Lynx Pass quad; Trails Illustrated Map 119; Routt National Forest Map.

Finding the trailhead: Take Colorado Highway 134 west about 18 miles from the junction with U.S. Highway 40 north of Kremmling or about 9 miles east from the junction just south of Toponas. Turn south on Forest Road 206 at the sign for Rock Creek, then go south about 1 mile and bear right at the fork and cattle guard onto Forest Road 225. In another 0.8 mile is an outhouse and parking area just before the road climbs up to the west of Rock Creek.

Parking and trailhead facilities: Parking and outhouse.

Key points:
- 0.8   Stream gauging station
- 1.3   Trail bends around small tributary
- 2.0   Enter canyon; trail disappears
- 2.3   First narrows

The hike: This hike follows beautiful Rock Creek, which meanders through a lush landscape of wet meadow and willows, then drops into a rugged, mid-elevation canyon. This is an easy hike with minimal elevation change for the first 2 miles—perfect for kids to explore the creek and wetlands or maybe fish. About 0.3 mile into the canyon, however, both the creek and the trail turn into a rugged adventure.

Begin your hike by following the jeep road that forks to the left (downstream) as the main road climbs a hill. The jeep road quickly turns into a trail, which follows the west side of the valley. It's a good trail down as far as the U.S. Geological Survey stream gauging station at 0.8 mile. This gauging station is part of a network of stream gauges located throughout the mountains that monitor stream flows for scientific research and water supply forecasting.

After the gauging station the trail is less traveled but still easy to follow. Continue along the west edge of the meadows. After 1.3 miles the trail swings briefly up into a side drainage to avoid a wet area and thick willows.

Around the next bend the valley narrows and turns into a canyon. Notice how the stream channel and valley change from a meandering stream bordered by wetlands to a classic rocky stream that steepens in the canyon.

Rock Creek.

Rock Creek

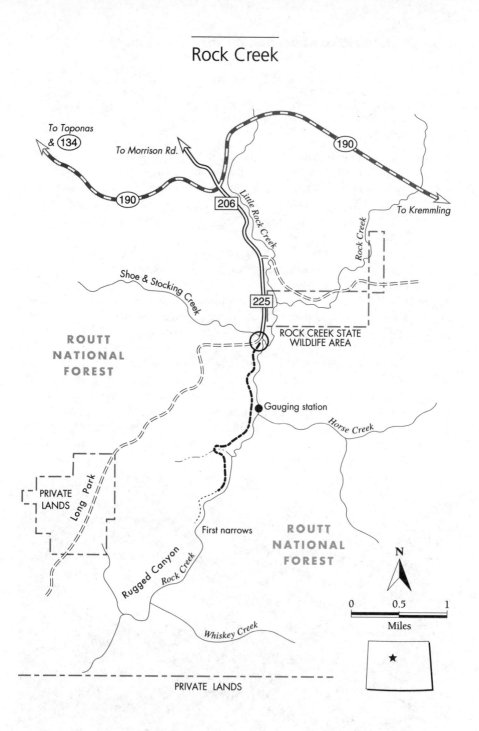

To Toponas & 134

To Morrison Rd.

190

190

To Kremmling

206

Little Rock Creek

Rock Creek

225

Shoe & Stocking Creek

ROCK CREEK STATE
WILDLIFE AREA

ROUTT
NATIONAL
FOREST

Gauging station

Horse Creek

PRIVATE
LANDS

Long Park

First narrows

ROUTT
NATIONAL
FOREST

Rugged Canyon

Rock Creek

N

Whiskey Creek

0   0.5   1

Miles

PRIVATE LANDS

The trail becomes fainter and more rugged and you begin to encounter rock talus. The trail eventually disappears, apparently for good reason, because at about 2.3 miles is the first of several narrows where the cliffs come down to the stream on both sides. It is not recommended to continue past this point unless you are prepared to cross the stream and do some rock scrambling to get around obstacles. Return as you came.

Options: The route beyond the first narrows is difficult and strenuous, best attempted during lower flows in late summer or fall. With a great deal of effort and slow going, you can continue another 2 miles to a point below Whiskey Creek before reaching the national forest boundary and private land. To whatever extent you attempt bushwhacking this lower canyon, keep in mind how long it takes and that you must get back out.

Camping and services: None.

For more information: Routt National Forest, Yampa Ranger District.

17 Picture Lake

Highlights:	Beautiful wildflowers and lake; introduction to the Castle Peak Wilderness Study Area.
Location:	North of Eagle.
Type of hike:	Bushwhack.
Total distance:	3.7 miles.
Difficulty:	Moderate.
Elevation gain:	800 feet.
Best months:	July–September.
Maps:	USGS Castle Peak quad; Trails Illustrated Map 120.

Special considerations: Check with the Bureau of Land Management on road conditions in the spring or after wet weather.

Finding the trailhead: From Interstate 70, go either east from Eagle or west from Vail to Exit 157 at Wolcott. Go north on Colorado Highway 131 to U.S. Highway 6, then turn left (west) and then right (north) on CO 131 at Wolcott and follow it for 3 miles; turn left (west) on County Road 54. At 2.2 miles turn right off the county road onto a dirt road. If you come to a sign that reads "Public Access Dead End," you went too far on the county road. You need a four-wheel-drive or high-clearance vehicle to reach the trailhead as described from here. However, in dry conditions, you should be able to get most of the way to the wilderness area boundary with a two-wheel-drive vehicle. At 4.3 miles from the county road the road forks and becomes much rougher as it climbs a steep slope. You can probably make it to this point with a two-wheel-drive vehicle. In four-wheel drive, go uphill 2 miles to a saddle called Coberly Gap. At the gap go left on another jeep road marked 8512. This road climbs and follows an open ridge for another mile. Park just below where the road reenters the aspen forest and meets a fence where it turns north.

Parking and trailhead facilities: None.

Key points:
- 0.3 Meadow and short climb
- 0.5 Pond below Picture Lake
- 0.7 Picture Lake
- 1.2 Switchback through meadows to ridge
- 1.7 Saddle on ridge
- 2.2 High point
- 3.0 Back to Picture Lake
- 3.7 Back to trailhead

The hike: When we hiked this in 1997 there were no formal trails within the Castle Peaks Wilderness Study Area. Although the Bureau of Land Management may have plans to construct a few trails through the area, take a topographic map and be prepared to find your own route.

At the beginning of this hike take a primitive trail, heading west at a gate through the fence. From the gate the trail continues to the top of the meadows along the ridge and then levels a short distance after it enters forest. It then bears northwest and in and out of forest and meadow. When you come to a steep meadow area, climb to the top of the hillside and then turn north, keeping the drop-off to your right and forest to your left. You will emerge into a large meadow with a small pond. Skirt the pond to the south and then

Picture Lake.

Picture Lake

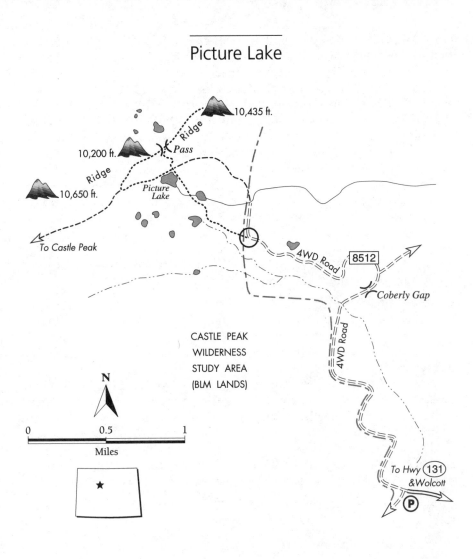

10,435 ft.

10,200 ft.

Ridge

Pass

Ridge

10,650 ft.

Picture Lake

To Castle Peak

4WD Road

8512

Coberly Gap

CASTLE PEAK
WILDERNESS
STUDY AREA
(BLM LANDS)

4WD Road

N

0   0.5   1

Miles

To Hwy (131)
&Wolcott

(P)

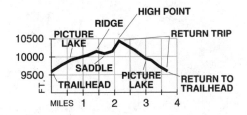

HIGH POINT

RIDGE

PICTURE
LAKE

RETURN TRIP

10500

10000

SADDLE

PICTURE
LAKE

9500

FT.

TRAILHEAD

RETURN TO
TRAILHEAD

MILES 1   2   3   4

cross the small creek. When we hiked this area in July the wildflowers were so thick we could have used a machete on our bushwhack. Picture Lake is 0.2 mile across the open meadows to the northwest. Picture Lake and many of the ponds in this area were created by landslides. In fact, the entire east side of Castle Peak has been formed this way.

From the lake we encountered a trail at the west edge, which led in the direction of Castle Peak. We followed this trail 0.5 mile and climbed the ridge to the north. We then turned back along the ridgetop and followed the ridge to a saddle where a trail crosses. From this saddle you can easily climb the triangular peak to the northeast for views of the entire area in all directions. From its vantage point—on the divide between the Colorado and the Eagle Rivers—you can see the Colorado River drainage to the north, and the Flat Tops to the northwest. To the southwest are spectacular views of the Holy Cross Wilderness.

After enjoying the views, return to the saddle where there's a trail that drops down to Picture Lake. Return as you came.

Options: An alternative route to Picture Lake is to go beyond the trailhead, following the jeep road north to its end and look for a trail that climbs west. Or use this as a different route back to your car, picking it up on the left as you descend from the saddle and triangular peak north of Picture Lake, and just before reaching the lake.

You can extend this hike into a backpack or longer day hike in many directions, including a climb of Castle Peak. There are numerous beautiful meadows and small ponds scattered throughout this area. If you don't have a four-wheel-drive vehicle, you can hike in from the fork preceding the jeep road climb to Coberly Gap. There are also jeep tours from Vail that regularly drive to the trailhead on the ridge. You might be able to make arrangements to have them drop you off and pick you up.

Camping and services: Camp at least 200 feet from lakes and streams; no services.

For more information: Bureau of Land Management, Glenwood Springs Office.

18 Wall Lake

Highlights:	Spectacular setting; views; open meadows and plateau near timberline.
Location:	Near Trappers Lake near the center of the Flat Tops Wilderness.
Type of hike:	Out-and-back day hike or backpack.
Total distance:	8 miles.
Difficulty:	Moderate.
Elevation gain:	1,310 feet.
Best months:	July–September.
Maps:	USGS Big Marvine Peak and Trappers Lake quads; Trails Illustrated Map 122; White River National Forest Map.

Finding the trailhead: This trail begins near Trappers Lake, which is almost an equal distance from Meeker and Yampa. From Meeker, go east on Colorado Highway 13 almost 2 miles and turn east (right) on County Road 8. Follow CR 8 up the White River Valley about 39 miles, the last 10 miles of which are gravel road. Turn right (southeast) on Forest Road 205 at the signs for Trappers Lake. You can also reach this same junction by taking gravel roads west from Yampa about 41 miles over Dunckley and Ripple Creek Passes, a more rugged but very scenic route. From the road juction, follow FR 205 for 10 miles to the Trappers Lake Recreation Area. Continue past the Trappers Lake Lodge and turn right at the signs for the campgrounds and

Wall Lake in the Flat Tops Wilderness.

Wall Lake

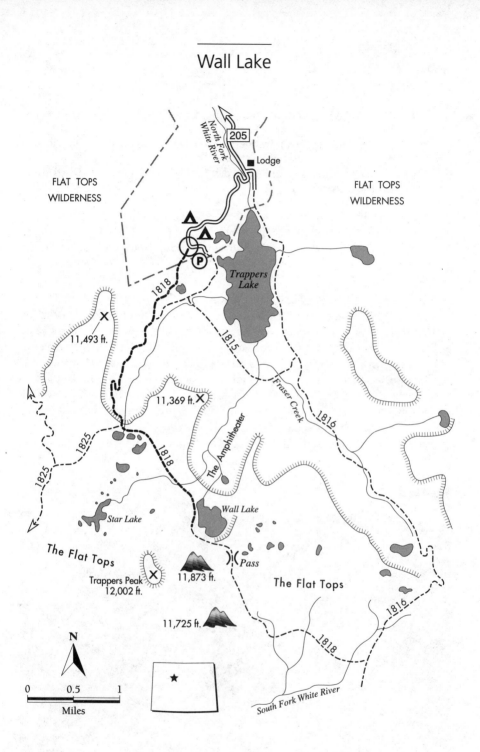

trailhead area. Wall Lake Trailhead and parking area is 1.7 miles past the lodge on the right after the campgrounds and just before Scots Bay.

Parking and trailhead facilities: Parking; facilities at nearby campgrounds or Trappers Lake Lodge.

Key points:
    0.5   Anderson Lake
    0.8   Junction with Trail 1815
    1.7   Switchbacks
    2.5   Top of rim and junction with Trail 1825
    4.0   Wall Lake

The hike: A trek up to Wall Lake takes you to the rim of the White River Plateau and then cross-country through meadows to this alpine lake named for a small cliff that forms the east edge.

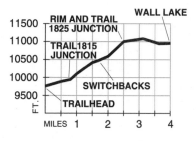

The hike starts in spruce-fir forest and climbs slowly into a valley near the west edge of Trappers Lake. At 0.5 mile you'll pass by small Anderson Lake, which you can see below you through the trees. The trail then opens into some meadows with views of the cliffs above. After a larger meadow and then another small meadow you come to the junction with Trail 1815 to the left. This junction is easy to miss on the way up. From here the trail climbs steadily again through forest until it emerges at the base of the cliffs where a trail traverses the rim at the head of the valley. There are a couple of short switchbacks: a long but only moderately steep climb. The views of Trappers Lake and the surrounding volcanic plateaus are rewarding through this stretch.

At the rim is a trail junction. Stay left, then cross the small creek at the head of the cliff; there are some small, shallow lakes here. Keep to the north (left) of the lakes as you climb over some rocks and head southeast across meadows. Some other game and hiking routes leading to Star Lake and other places can be mistaken for the main trail. Once you head off through the meadows on the top of the plateau, it is an easy 1.5 miles farther to Wall Lake.

The lake sits on top of the main plateau, not far from the rim of the much photographed Amphitheater, which drops down to Trappers Lake. Nearby Trappers Peak, southwest of Wall Lake, has some spectacularly colored volcanic rock. Because this is a popular destination, please camp well away from the lake.

Options: Once you are on top of the plateau there are numerous cross-country routes to any number of lakes. One option is to continue on the Wall Lake Trail through a saddle notch and connect with Trail 1816, the Trappers Lake Trail, which drops into Fraser Creek, then connect back to the trailhead by way of Trail 1815 near the south end of Trappers Lake.

Camping and services: Many camping possibilities exist on the plateau. Services are available at campgrounds and the Trappers Lake Lodge.

For more information: White River National Forest, Blanca Ranger District.

The Central Mountains

Central Mountains

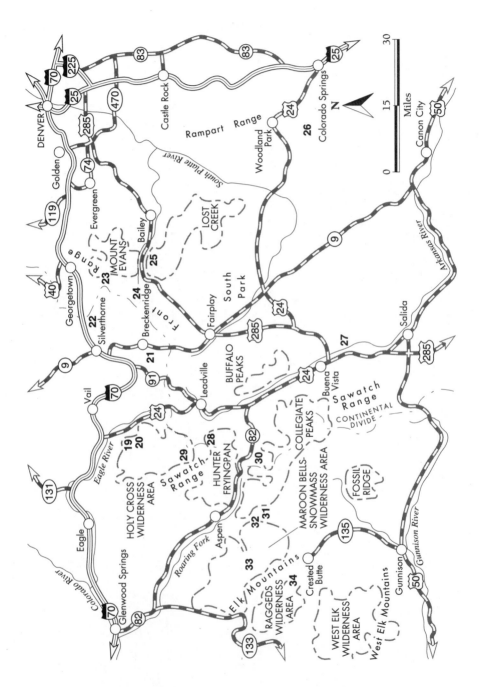

19 Cross Creek

Highlights: Pretty wildflowers and creek; views.
Location: South of Minturn in the Holy Cross Wilderness.
Type of hike: Out-and-back day hike.
Total distance: 4.4 miles.
Difficulty: Easy.
Elevation gain: 500 feet.
Best months: July–September.
Maps: USGS Minturn quad; Trails Illustrated Map 108; White River National Forest Map.

Special considerations: Heavily used trail. Hike on weekdays. Pets must be leashed.

Finding the trailhead: From the south end of Minturn, drive south on U.S. Highway 24 about 2 miles, and just past mile marker 143 turn right (west) on Tigiwon Road (Forest Road 707), which is signed. Travel through an area of old mine tailings being reclaimed, going 1.7 miles to the trailhead. (The road becomes kind of rough, but you can still make it in a passenger car.)

Parking and trailhead facilities: Two small parking lots are provided; no facilities.

Mount of the Holy Cross. W. H. JACKSON PHOTO. COURTESY USGS.

Cross Creek

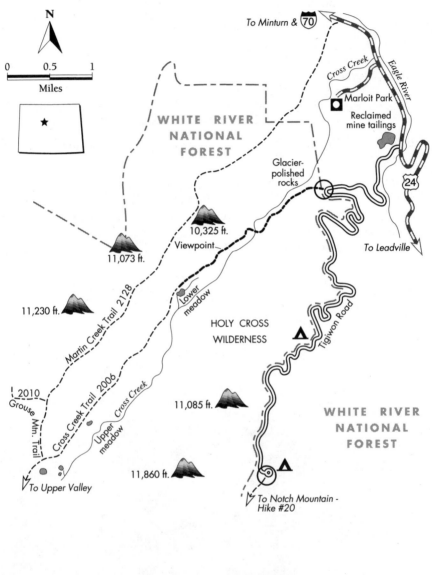

N

0   0.5   1
Miles

WHITE RIVER
NATIONAL
FOREST

To Minturn & 70

Cross Creek

Eagle River

Marloit Park

Reclaimed
mine tailings

24

Glacier-
polished
rocks

To Leadville

10,325 ft.
Viewpoint

11,073 ft.

11,230 ft.

Lower
meadow

Martin Creek Trail 2128

HOLY CROSS
WILDERNESS

Tigiwon Road

2010
Grouse Mtn. Trail

Cross Creek Trail 2006

Cross Creek

Upper
meadow

11,085 ft.

WHITE RIVER
NATIONAL
FOREST

To Upper Valley

11,860 ft.

To Notch Mountain -
Hike #20

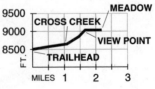

9500
9000
8500
FT.

MEADOW
CROSS CREEK
VIEW POINT
TRAILHEAD

MILES   1   2   3

Key points:
- 1.1 Bridge over Cross Creek
- 1.7 View of Mount of the Holy Cross from rocks
- 2.2 Lower meadow

The hike: This hike describes the beginning section of the Cross Creek Trail (Trail 2006), which follows the length of Cross Creek, one of the largest tributaries to the Eagle River. You will walk by an interesting geologic feature, down to a pretty creek, and on to see views and meadows.

Begin your hike at the northwest end of the parking lot on the west side of the road at the USDA Forest Service sign. Note the rules for the Holy Cross Wilderness. Right away you will be in an aspen grove, which is especially pretty when in its late-September gold. All along this trail, the understory of the groves and forest is dominated by thimbleberry, a plant with saucer-size leaves shaped like maple leaves.

The trail follows the base of a ridge, dropping down to Cross Creek. As you follow the ridge, look across the creek to the north and you will see a long stretch of smooth, hummocky rock; this is evidence of an enormous glacier that once moved down the valley carrying rocks in its load, which it dumped at the end of the valley in end moraines. The glacier polished the uphill side of rock as it moved along, then plucked chunks out of the downhill side, leaving the smooth hummocks of rock behind.

Walk on down to the creek at mile 1.1 and cross a bridge. The cascades here are especially spectacular during the snowmelt, which lasts well into summer due to the snowpack in the upper basins and tributaries of Cross Creek. Continue up the trail, climbing along some of the glacially polished rocks until at about 1.7 miles you can see Mount of the Holy Cross. Find a comfortable spot on a rock and enjoy the view. Although you can't see it from here, on the east side of the mountain is the shape of a cross defined in the rock by a permanent snowfield. If you want to see the cross, take the Notch Mountain hike (Hike 20).

Return as you came or continue another 0.5 mile to the lower meadows of Cross Creek, with beautiful wetlands and a gentle meandering section of the creek. Because this is a popular destination, please do not camp here, and avoid creating new trails. If you choose to backpack, it is recommended that you camp at points farther along the trail, and at least 200 feet from the stream or the trail.

Options: Make this into a backpacking trip, either as a longer out-and-back hike to the upper portions of the valley, or with a car shuttle to the destination of your choice. Some good intermediate destinations include upper meadows at 4.2 miles and Harvey Lake at 13 miles. At 10.5 miles are some spectacular cascades where the creek drops down across smooth rock, above the junction with West Cross Creek. The total length of the Cross Creek valley is about 15 miles, where you exit the valley at Fancy Pass. From there you can connect to Holy Cross City, reached via a jeep road (759) from FR 704 and the Homestake Road (703). Or continue east on Trail 2006 down

Fancy Creek, or go southeast on Trail 2003 along Missouri Creek—both eventually arrive at FR 704.

You can also hike the Cross Creek Trail to meet the Grouse Mountain Trail at about mile 5 and then hike northwest on Trail 2010. Then you have a few choices: go right in 0.7 mile and head northeast on Trail 2128 to Minturn, or go left (northwest) at this junction for another 2 miles, passing Grouse Mountain on your left, and connecting with Trail 2129 along West Grouse Creek. Hiking northeast will take you to US 24 north of Minturn. Hiking southwest will take you to Turquoise Lakes and Trail 2109 to Beaver Creek Resort.

Camping and services: Because this is a popular trail, it is best to camp in the upper portions of the valley and away from the trail and stream; no services.

For more information: White River National Forest, Holy Cross Ranger District.

20 Notch Mountain

Highlights:	View of the snow-filled cross on Mount of the Holy Cross; wildflowers.
Location:	Southwest of Minturn in the Holy Cross Wilderness.
Type of hike:	Out-and-back day hike.
Total distance:	10.6 miles.
Difficulty:	Strenuous.
Elevation gain:	2,800 feet.
Best months:	July–September.
Maps:	USGS Minturn and Mount of the Holy Cross quads; Trails Illustrated Map 109; White River National Forest Map.

Finding the trailhead: Drive south from the south end of Minturn on U.S. Highway 24 for about 2 miles. Turn right on Tigiwon Road (Forest Road 707), which is signed. Drive to the end of Tigiwon Road in 8.6 miles.

Parking and trailhead facilities: Parking available.

Key points:

1.5   Cross small creek
2.2   Trail junction
3.6   Overlook into steep gully
5.3   Notch Mountain shelter

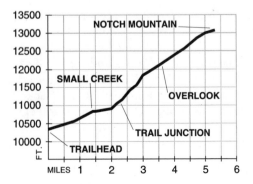

Notch Mountain

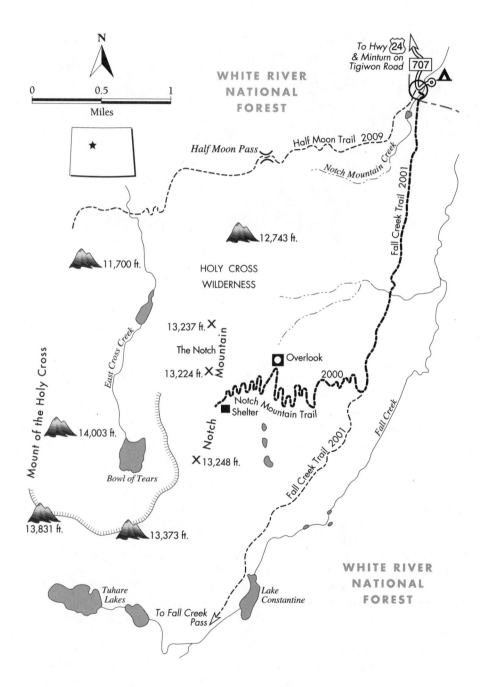

N

0   0.5   1
Miles

WHITE RIVER NATIONAL FOREST

To Hwy 24 & Minturn on Tigiwon Road

707

Half Moon Pass

Half Moon Trail 2009

Notch Mountain Creek

Fall Creek Trail 2001

12,743 ft.

11,700 ft.

HOLY CROSS WILDERNESS

East Cross Creek

13,237 ft.

The Notch

13,224 ft.

Notch Mountain

Overlook

2000

Notch Mountain Trail

Notch Mountain Shelter

Mount of the Holy Cross

14,003 ft.

Bowl of Tears

13,248 ft.

Fall Creek Trail 2001

Fall Creek

13,831 ft.

13,373 ft.

WHITE RIVER NATIONAL FOREST

Tuhare Lakes

To Fall Creek Pass

Lake Constantine

Shelter on Notch Mountain.

The hike: Henry Wadsworth Longfellow wrote:
> *"There is a mountain in the distant west,*
> *That, sun-defying, in its deep ravines,*
> *Displays a cross of snow upon its side...."*

This hike takes you up to the summit of Notch Mountain from where you will get a glimpse of Mount of the Holy Cross. You will be following a route many have followed before you.

Begin your hike at the south end of the parking area where there is a trailhead sign. Do not take the Half Moon Trail, which begins at the southwest end of the parking area and uphill. Immediately cross Notch Mountain Creek, then bear right on the Fall Creek Trail (Trail 2001).

The trail climbs gradually through spruce-fir and lodgepole pine forest and then begins to traverse along the ridge above Fall Creek. There are a few points where you'll cross steep, open areas and have views down into the meadows along the creek. At 1.5 miles cross a creek, which originates near the notch on Notch Mountain and plunges steeply into Fall Creek.

At 2.2 miles you gain a small bench where the trail splits—a good resting spot before beginning the steep climb to the summit. If you continue straight on the Fall Creek Trail, you'll reach Lake Constantine and Fall Creek Pass. Go right (west) and begin climbing through intermittent forest and meadows and over several small switchbacks. The trail first heads north and then swings west and climbs and climbs and climbs. After a climb through forest, you emerge into a broad bowl at timberline. Enjoy the beautiful wildflowers here.

At 3.6 miles is an overlook point at the edge of a steep gulch. To the west is a good view of the notch in Notch Mountain. Keep climbing the innumerable switchbacks, which can be tedious at times, but are ingenious in their design, giving you a moderate grade on which to climb. (It would be a good pastime for kids to count the number of switchbacks on this climb. It may be a record number!)

At 5.3 miles is a beautiful stone shelter, which was built in 1924 to give hikers and religious pilgrims a place out of the wind and cold. From the shelter look directly across the Bowl of Tears to the east face of Mount of the Holy Cross. Although slightly eroded, the cross is still visible and best viewed in July.

Options: Instead of climbing Notch Mountain continue on the Fall Creek Trail about 2 miles to Lake Constantine, or beyond to Fall Creek Pass where the trail drops down to FR 759 (four-wheel-drive vehicle needed) and the Homestake Road (FR 703) near Gold Creek Campground. Many people also use the Half Moon Trail to climb Mount of the Holy Cross from the north end of Holy Cross Ridge.

Camping and services: This is a popular trail, so please do not use the shelter for camping, except in an emergency. The best camping spots are below timberline near the beginning of the hike.

For more information: White River National Forest, Holy Cross Ranger District.

21 Crystal Lakes

Highlights:	Wildflowers and pretty creek; alpine lakes; views; mining history.
Location:	South of Breckenridge in the Ten Mile Range.
Type of hike:	Out-and-back day hike.
Total distance:	5.2 miles.
Difficulty:	Moderate.
Elevation gain:	1,800 feet.
Best months:	July–September.
Maps:	USGS Breckenridge quad; Trails Illustrated Map 109; Arapaho National Forest Map.

Special considerations: This trail can be heavily used. You may want to hike it on a weekday.

Finding the trailhead: From the tower at the south end of Breckenridge, take Colorado Highway 9 for 2.5 miles south to the south end of the lake on your left (east), which is Goose Pasture Tarn. At the same point on your right you'll see a sign for The Crown, a subdivision. Turn right on Spruce Creek Road (County Road 800) and follow it through the subdivision, keeping left at intersections and heading south. The Spruce Creek Trailhead is 1.2 miles from CO 9.

Crystal Lakes

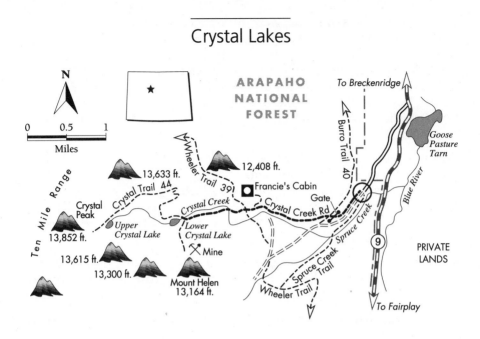

Parking and trailhead facilities: Parking is available; no facilities.

Key points:
- 0.6   Crystal Creek Road
- 1.7   Junction with Wheeler Trail
- 2.0   Creek crossing
- 2.6   Lower Crystal Lake

The hike: Begin your hike by walking 0.6 mile south on Spruce Creek Road to Crystal Creek Road (Forest Road 803), an old jeep road that goes west off Spruce Creek Road. There is a gate across Crystal Creek Road right away, which is meant to keep motorized vehicles out. You will climb through spruce-fir forest and soon cross the Burro Trail (Trail 40), which goes north into Breckenridge and south to Spruce Creek Road.

Burros were very important to the miners who worked this part of Colorado. Prunes was a burro who carried supplies to many mines in the area around Fairplay. So important was this animal to his last owner that when Prunes was dying, his owner asked to be buried with him—and he got his wish. The partnership of burros and miners is celebrated each year during the Get Your Ass Up the Pass Race from Fairplay to the top of Mosquito Pass.

A fairly steep climb takes you up and out of the forest at timberline then through a krummholz area with mostly Engelmann spruce. Along the creek are willows and lots of wildflowers. Continue climbing along the jeep road, crossing the Wheeler Trail, which goes north past Francie's Cabin. Forest Service signs warn you to keep dogs away from the cabin.

Once up on the tundra it is a short walk to Lower Crystal Lake, which lies at the base of Crystal Peak (13,852 feet). The remains of an old cabin sit at the point where the Crystal Creek Road ends and the Crystal Trail (Trail 44) begins. Enjoy the setting of Lower Crystal Lake. To the south is Mount Helen (13,164 feet) with the southbound fork of the road going to old mine tailings at the base of the mountain. Though gold was the most sought-after mineral from Fairplay to Breckenridge in the 1800s, some miners found other metals.

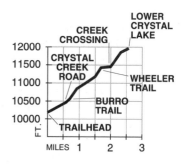

Al Look tells a story in his book, *Colorado Sidelights*, which surely could be a tale about the start of mining around Crystal Peak: "Silver also is where you find it. A gold miner in 1880 was getting a two-bit hair cut in Breckenridge, a placer gold camp, and the barber noticed that he had silver dust in his hair. The prospector visited the place where he slept the night before and a new silver camp was born." In the late 1800s, Crystal was a busy mining community from which much silver was taken. Abandoned mines can be dangerous, so don't go poking around looking for your own treasure.

When you're ready, hike on down the trail the way you came. On your return, you'll get a good look at the mountains to the east: Bald Mountain is on the left (north), Boreas Mountain is east of it; Mount Silverheels rises to your right (south), and Palmer Peak is south of it.

Lower Crystal Lake.

Options: Hike to Upper Crystal Lake in another 1.9 miles. Cross the creek and follow Crystal Trail northwest around the lake, then head east up the ridge of Peak 10. Switchback west to the shelf where Upper Crystal Lake rests. Then return as you came.

Another option is to make a loop by connecting with the Wheeler National Recreation Trail at timberline—after visiting Crystal Lakes—and heading northwest to Peak 10 Road. Hike that road northeast to its connection with Burro Trail, which is just before Peak 10 Road becomes paved. Then hike Burro Trail south to your car. You could also hike Wheeler Trail all the way to Interstate 70 near Copper Mountain, if you arrange for a car shuttle or for someone to pick you up.

Camping and services: The best camping is above timberline in the vicinity of Lower Crystal Lake. Please camp at least 200 feet away from the lake; no services.

For more information: Arapaho National Forest, Dillon Ranger District.

22 Porcupine Gulch

Highlights:	Pristine watershed, wildflowers.
Location:	East of Keystone in the Front Range south of the Eisenhower Tunnel.
Type of hike:	Out-and-back day hike.
Total distance:	3 miles.
Difficulty:	Moderate.
Elevation gain:	650 feet.
Best months:	July–September.
Maps:	USGS Loveland Pass quad; Trails Illustrated Map 104.

Finding the trailhead: Drive east from the junction of Swan Mountain Road (County Road 1) and U.S. Highway 6, which is east of Dillon, for about 8 miles to the stone drinking fountain on the north side of the highway (a spring feeds the fountain). Park in the small area provided at the fountain.

Parking and trailhead facilities: Parking and water are available; no facilities.

Key points:
- 0.8   Cross creek
- 1.5   Meadow at fork of creeks

The hike: This hike takes you into a lush, pristine watershed along Porcupine Creek to a pretty meadow. Hike for about 10 minutes and

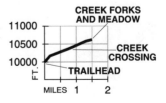

Porcupine Gulch

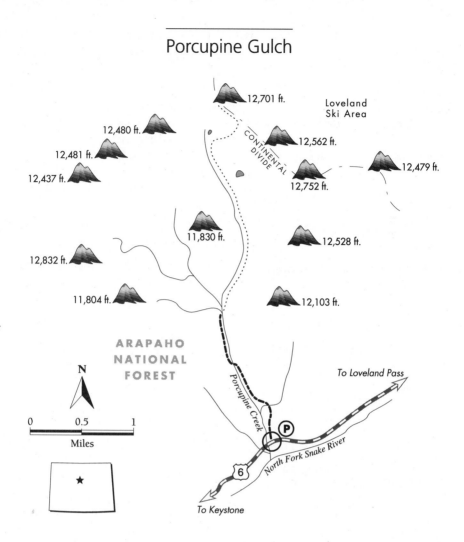

you're in a quiet world apart from the traffic between Summit County ski areas. Along the way are some nice wildflowers.

Begin by walking east along the north side of the highway for 0.2 mile. Cross a small creek that goes under the highway. The second and larger drainage is Porcupine Creek.

The trail begins as a jeep road with the first steep pitch being the most strenuous. It goes away from the creek, through lodgepole forest, narrows to a trail, and crosses a couple of small drainages before coming back to the beautiful tumbling creek. The trail becomes faint as it climbs again into spruce-fir forest. Cross a very wet little meadow and go toward the creek (you'll need to ford the creek), then follow the left bank uphill. Keep following it until you come to a small meadow where several drainages run together to form Porcupine Creek.

Enjoy the sound of the creek while you look at lichen and moss. Wild-flowers here include columbine, Indian paintbrush, larkspur, chiming bells, elephanthead, and tiny lilies growing near the trunks of evergreens. Return as you came.

Options: Bushwhack along the right (east) fork of the creek above treeline for a look at the surrounding ridges, peaks, and snowfields, which are the source of the creek. You can get up to the Continental Divide and a high point (12,701 feet) where you can look down on both ends of the Eisenhower Tunnel, Loveland Ski Area, and Porcupine Gulch. If you take the left fork from the meadow, again a bushwhack, you'll come to a broad basin with lots of wildflowers.

Camping and services: Camping is good in some of the meadows above where this hike ends. The lower meadows are pretty wet; no services.

For more information: Arapaho National Forest, Dillon Ranger District.

23 Square Top Lakes

Highlights: Alpine lakes; views; wildflowers; tundra.
Location: South of Georgetown at Guanella Pass in the Front Range.
Type of hike: Out-and-back day hike.
Total distance: 5.4 miles.
Difficulty: Moderate.
Elevation gain (loss): 700 feet (200 feet).
Best months: July–September.
Maps: USGS Mount Evans quad; Trails Illustrated Map 104; Pike National Forest Map.

Finding the trailhead: Drive south from Georgetown (or north from Grant) on Colorado Highway 62 (Forest Road 118) to Guanella Pass. Park here.

Parking and trailhead facilities: There are two parking lots on the east side of the highway and parking along the road on the west side. No facilities.

Key points:
   2.0   Lower Lake
   2.7   Upper Lake

The hike: A hike to Square Top Lakes by way of the South Park Trail (Trail 600) begins with views and wildflowers, and culminates at a peaceful setting in the crook of the arm of Square Top Mountain. It is a good introductory hike to an alpine lake.

Square Top Lakes

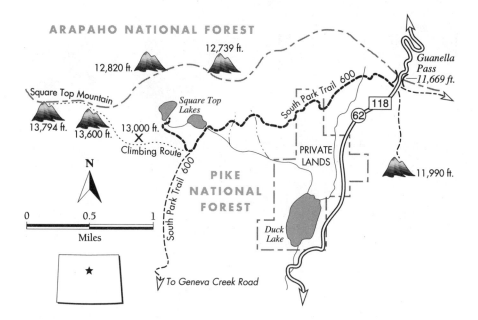

Begin on the west side of the road by following an old jeep road, which turns into a trail. Cross the broad saddle of Guanella Pass and drop down to a little creek, which drains down to Duck Lake.

Traverse a slope with alternating willows and meadows, then begin a series of short climbs to benches, each of which you think may hold the lake, but doesn't. After stream crossings, you finally come to the lower lake—a good shorter destination.

To reach the upper lake, cross below the outlet from the lower lake and climb the jeep road to a saddle to the south. Then look for the trail going back to the northwest to the bench with Upper Square Top Lake.

After enjoying the upper lake, return as you came. While descending be sure to notice the great views across Guanella Pass of Mount Bierstadt and the Sawtooth, a ridge connecting to Mount Evans.

Options: Many use this trail to climb Square Top Mountain (13,794 feet), so named because of its flat ridge when viewed from the south. The easiest route is to follow the ridge from the saddle on the trail between the two lakes. Go west and northwest to the summit, which is at the west edge of the mountain.

Another option is to continue on the South Park Trail to Geneva Creek Road.

Crossing the tundra below Square Top Lakes.

Camping and services: You may camp at Upper Square Top Lake, but camp at least 200 feet away from the lake in a secluded spot; no services.

For more information: Pike National Forest, South Platte Ranger District.

24 Gibson Lake

Highlights: Rugged terrain; views; alpine lake.
Location: West of Grant in the Front Range.
Type of hike: Out-and-back day hike.
Total distance: 4.8 miles.
Difficulty: Moderate.
Elevation gain: 1,550 feet.
Best months: July–September.
Maps: USGS Jefferson quad; Pike National Forest Map.

Special considerations: Take a high-clearance or four-wheel-drive vehicle to the trailhead if you can. If you take a passenger car, add about 3 miles total to your hike as the last mile and a half require four-wheel-drive.

Finding the trailhead: Take U.S. Highway 285 for 2.9 miles west of Grant to Hall Valley Road (Forest Road 120, Park County Road 60). Take this road up the main valley to the west. After about 3 miles keep right at the fork and follow the signs to Hall Valley Campground; go another 1.8 miles to Handcart

Gibson Lake

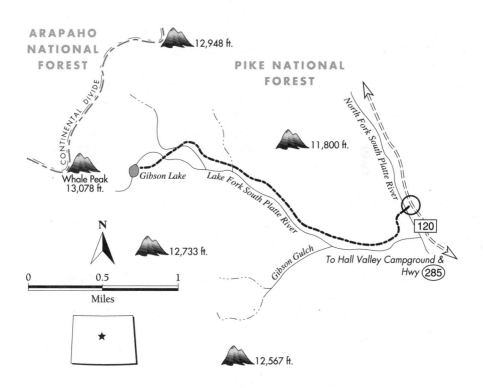

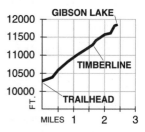

Campground. At the fork just beyond the campground bear left and travel another 0.3 mile to Hall Valley Campground. The last 1.5 miles to the trailhead are very rough—use a high-clearance or four-wheel-drive vehicle. You will come to the Gibson Lake Trailhead, which is on the left, at mile 6.6.

Parking & trailhead facilities: There is a small parking area; no facilities.

Key points:
- 1.6 Timberline
- 2.4 Gibson Lake

The hike: This adventure takes you to an alpine lake at the base of Whale Peak. Along the way you'll see evidence of glacial activity and enjoy vistas and wildflowers.

Begin by going southwest of the parking lot, following the USDA Forest Service signs. You'll go through willows and cross a bridge over the North

Fork of the South Platte, then follow the right (north) bank of the Lake Fork, hiking northwest. The trail climbs steadily through spruce-fir forest to timberline at 1.6 miles. Along the way it is very rocky in places. The Forest Service says there is a trail junction along this reach, with the right fork an unmarked trail going to the Continental Divide (we did not notice it when we hiked it in 1998). Continue following the Lake Fork northwest to stay on the trail to Gibson Lake.

Above timberline lie big boulders—evidence of glacial activity—and a Krummholz area with Engelmann spruce. Wildflowers grow profusely here, especially in midsummer.

After crossing tributaries to the Lake Fork a few times, head southwest through willows and tundra up to Gibson Lake. At the south end of the lake waterfalls spill down from a small upper lake. Enjoy the setting, then return as you came.

Options: Climb Whale Peak from Gibson Lake by either of its flanking ridges. The climb is about another mile to the summit at 13,078 feet on the Continental Divide. Return to the lake and hike down along the Lake Fork as you came.

Camping and services: There are very few camping spots along this hike; no services.

For more information: Pike National Forest, South Platte Ranger District.

25 Ben Tyler Gulch

Highlights:	Views from pass; wildflowers; pretty stream; Lost Creek Wilderness. Great hike in autumn.
Location:	West of Bailey in the Platte River Mountains.
Type of hike:	Out-and-back day hike.
Total distance:	12.8 miles.
Difficulty:	Strenuous.
Elevation gain:	3,390 feet.
Best months:	June–October.
Maps:	USGS Shawnee and Mount Logan quads; Trails Illustrated Map 105; Pike National Forest Map.

Finding the trailhead: Drive west from Bailey on U.S. Highway 285 for about 6.5 miles. The trailhead is located on the south side of the highway.

Parking and trailhead facilities: Limited parking is available on both sides of the highway; no facilities.

Ben Tyler Gulch

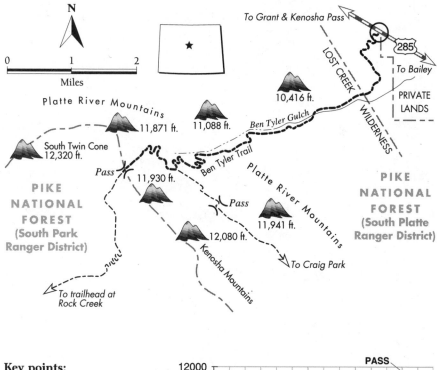

Key points:

0.3	End of switchbacks
1.4	Begin hiking Ben Tyler Gulch, wilderness boundary
2.1	Creek crossing
4.0	Start switchbacks at upper meadow
5.1	Junction with Craig Park Trail
5.7	Final switchbacks to timberline
6.4	Pass

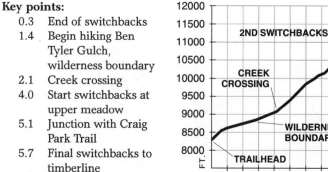

The hike: This long day hike takes you up Ben Tyler Gulch, which was named for a resident of the gulch who operated a lumber mill during the days when gold was king in Colorado. He transported his lumber—over a pass in the Kenosha Mountains and down the other side to Fairplay in South Park—for the miners to use. This trek goes up into the Lost Creek Wilderness and to the top of the pass Ben Tyler used, then returns.

Begin your hike at the east end of the parking area. The trail takes you up and up for the first 0.3 mile as you switchback many times. It then levels.

Time out for investigation.

Start up Ben Tyler Gulch, entering the Lost Creek Wilderness. You will come to a stream crossing at mile 2.1. When our kids were young, we enjoyed spending a little time by the stream and playing in the water. It was a good destination hike just to the stream. Notice the wild roses near the water.

From here the trail is a steady climb to the pass. Hike through some aspen groves to nice meadows with lots of wildflowers at mile 4, then start up the second series of switchbacks. At 5.1 miles is the junction with the Craig Park Trail (Trail 608); Craig Park is to the left (east). Keep right (west), continuing along the Ben Tyler Trail. At 5.7 miles start up the final set of switchbacks to timberline and the pass at 11,650 feet. The center of the pass—a broad, open saddle above timberline—is at 6.4 miles. From here are views down into the more rugged Rock Creek drainage and beyond into South Park. South Twin Cone Peak is immediately to the east.

Enjoy your accomplishment in reaching the pass, then return as you came.

Options: Shorten this hike for a family outing, if you like. A hike to the stream with a picnic is good, or for a fall hike, continue into the aspens beyond the stream crossing.

There are two other options for continuing on from the pass. Stay on the Ben Tyler Trail down into the Kenosha Mountains and to the Rock Creek Trailhead, about 4 miles farther, or go east on the Craig Park Trail to another saddle and into Craig Park, a beautiful, long, high mountain valley.

Camping and services: Some camping is available in the upper valley before the trail makes its steep climb from the meadows to the pass.

For more information: Pike National Forest, South Platte Ranger District.

26 The Crags

Highlights:	Rock formations; great views; geology. Good family hike.
Location:	Southeast of Divide on the northwest side of Pikes Peak.
Type of hike:	Out-and-back day hike.
Total distance:	4 miles.
Difficulty:	Easy.
Elevation gain:	710 feet.
Best months:	May–October.
Maps:	USGS Woodland Park and Pikes Peak quads; Trails Illustrated Map 137; Pike National Forest Map.

Special considerations: This hike receives heavy use. You might want to hike on a weekday.

The Crags

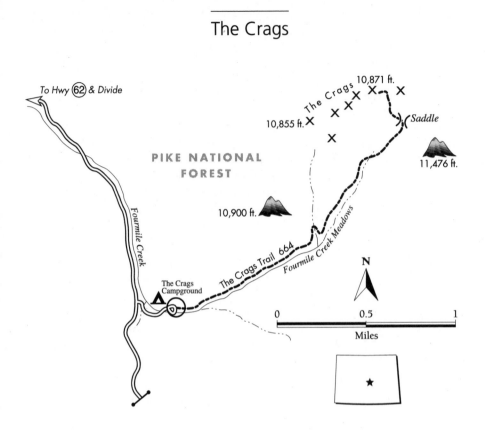

Finding the trailhead: From the town of Divide at the junction of U.S. Highway 24 and Colorado Highway 67, go south on CO 67 for 4.4 miles. You will pass Mueller State Park on the right (west) at mile 3.9. Turn left (east) on Teller County Road 62 and go 0.6 mile. Turn right at the Mennonite Camp and travel 2.6 miles to the Crags Campground.

Parking and trailhead facilities: Do not park in campground spots. If the parking area is full, go back to the road and park. Restroom facilities at the campground.

Key points:
    0.9   Cross small creek
    1.8   Saddle
    2.0   The Crags

The hike: This easy hike to the Crags, spectacular rock formations at the northwest end of Pikes Peak, offers great views of the rocks as well as distant landscapes. This is an excellent hike for families because of the interesting creek, meadows, and easy-to-reach destination.

Begin your hike up a little steep pitch for the first quarter mile. The trail then becomes very easy for the next mile as you follow along meadows by beautiful Fourmile Creek. Cross a small side creek at 0.4 mile and reenter the forest at about 1.5 miles for a short climb to a saddle. At the saddle the trail bends to the northwest along a rocky ridge to the top of the Crags—rounded domes and pinnacles formed of Pikes Peak granite.

From here you can see Wilkerson Pass to the west; to the east and southeast is the west flank of Pikes Peak. The first of Colorado's peaks above 14,000 feet to be named, this landmark was designated not for the first man to ascend to the summit, as you might expect. Zebulon Pike climbed a mountain in 1806, but it is believed the mountain was not Pikes Peak. Dr. Edwin James, a botanist with the Long expedition, was the first white man to climb the mountain, in 1820.

Below and to the northeast are the Catamount reservoirs. Far to the north is Devils Head, rising above surrounding foothills. This is an old Eocene erosion surface, leveled to a plain millions of years ago. The same ancient land surface forms much of the closer country to the north and west, but at lower elevation due to faulting. Within this area were the Florissant Fossil Beds lakes.

After enjoying the view, return as you came.

Camping and services: Camping at the trailhead; no services.

For more information: Pike National Forest, Pikes Peak Ranger District.

The Crags.

27 Little Cottonwood Creek

Highlights: Rugged rock formations; mid-elevation canyon; aspens; views; wildflowers.
Location: Southeast of Buena Vista in the Browns Canyon Wilderness Study Area.
Type of hike: Out-and-back day hike.
Total distance: 3.2 miles
Difficulty: Moderate.
Elevation gain (or loss): 350 feet.
Best months: May–October.
Maps: USGS Buena Vista East and Nathrop quads; Trails Illustrated Maps 129 and 130; San Isabel National Forest Map.

Special considerations: Daily use fee.

Finding the trailhead: From Buena Vista, go south on U.S. Highway 24 to the junction with US 285 at Johnson Village. From this intersection, continue south on US 285 about 3.5 miles and look for County Road 301 on the left, just past mile marker 145. Turn north on CR 301 for 0.6 mile, then right (east) on Chaffee County Road 300. Follow this road 2.6 miles to the Arkansas Headwaters Recreation Area site at Ruby Mountain. Stop at the pay station by the campground and rafting put-in and pay the daily use fee, then continue on up the road east, left past the entrance to a private campground,

One of the drops along Little Cottonwood Creek.

Little Cottonwood Creek

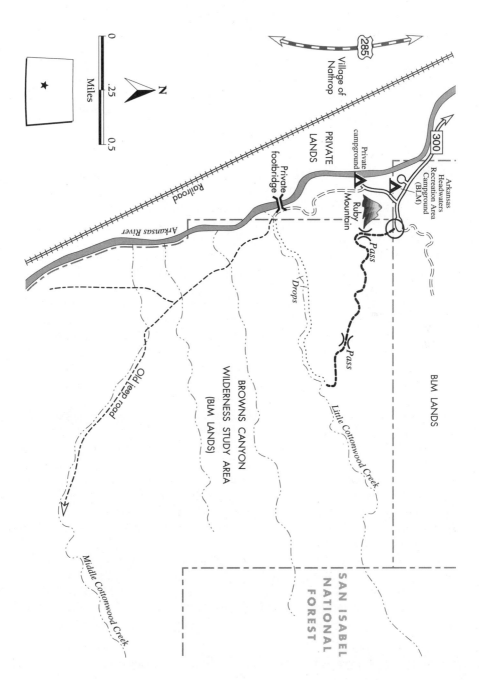

Village of Nathrop

285

300

N

Miles
0   .25   0.5

Railroad

Arkansas River

PRIVATE LANDS

Private footbridge

Private campground

Ruby Mountain

Arkansas Headwaters Recreation Area Campground (BLM)

Pass

Pass

Drops

Old Jeep road

BROWNS CANYON WILDERNESS STUDY AREA (BLM LANDS)

Little Cottonwood Creek

BLM LANDS

Middle Cottonwood Creek

SAN ISABEL NATIONAL FOREST

to the trailhead on the northeast side of Ruby Mountain. A fence and signs for the wilderness study area mark the trailhead.

Parking and trailhead facilities: Limited parking; facilities are at the nearby recreation site.

Key points:
- 0.2 First saddle at Ruby Mountain
- 0.8 Second saddle into Little Cottonwood drainage
- 1.1 Little Cottonwood Creek; head downstream
- 1.6 Drops in canyon

The hike: This short hike provides an introduction to the Browns Canyon Wilderness Study Area, a rugged area with a number of small canyons running down to the Arkansas River. The hike as described takes you to some spectacular drops in the canyon of Little Cottonwood Creek, but there are many other options for longer hikes, including backpacks.

Begin by heading south up an old jeep road to a saddle next to Ruby Mountain. Many people continue right at the saddle, along the old road that climbs some switchbacks to a mine on the east side of the mountain. Take the less distinct trail up the ridge to the left (east) and follow an old fenceline to a gate. Go through the gate and follow the trail down and then up through ponderosa pine and aspen stands to another saddle at 0.8 mile. Continue over this saddle into the Little Cottonwood Creek drainage. You will pass through some nice meadows and past two large, dead, ponderosa pines about 3 feet in diameter. At 1.1 miles, the trail drops down to Little Cottonwood Creek.

At this point you can go upstream or downstream along the creek bed—there is no formal trail. Upstream the canyon is less enclosed, and there are opportunities to climb some of the surrounding rocks for views of the area and of the Arkansas River valley and Collegiate Range to the west. Whichever route you take, keep in mind that there are large concentrations of mountain lions in this area. Do not hike alone or allow children to run ahead of you or tag behind. Avoid hiking at dawn, dusk, or after dark when lions are most active. The many deer bones you will find are evidence of the mountain lion's favorite food.

For this short hike, however, we recommend going downstream instead, where the canyon is more rugged. Follow the creek bed and primitive trail downstream about half a mile until you come to two rugged drops in the canyon with cliffs and large boulders. With a little effort, you can find faint trails leading around these obstacles. After enjoying the canyon, return as you came.

Options: Continue on down the canyon of Little Cottonwood Creek almost to its confluence with the Arkansas River. You can follow an old jeep road south across an open bench to explore other side canyons, including the larger canyon of Middle Cottonwood Creek, which the jeep road follows.

Please note that you immediately enter private land if you take the jeep road north from Little Cottonwood Creek. This route and the footbridge across the Arkansas River are not public access. However, at the time of our visit in 1997, a daily use fee at the private campground allowed access via this route, which provides an easy loop back to your car. Check with the BLM or the signs at the private campground entrance regarding the status of this land before you hike.

Camping and services: Camping near the trailhead in the BLM and private campgrounds; no services.

For more information: Bureau of Land Management, Arkansas Headwaters Office.

---

28 Native Lake

Highlights:	Alpine lake; views of Mount Massive.
Location:	West of Leadville in the Mount Massive Wilderness.
Type of hike:	Backpack or day hike.
Total distance:	6 miles.
Difficulty:	Moderate.
Elevation gain (or loss):	1,100 feet (650 feet).
Best months:	July–September.
Maps:	USGS Mount Massive quad; Trails Illustrated, 127; San Isabel National Forest Map.

Special considerations: Fishing restrictions to protect native trout.

Finding the trailhead: From Leadville, go west on the Turquoise Lake Road (County Road 4) to Turquoise Lake. Cross the dam and continue along the south side of Turquoise Lake and bear left at the fork about 3 miles past the dam. Continue on about 3.4 miles and look for the Native Lake trailhead on the left (south) side of the road just before a big bend and the Busk-Ivanhoe Tunnel.

Parking and trailhead facilities: Parking. No facilities.

Key points:
- 1.6   Top of pass
- 3.0   Native Lake

The hike: This hike goes up and over a steep pass to beautiful Native Lake located at the base of Mount Massive. Begin from the south side of the road and note the signs at the trailhead; in particular, the restrictions on fishing to protect the native greenback cutthroat trout. The nearby fish hatchery and some of the local high mountain lakes and streams are important to the

Native Lake

CONTINENTAL DIVIDE

Windsor Lake

To Turquoise Lake & Leadville

Native Lake Trail

11,980 ft.

12,654 ft.

Busk Creek

MOUNT MASSIVE WILDERNESS

12,875 ft.

12,267 ft.

12,080 ft.

Pass

11,848 ft.

13,000 ft.

Notch Lake

Three Lakes

1489

Rainbow Lake

Rock Creek

Pear Lakes

Native Lake

13,125 ft.

1382

LEADVILLE NATIONAL
FISH HATCHERY

Highline Trail

13,801 ft.

14,169 ft.

SAN ISABEL
NATIONAL
FOREST

12,528 ft.

N

★

0   1   2

Mount Massive
14,421 ft.

Miles

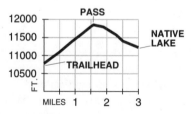

12000

11500

11000

10500

PASS

NATIVE
LAKE

TRAILHEAD

FT.

MILES 1   2   3

recovery of this threatened species, which was once found throughout the mountains east of the Continental Divide in Colorado.

After traversing the slope back to the east for about the first half mile, the trail begins a series of several switchbacks through forest to timberline along a small, steep drainage. Above timberline the slope lessens until at about 1.6 miles, you reach the top of a pass, halfway to your destination but with most of the effort behind you. Continue across the pass to the south and follow the trail as it drops into a large basin, which drains the north side of Mount Massive and the Continental Divide to the west. As you descend along two long switchbacks, you will have glimpses of Native Lake below.

If you are backpacking, please choose a campsite well away from the lake; if not, enjoy this special place and return as you came.

Options: Continue on the Highline Trail (Trail 1382) past Native Lake to the Colorado Trail or to a trailhead at the entrance to the fish hatchery. You could also continue up the basin to Three Lakes, Rainbow, and Notch Lakes, and an unnamed lake. The easiest way to reach these upper lakes is to go back up the trail to the last bend before the pass, and then up and to the southwest along a bench. From Notch Lake loop back to the trailhead by dropping down a creek to the Windsor Lake Trail. A few people also use Native Lake as a base camp for climbing Mount Massive via one of the slopes to the southwest of the lake. This is a very long route that earns this mountain its name.—*Michael Kephart*

Camping and services: Camp at least 200 feet from lakes and streams in this area; no services.

For more information: San Isabel National Forest, Leadville Ranger District.

29 Lyle Lake

Highlights:	Alpine lake; meadows; wildflowers; tundra.
Location:	Southeast of Basalt and the Ruedi Reservoir in the Holy Cross Wilderness.
Type of hike:	Out-and-back day hike.
Total distance:	2.6 miles.
Difficulty:	Easy.
Elevation gain:	650 feet.
Best months:	July–September.
Maps:	USGS Nast quad; Trails Illustrated Map 126; White River National Forest Map.

Special considerations: It is a long drive to the trailhead. You may want to do this hike as a diversion on a four-wheel-drive trip over Hagerman Pass.

Lyle Lake

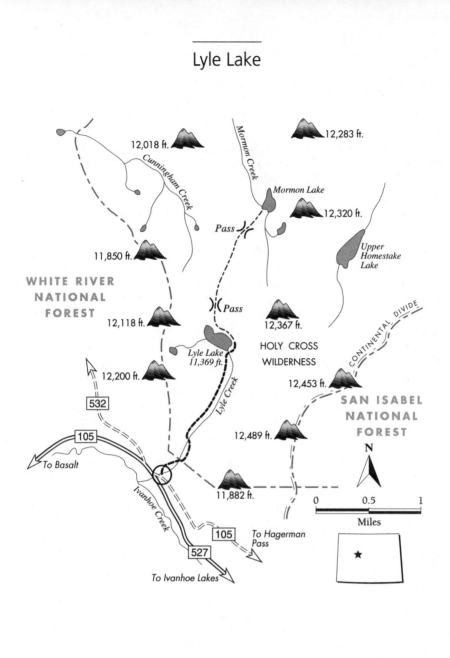

12,018 ft.

12,283 ft.

Cunningham Creek

Mormon Creek

Mormon Lake

12,320 ft.

Pass

Upper Homestake Lake

11,850 ft.

WHITE RIVER NATIONAL FOREST

)(*Pass*

12,367 ft.

12,118 ft.

Lyle Lake 11,369 ft.

HOLY CROSS WILDERNESS

CONTINENTAL DIVIDE

12,200 ft.

Lyle Creek

12,453 ft.

532

SAN ISABEL NATIONAL FOREST

105

To Basalt

12,489 ft.

N

Ivanhoe Creek

11,882 ft.

0   0.5   1
Miles

105
To Hagerman Pass

527
To Ivanhoe Lakes

★

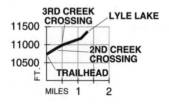

3RD CREEK CROSSING   **LYLE LAKE**

11500

11000

2ND CREEK CROSSING

10500

TRAILHEAD

FT.

MILES   1   2

Finding the trailhead: Take Midland Avenue through the town of Basalt east onto Frying Pan Road (Colorado Highway 4), following signs for Ruedi Reservoir. Drive 34.6 miles on this road, going through Thomasville and straight at all forks. Turn left on Hagerman Pass Road (Forest Road 105) and make a sharp turn so you're going northwest. After turning southeast again, go straight at the road to Diemer Lake. Continue to a fork with the road to the right going to Ivanhoe Lakes. Go straight for a short distance and you will come to the trailhead on your left—you will have driven about 42 miles to the trailhead from Basalt. You can get to the trailhead in a passenger car as we did but, it's probably not a good idea to drive over Hagerman Pass without a four-wheel-drive vehicle.

With a four-wheel-drive vehicle you can reach the trailhead by driving northwest from Turquoise Lake over Hagerman Pass on Hagerman Pass Road, which connects with Turquoise Lake Road (FR 104) about 2.5 miles west of Abelee Fishing Park. Continue northwest of the pass to the trailhead. If you see the intersection with FR 527, which is the road to Ivanhoe Lakes, you've gone too far. To reach Turquoise Lake, go to Leadville and follow the signs west.

Parking & trailhead facilities: Minimal parking; no facilities.

Key points:
- 0.3   Second creek crossing
- 0.5   Third creek crossing
- 1.3   Lyle Lake

The hike: Begin hiking at the north end of the parking lot at the sign. Cross Lyle Creek right away for a gentle climb on a clear trail through lodgepole forest, then willows, then spruce-fir forest. You will cross the creek two more times in the first 0.5 mile. Along the way you can see monkshood, elephanthead, American bistort, Indian paintbrush, wild parsley, forget-me-not, mountain aster, fireweed, marsh marigold, violet, primrose, penstemon, and chiming bells.

After hiking through a Krummholz area, you will emerge on the tundra at the cirque in which Lyle Lake sits. We hiked to Lyle Lake in late July and saw a snow cornice up on the ridge to the east of the lake.

Enjoy the lake and then return to your car as you came.

Options: This is a terrific first backpack. A good side trip from Lyle Lake is to hike northeast on Lyle Lake Trail beyond the lake for another 1.5 miles to Mormon Lake, which sits just beneath the Continental Divide. This hike takes you to the headwaters of three separate drainages within the Holy Cross Wilderness.

Camping and services: You'll find some good camping spots at your destination. Please camp at least 200 feet away from the lake.

For more information: White River National Forest, Mount Sopris Ranger District.

30 Graham Gulch

Highlights:	Spruce-fir forest; pretty creek; views.
Location:	At the foot of Independence Pass on the east side.
Type of hike:	Out-and-back day hike.
Total distance:	3 miles.
Difficulty:	Moderate.
Elevation gain:	750 feet.
Best months:	July–September.
Maps:	USGS Independence Pass quad; Trails Illustrated Map 127; White River National Forest Map.

Finding the trailhead: From the winter gate at the bottom of the east side of Independence Pass on Colorado Highway 82, drive 0.3 mile east. Turn right (south) on a dirt road. Follow the road around to the right (west) until it crosses the North Fork of Lake Creek where it meets the main fork of Lake Creek.

Parking and trailhead facilities: Parking is available near the water diversion structure; no facilities.

Key points:
- 0.7   Cross side creek
- 1.5   Collegiate Peaks Wilderness boundary

The hike: This hike follows Graham Gulch as it spills down from the Continental Divide.

Begin at the west end of the parking lot, following signs to the trail. Start hiking on a jeep road. The trail makes a loop to the northwest, then swings back around the ridge into Graham Gulch, going south. Follow a side gulch, separated from Graham Gulch by a low ridge. At 0.7 mile cross a side gulch.

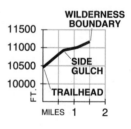

We hiked to a high point along this ridge where we could get some good views. We could look down on Graham Gulch, which continues southwest. A tributary comes down to join it from Ouray Peak to the south; southwest down the line of Graham Gulch is the Continental Divide. La Plata Peak is visible to the far left (southeast) beyond Star Mountain, which is in the near distance, to the southeast. We returned to our car from this high point, going back the way we came.

You can continue along the jeep road, which crosses the low ridge and drops down to follow Graham Gulch. At 1.5 miles is the wilderness boundary for the Collegiate Peaks Wilderness and an open meadow with views of the upper drainage. Beyond this point, the trail becomes less distinct as it climbs above timberline.

Explore as far as you want, then return as you came.

Graham Gulch

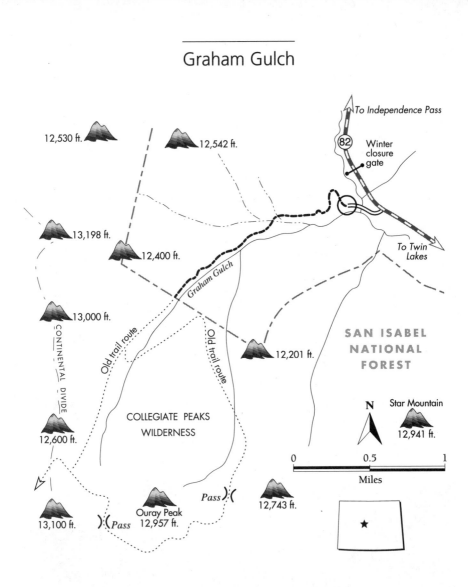

Options: Follow old trail routes up and over a saddle at the end of Graham Gulch, then around the south side of Ouray Peak to another saddle into the gulch that drains the northeast side of Ouray Peak. From there you can drop down that drainage and around the nose of a ridge back into Graham Gulch at timberline.

An old trail route takes off to the west near the top of Graham Gulch and crosses over the Continental Divide into the Grizzly Creek drainage.

Camping and services: At the upper end of the Graham Gulch Trail, in the wilderness, there are probably some good camping spots but no services.

For more information: San Isabel National Forest, Leadville Ranger District.

31 Ashcroft

Special considerations: No pets allowed. You might want to bring a picnic along to share by Castle Creek after your hike.

Finding the trailhead: From the Forest Service ranger station at the west end of Aspen, drive west on Colorado Highway 82 over a bridge. Turn left on Maroon Creek Road at a stone church. Make an immediate left onto Castle Creek Road (Forest Road 102). In 10.7 miles turn left into the parking lot for Ashcroft.

Parking and trailhead facilities: Parking and restrooms are provided.

The hike: This hike takes you through the ghost town of Ashcroft and gives you an introductory look at the natural history of the area. It is a fun, short hike with lots of historical interest and a packed trail, which is just right for young children and others who need a smooth trail with no obstacles.

Ashcroft.

Ashcroft and American Lake

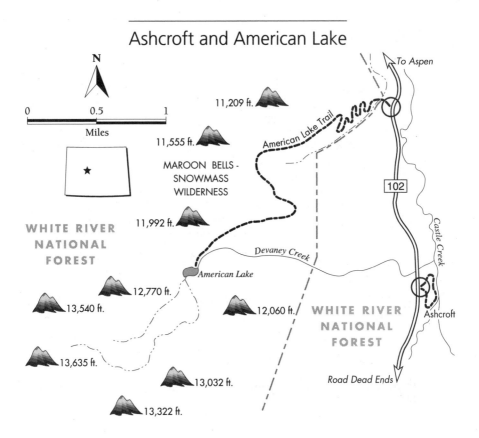

Begin at the south end of the parking lot by taking a moment to read about the history of Ashcroft and the people who inhabited it. Silver—discovered here in 1879—was the magnet that drew settlers into this valley. Peaking in 1885, the population swelled in the summers to 2,500, and was served by 6 hotels, 17 saloons, a bowling alley, a doctor, a jail, and even a suburb named Hanley's Addition. The town was first named Castle Forks, then Chloride, then Ashcroft. It lasted only until 1893, when silver was devalued.

Walk along the boardwalk into the ghost town, and imagine what it must have been like in its heyday. At the hotel go left down the hill along the path that follows Castle Creek. Look for tree stumps—evidence of the work of beavers along the creek. Picnic areas are provided.

Follow the trail through a meadow—where there are wildflowers such as mountain asters and yellow cinquefoil—back to the parking area.

Options: None.

Camping and services: No camping is available on the Ashcroft site. Guided nature tours and ghost tours are provided on a regular basis. Check the information on the signs at the south end of the parking area.

For more information: White River National Forest, Aspen Ranger District.

32 American Lake

See map on page 123

Highlights:	Pretty aspen groves; wildflowers; alpine lake. Good fall hike.
Location:	Southwest of Aspen in the Maroon Bells–Snowmass Wilderness.
Type of hike:	Out-and-back day hike.
Total distance:	6.4 miles.
Difficulty:	Strenuous.
Elevation gain:	1,975 feet.
Best months:	July–September.
Maps:	USGS Hayden Peak quad; Trails Illustrated Map 127; White River National Forest Map.

Special considerations: Area is heavily used and best hiked on weekdays. Dogs must be leashed.

Finding the trailhead: From the west end of Aspen, drive west on Colorado Highway 82 over a bridge. Turn left on Maroon Creek Road at a stone church. Make an immediate left onto Castle Creek Road (Forest Road 102). Drive 10 miles until you see the Elk Mountain Lodge. The trailhead is on the right.

Parking and trailhead facilities: Parking is provided. No restrooms or other facilities.

Key points:
- 0.3 Start switchbacks
- 1.7 Small meadow
- 2.6 Rock slide
- 3.2 American Lake

The hike: This hike is challenging but rewarding. Begin at the trailhead to climb steeply through pretty aspen groves on many switchbacks. Notice the purple clover and blue penstemon as you cross the small creek and start up through old-growth aspen forest. You'll come upon columbine as you enter the Maroon Bells–Snowmass Wilderness. Other wildflowers include monkshood, Queen Anne's lace, mountain aster, and wild geranium.

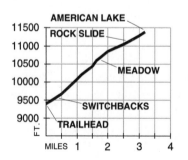

Switchback for about 1.5 miles when you come to some spruce trees. The trail gains elevation at a more moderate grade. You will come to a meadow and walk along its lower edge, go south and into the forest again, and continue a gentle climb. At about 2.3 miles, round a ridge and turn southwest into the basin containing American Lake. The trail climbs along the base of a steep ridge, with views of the Castle Creek valley below and the high alpine basins and peaks above American Lake. When you cross a rock slide area, you are about half a mile from the lake, which sits below timberline on a small bench to the southwest.

Enjoy American Lake, then return as you came.

Options: This hike is a good short backpack. Please camp away from the lake and practice Leave No Trace techniques if you do. You can also continue on above the lake and explore the higher basin.

Camping and services: The best camping is away from the lake on a bench; no services.

For more information: White River National Forest, Aspen Ranger District.

---

33 Buckskin Pass

Highlights:	Maroon Bells–Snowmass Wilderness; views; wildflowers.
Location:	Southwest of Aspen in the Elk Mountains.
Type of hike:	Out-and-back day hike.
Total distance:	9.6 miles.
Difficulty:	Strenuous.
Elevation gain:	2,900 feet.
Best months:	July–September.
Maps:	USGS Maroon Bells quad; Trails Illustrated Map 128; White River National Forest Map.

Special considerations: From mid-June through August, and on weekends in September, the Maroon Creek Road is closed from 8:30 A.M. to 5 P.M., and trailhead access is by shuttle bus from Aspen only.

Finding the trailhead: Drive west of Aspen on Colorado Highway 82 for about a half mile, then bear south at the Maroon Creek Road turnoff. Turn right and continue 9.5 miles to the Maroon Lake parking area; parking for day use is in the upper parking lot. The hike description is written based on this upper trailhead. If you take the shuttle bus, you will start your hike at the trailhead next to Maroon Lake, which shortens your hike by 0.3 mile. The shuttle bus picks up at either Ruby Park in downtown Aspen, or the Aspen Highlands Ski Area parking lot located near the lower end of Maroon Creek Road. Check with the Aspen Ranger District for current shuttle information.

Parking and trailhead facilities: Parking and restrooms are available.

Buckskin Pass

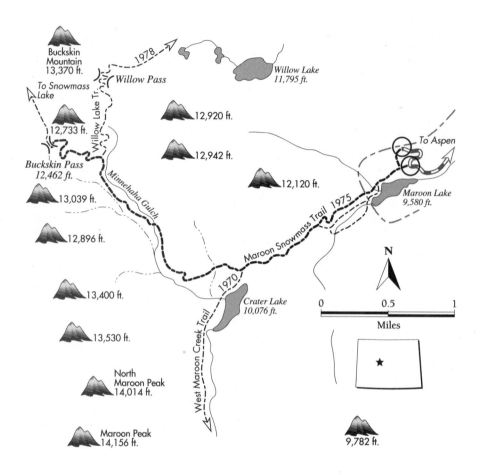

Key points:

The hike: No doubt, you have seen the Maroon Bells on many a calendar and book, but they are even more spectacular in person: They are classic Colorado! This trail will take you past the Maroon Bells and along a some-times-steep trail to Buckskin Pass, where you will be rewarded with more beautiful views of the Elk Mountains.

Start down the trail at the west end of the parking lot toward the lake. You'll walk through a meadow of tall grasses, then through stands of aspen mixed with evergreen to the far end of Maroon Lake. As you begin, consider how careful management has preserved this popular area for you to enjoy.

At the fork at a Forest Service bulletin board, one trail goes to a scenic loop. Go right on the other, which is the Maroon-Snowmass Trail.

Hike through a grove of tall aspen, noticing the Rocky Mountain maple along the way, and the beaver dam at the lake; you may even see beavers swimming. Also notice the trees along the trail, which beavers have marked while pursuing their heavy-duty construction work.

You'll walk through a glacial moraine. Here little pikas, which look like baby rabbits with round ears, come very near the trail, then duck into the boulder fields to follow their secret paths away from you. They are usually very shy and often impossible to spot. You might only hear their chirps elsewhere, but they have become used to the presence of humans in this wilderness area.

You will come to the junction with West Maroon Creek Trail, which goes left (south) to Crater Lake and beyond. No dogs are allowed at the lake.

Take the right-hand trail on Maroon-Snowmass Trail 1975, which climbs Minnehaha Gulch to Buckskin Pass. Sign in at the Forest Service register both going up and coming down from Buckskin Pass. The aspen grove gives way to spruce and fir before you ascend a long and very steep hill. A series of switchbacks takes you up the valley toward the pass. Richardson's ground squirrels may cross your path or run ahead with tails up. When you take a rest, take some time to look closely at the Maroon Bells to the south and Pyramid Peak to the east.

The Maroon Bells are of the Maroon Formation, consisting of sandstones and shales that have been changed by heat and pressure into quartzite and slate. The degree of alteration varies throughout the Elk Mountains. The two Maroon Bells (North Maroon Peak and Maroon Peak) and Pyramid Peak are all "Fourteeners" (peaks more than 14,000 feet high). The Bells are some of the more difficult Fourteeners to climb, and a few hikers have died there.

Hike out of the spruce-fir forest to a lush drainage, and cross a small creek, which is Minnehaha Gulch. Chiming bells, wild geraniums, larkspur, and other wildflowers love the water, and thrive here. This is a nice spot for a rest.

Hike through a little krummholz area with its wind-shaped Engelmann spruce. As you hike uphill, you'll see snow and a rock outcropping up ahead before coming to a fork in the trail. Keep to the main trail on the right bank of the little creek, which takes you to a larger, signed fork in the trail. The Maroon-Snowmass Trail leads left to your destination: Buckskin Pass. The trail to the right is Willow Lake Trail, leading to Willow Pass and Willow

Lake. The last pitch to the pass is very steep, but the trail switches back and forth. As you trudge upward, notice the red, magenta, and pink Indian paintbrush, mountain asters, white American bistorts, buttercups, harebells, and several species of grass that grace the tundra. Before you know it you'll have arrived!

Drink in the solitude and the view. Looking west from the pass and down you'll see Snowmass Lake, fed by Snowmass Creek. Snowmass Peak is on your left, and behind it is Hagerman Peak; to the northwest is Snowmass Mountain.

Enjoy this bird's-eye view of the wilderness and then return as you came.

Options: Climb from Buckskin Pass to the summit of Buckskin Mountain (13,370 feet) to the north.

Some people like to use this hike as a starter for a longer backpack into the Maroon Bells–Snowmass Wilderness. If you want to do this, plan to leave a car at the Snowmass Creek Campground above Snowmass Village, then travel to Maroon Lake via another car. You can hike up and over Buckskin Pass and down to the Snowmass Campground.

Camping and services: Camping is available at Crater Lake in designated places, and in the basin before the final pitch to Buckskin Pass; no services.

For more information: White River National Forest, Aspen Ranger District.

---

34 Oh-Be-Joyful Pass

Highlights:	Views; forest and tundra; wildflowers.
Location:	North of Crested Butte in the Ruby Range and Raggeds Wilderness.
Type of hike:	Out-and-back day hike or backpack.
Total distance:	13.8 miles.
Difficulty:	Strenuous.
Elevation gain:	2,800 feet.
Best months:	July–September.
Maps:	USGS Oh-Be-Joyful quad; Trails Illustrated Map 133; Gunnison National Forest Map.

Finding the trailhead: From the center of the town of Crested Butte, take Colorado Highway 135 east toward the ski area for 0.8 mile. Just before you start the climb to the ski hill, go left on Slate River Road (County Road 734). Take this road northeast, passing a lake, and going straight at a fork in 2.5 miles. At 3.5 miles is a junction with the road that goes to Gunsight Pass. Continue straight. At mile 4.6 turn left at the sign for Oh-Be-Joyful. Drive down through a primitive camping area, cross the river, and turn left, following the right bank of the river. You will need a four-wheel-drive vehicle for this last stretch. If you have a passenger car, park at the campground and walk the road from there. The wilderness boundary is in 1 mile. You must park before it.

Parking and trailhead facilities: Parking is available; no facilities.

Key points:
    1.0   Wilderness boundary
    4.9   Junction with trail from Blue Lake
    6.4   Pond
    6.9   Pass

The hike: This hike gives you joy for the views it offers once you hike up the long, long valley to Oh-Be-Joyful Pass on the Ruby Range.

Begin by heading west up a jeep road and register at the Forest Service sign. You'll be hiking the right (north) bank of Oh-Be-Joyful Creek and following the long east ridge of Schuykill Mountain, which rises to the north of the trail.

The pitch up the jeep road is steep at first. The road jogs to the right around timber blocking the road, then heads into the wilderness. A fairly moderate grade goes through spruce-fir mixed with a few aspen, and the jeep road soon becomes more of a single-track trail.

You'll hike away from the creek a bit and see Purple Peak to your left. Then the trail leads back to the creek, crosses a couple tributaries, then climbs into the forest and up steeply (a little waterfall is to your left). Just below timberline, Trail 404 comes from Blue Lake to the south. Go right

View east from Oh-Be-Joyful Pass.

Oh-Be-Joyful Pass

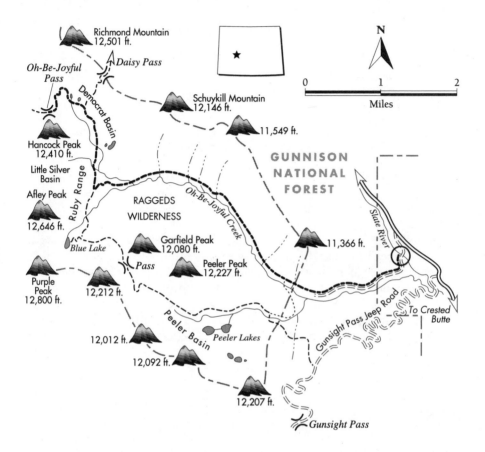

Richmond Mountain
12,501 ft.

Daisy Pass

Oh-Be-Joyful Pass

Schuykill Mountain
12,146 ft.

11,549 ft.

Hancock Peak
12,410 ft.

Little Silver Basin

Afley Peak

12,646 ft.

Democrat Basin

Ruby Range

RAGGEDS
WILDERNESS

Oh-Be-Joyful Creek

**GUNNISON
NATIONAL
FOREST**

Slate River

Garfield Peak
12,080 ft.

Blue Lake

Pass

Peeler Peak
12,227 ft.

11,366 ft.

Purple Peak
12,800 ft.

12,212 ft.

Peeler Basin

Peeler Lakes

12,012 ft.

12,092 ft.

12,207 ft.

Gunsight Pass Jeep Road

To Crested Butte

Gunsight Pass

N

0   1   2
Miles

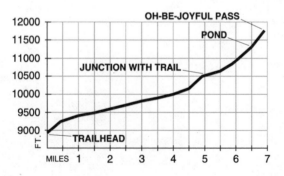

OH-BE-JOYFUL PASS

POND

JUNCTION WITH TRAIL

TRAILHEAD

FT.

MILES 1   2   3   4   5   6   7

and up the hill and you should emerge from the trees just beneath the triangular rock formation that hides Little Silver Basin.

Walk north into Democrat Basin, crossing the creek where it forks. As you look to the northeast you can see the switchbacks of the Daisy Pass Trail, going the opposite direction of Oh-Be-Joyful Pass. Switchback up some hummocky stuff, come to another small waterfall and a little pond, and cross the creek with its pretty wildflowers, which in summer include Queen Anne's lace, fireweed, and mountain asters. At the top of a terrace the trail bends south. Follow the switchback south, then turn up through a seam of black rock to the pass. There is a wooden sign for Oh-Be-Joyful Pass on the west side of the pass.

Enjoy the views! To the west are the Raggeds; Daisy Pass is straight across to the northeast. Along the ridge to the southeast of Daisy Pass is Schuykill Mountain. The pointy mountain to the southeast is Gothic Mountain. The ridge south from the pass goes to Hancock Peak. The mountain with the big cirque off to the south is Garfield Peak.

Enjoy the pass, then head on down as you came.

Options: Make this into a loop hike by connecting with the trail over Daisy Pass and hiking it to the northeast to connect with Baxter Basin Road (Forest Road 552). Then follow it to the Poverty Gulch Road (FR 734.2A), heading southeast (right) along the creek to the Slate River and the road by the same name. Then follow Slate River Road back to your car.

You could also go back down through Democrat Basin, and instead of following Oh-Be-Joyful Creek down, take Trail 404 south to Blue Lake, then hike south of Garfield Peak and reconnect with the Oh-Be-Joyful Trail, and return to your starting point.

Camping and services: Camping is good in Democrat Basin; no services.

For more information: Gunnison National Forest, Taylor River–Cebolla Ranger District.

The Southern Mountains

The Southern Mountains

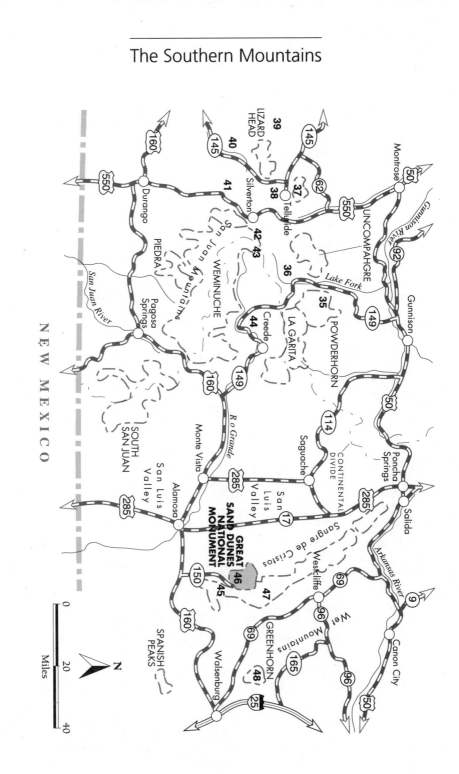

35 Powderhorn Lakes

Highlights:	Lakes; meadows; wildflowers; wildlife; tundra; views.
Location:	Northeast of Lake City in the Powderhorn Wilderness.
Type of hike:	Out-and-back day hike.
Total distance:	9.8 miles.
Difficulty:	Moderate.
Elevation gain (loss):	850 feet (400 feet).
Best months:	July–September.
Maps:	USGS Powderhorn Lakes quad; Gunnison National Forest Map.

Finding the trailhead: From Lake City take Colorado Highway 149 north about 23 miles or from the junction of U.S. Highway 50 and CO 149 west of Gunnison, south about 20 miles to Indian Creek Road (County Road 58). Drive south on Indian Creek Road 10.5 miles to its end in a timber sale. Stay on the main road the entire way, passing the YLL Camp. The road gets a little rough but most passenger cars can make it.

Parking and trailhead facilities: Parking is available; no facilities.

Key points:

1.4	Saddle
1.8	Meadow
2.9	Pond
3.6	West Fork drainage
4.1	Lower lake
4.9	Upper lake

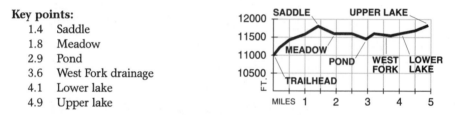

The hike: This hike will take you into the Powderhorn Wilderness, an area of rolling tundra and two lakes located in a glacial valley carved into the Calf Creek Plateau. The plateau is one of the largest flat expanses of alpine tundra in Colorado and was a summer hunting ground of the Ute Indians.

From the trailhead climb steadily for about 1.5 miles to a saddle. You will come to a beautiful meadow at 1.8 miles where we came upon a sheep-herder. If you encounter a sheepherder with his animals, please keep your dogs under control around them.

The trail descends into spruce-fir forest. When you come upon a pond you are a little more than halfway through the hike. Beyond the pond, the trail loses a little elevation; then there is a short, steep section, after which you emerge into the drainage of West Fork Powderhorn Creek and the intersection with the West Fork Trail. Go right up the valley for about half a mile to the lower lake. For many people the lower lake is a good destination, but the much larger upper lake sits in an even more spectacular setting and is well worth the extra 0.8-mile effort. To reach the upper lake hike around the north and west sides of the lower lake and look for the trail entering the timber at the southwest end of the lake. The trail follows the creek closely to the upper lake.

Enjoy the setting and return as you came.

Powderhorn Lakes

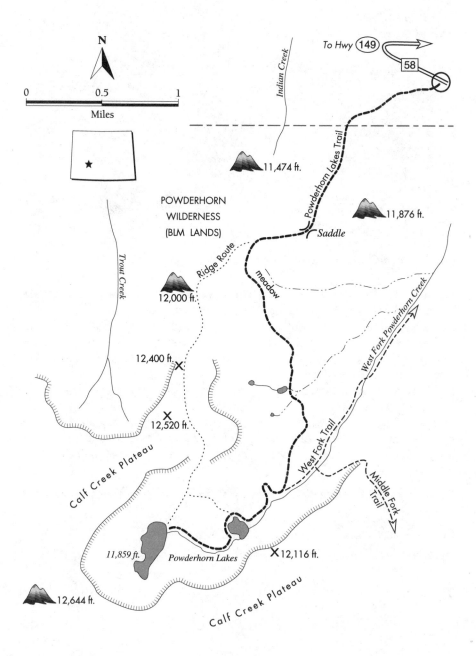

N

0   0.5   1
Miles

To Hwy (149)

58

Indian Creek

11,474 ft.

POWDERHORN
WILDERNESS
(BLM LANDS)

11,876 ft.

Saddle

Powderhorn Lakes Trail

Ridge Route

meadow

Trout Creek

12,000 ft.

West Fork Powderhorn Creek

12,400 ft. X

12,520 ft. X

West Fork Trail

Calf Creek Plateau

Middle Fork Trail

11,859 ft.

Powderhorn Lakes

X 12,116 ft.

12,644 ft.

Calf Creek Plateau

Resting on the tundra above Upper Powderhorn Lake.

Options: One option, which we highly recommend, is to take an alternate route on the way in or out across the tundra of the Calf Creek Plateau. It's about the same distance, but another 600 to 800 feet in elevation gain. To take this route, on the way in look for the ridge at the west edge of the meadow after the saddle. Follow this ridge up above timberline to the Calf Creek Plateau. You will reach the broad expanse of the plateau in about 1.3 miles. Head south, keeping a group of rocks to your right, and look for an easier route down the slopes to the lakes. This route is easier to see if you take it from the lakes to return to your car, as we did. It is located to the north about halfway between the two lakes. If you take this route, use Leave No Trace techniques so you don't impact the tundra too much. This is the ultimate tundra hike!

Camping and services: Camp away from the lakes in the area between them.

For more information: Bureau of Land Management, Gunnison Resource Area office.

36 Alpine Gulch

Highlights:	Beautiful creek; aspens; wild basin with avalanche chutes; raspberries.
Location:	Southwest of Lake City in the Redcloud Peak Wilderness Study Area.
Type of hike:	Out-and-back day hike or backpack.
Total distance:	7.2 miles.
Difficulty:	Moderate.
Elevation gain:	1,500 feet.
Best months:	July–September.
Maps:	USGS Lake City, Lake San Cristobal, and Redcloud Peak quads; Trails Illustrated Map 141; Gunnison National Forest Map.

Special considerations: Bring a good walking stick for stream crossings.

Finding the trailhead: From Colorado Highway 149 near the south end of Lake City, go right (west) on Second Street at the sign for Engineer Pass. Go two blocks and turn left (southwest) on Henson Creek Road, which is part of the Alpine Loop Scenic Byway. Follow this road 2.3 miles through the narrow canyon of Henson Creek to the trailhead located on the left (south) side of the road.

Parking and trailhead facilities: Parking; no facilities. Note the posted private property.

West Fork Trail in Alpine Gulch.

Alpine Gulch

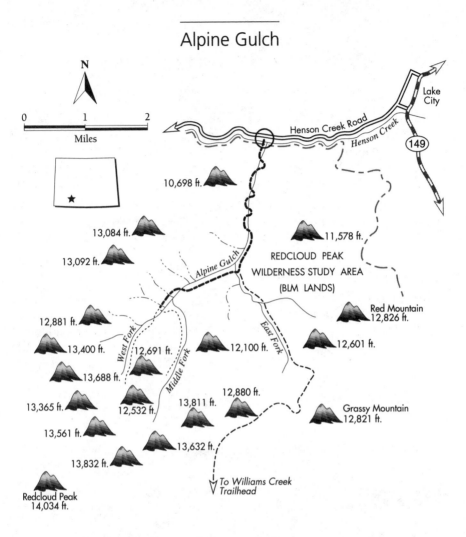

Key points:

0.3	First of several stream crossings
2.1	Junction with East Fork Trail
3.1	Upper stream crossing
3.6	Old cabin across from Middle Fork; end of good trail

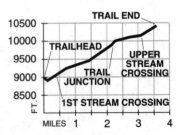

The hike: This hike, which can be done as an out-and-back day hike or backpack, takes you along Alpine Gulch into a high mountain basin surrounded by 13,000-foot peaks within the Redcloud Peak Wilderness Study Area. The described hike ends at a point where the trail becomes rugged and indistinct, but there are many opportunities for exploring in the upper basin of Alpine Gulch.

Begin by hiking down and around the posted private property and crossing Henson Creek on the footbridge. Stop and sign in at the trail register, then follow the trail into Alpine Gulch. All along the first 0.2 mile of this hike you will find raspberries, which ripen in late summer. Pick them as you go, but leave some for other hikers and for bears. At 0.3 mile is the first of seven creek crossings (if we counted correctly) in the lower canyon of Alpine Gulch. Both times we hiked this trail there were logs set at the crossings, but some were pretty precarious and looked like they might not survive the next high water. Bring a good walking stick for balance and be prepared to wade the stream if the logs are gone. Because of the many crossings, we recommend doing this hike after the peak snowmelt.

Not too long after the seventh stream crossing, pass through some posted private property to a trail junction at 2.1 miles. One trail goes straight and follows the East Fork of Alpine Gulch, then up and over Grassy Mountain. Go right on the trail marked West Fork and follow it across the creek (East Fork) and into the main drainage of Alpine Gulch. Immediately pass a site for a hunting camp, which, although a tempting spot to pitch a tent, is really too close to the trail. It's better to continue on up the valley.

After the campsite, climb steadily through a beautiful aspen forest for 0.8 mile. At 3 miles is the first of several meadows, a good resting spot with views of the high ridge to the north. This meadow sits on top of an old rock slide that came down the mountain from the south, but it is kept free of trees because of avalanches from the opposite side of the valley. Shortly after the meadow, the trail drops, and you cross Alpine Gulch as it climbs along the more open south-facing slope of the valley. After crossing some small side drainages, you will come to an old cabin across from the hanging valley of the Middle Fork, just before the trail enters a stretch of forest. This is the end of the good trail.

Beyond this point, the trail divides into elk trails, is blocked by downed timber, and in many places is filled with sticks and rocks, which make for difficult footing. At first we were puzzled by the debris in the trail, which at one time had been an old wagon or jeep road. But when we came to a 20-foot-deep pile of snow still covering the creek in late August, we realized that avalanches rule this upper valley, constantly assaulting any vegetation and leaving rocks and trees to clog the creek and trail.

From the trail end at the old cabin, you can drop down across the creek and climb to a bench at the base of the Middle Fork Valley; another bench above marks the entrance to the hanging valley. Between the two benches, the Middle Fork drops more than 350 feet through a series of cascades. Enjoy this area, or explore more of this wild alpine valley, then return as you came.

Options: Continue on the more primitive trail into upper basins of the West Fork of Alpine Gulch, or bushwhack into the Middle Fork Basin. If you are an experienced hiker, you might also want to camp up high and then make a difficult climb of Redcloud Peak (14,034 feet) via a connecting ridge from the divide at the top of either the West Fork or the Middle Fork. Two other options are also possible via the East Fork Trail: a climb of Grassy

Mountain (12,821 feet) and return, or a longer hike over Grassy Mountain to the Williams Creek Trailhead on Alpine Loop Road (County Road 3) above Lake San Cristobal.

Camping and services: The best camping is in the meadows and high basins near the end of the trail; no services.

For more information: Bureau of Land Management, Gunnison Resource Area Office.

37 Sneffels Highline Loop

Highlights:	Fabulous views of the San Juans; wildflowers and wildlife; waterfalls; good trail for viewing aspen gold.
Location:	North of Telluride in the San Juan Mountains.
Type of hike:	Loop hike or backpack.
Total distance:	12.2 miles.
Difficulty:	Strenuous.
Elevation gain (or loss):	2,900 feet (250 feet).
Best months:	July–October.
Maps:	USGS Telluride quad; Trails Illustrated Map 141; Uncompahgre National Forest Map.

Finding the trailhead: From the high school at the west end of Telluride, drive west on Colorado Highway 145 for 0.4 mile. Turn right (north) on a dirt road (Forest Road 637), which meets the highway with a big dip. The road is a bit hard to see, but look carefully and you'll find it. Follow FR 637 as it heads west and forks. Take it right (northeast) as it switches back to follow Mill Creek up to the trailhead, which is just before the road ends at a water treatment facility—this should be about 1.8 miles. Maps say this is the Mill Creek Trailhead, but it is not posted that way at the site. It is signed as the trailhead for the Deep Creek Trail (Trail 418).

Parking and trailhead facilities: Minimal parking is available on the road; no facilities.

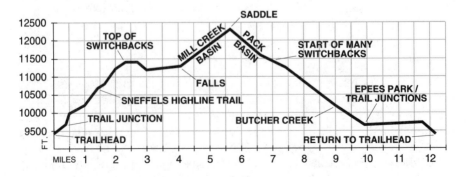

Mill Creek Basin and waterfall below Mount Emma.

Key points:

The hike: This trek takes you up into two alpine basins on trails that will reward you for much of their length with fabulous vistas and views of the San Juan Mountains.

Begin by walking the Deep Creek Trail north from the trailhead. You will pass the water treatment facility for Telluride right away. At 0.4 mile is the junction with the waterline section of the Deep Creek Trail. The sign indicates Last Dollar Road to the left and the Jud Wiebe Trail to the right. Go left and uphill. No doubt wildflowers are gorgeous here in summer, including Queen Anne's lace, columbines, fireweed, mountain asters, and Indian paintbrush.

You'll come to a meadow where there are views of Iron Mountain (11,413 feet) to the northwest. East of it is Campbell Peak (13,213 feet). (Two deer ran out ahead of us here.) Then walk down into another meadow and begin to switchback up to the end of a ridge. A good view to the southeast becomes visible: From east to west you can see U.S. Grant Peak (13,767) and Yellow Mountain.

Enter spruce-fir forest, climbing a little as you turn northwest. Walk back into some aspen groves, still climbing by way of many long switchbacks. Look for Mount Sneffels to the east through the trees. On top of the ridge you'll come to a sign. Leave the Deep Creek Trail, which goes west to Last Dollar Road, and go right (north) on Sneffels Highline Trail (Trail 434).

Hike the ridge due north into the Mount Sneffels Wilderness and switchback up the south-facing slope. (Here we came upon three cow elk that ran downhill as we came into their view.)

At the top of the switchbacks the trail heads east again. It is a good idea to check the skies before continuing, because in the event of an electrical storm you will be exposed for most of the next 4 miles.

Walk down to and cross a tributary to Mill Creek at the base of Dallas Peak (13,809 feet). It's easy walking here and you can see the Telluride Ski Area to the south. To the left (east) of the ski area is Ballard Mountain and the smaller La Junta Peak. South of the ski area is Palmyra Peak.

As you walk east, the peaks (from left to right) are Gilpin Peak to the north; Greenback Mountain and Mount Emma in the middle; and Mendota Peak to the south at the end of St. Sophia Ridge. As you continue east and

Sneffels Highline Loop

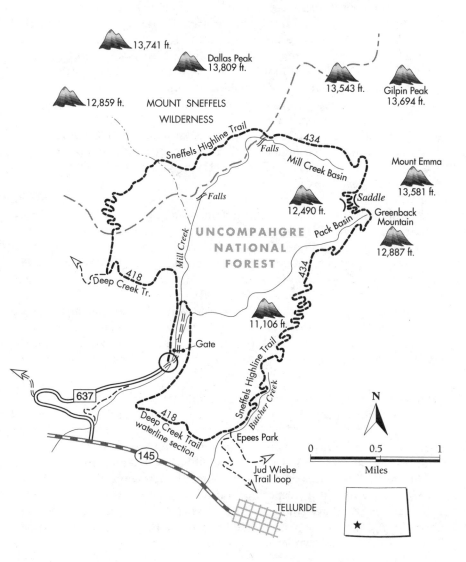

13,741 ft.

Dallas Peak
13,809 ft.

13,543 ft.

Gilpin Peak
13,694 ft.

12,859 ft.

MOUNT SNEFFELS
WILDERNESS

Sneffels Highline Trail

Falls

434

Mill Creek Basin

Mount Emma
13,581 ft.

Falls

12,490 ft.

Saddle

Greenback
Mountain

UNCOMPAHGRE
NATIONAL
FOREST

Mill Creek

Pack Basin

12,887 ft.

418

Deep Creek Tr.

434

11,106 ft.

Gate

Sneffels Highline Trail

637

418

Deep Creek Trail
waterline section

Butcher Creek

Epees Park

N

0   0.5   1

Miles

145

Jud Wiebe
Trail loop

TELLURIDE

★

northeast below Dallas Peak, you will come to a beautiful waterfall at the mouth of Mill Creek Basin, a good place for a rest or lunch.

Climb into the basin, following the posts and rock cairns at the base of Mount Emma and Greenback Mountain. Switchback up the talus slope to the saddle that separates Mill Creek and Pack Basins. The high point of the hike is here between stone points. From the top you can see Lizard Head Peak and Sunshine Mountain to the southwest; in front is San Bernardo Mountain; Wilson Peak, Mount Wilson, and El Diente are farther west; southeast of Pack Basin is Greenback Mountain.

Take a moment to savor your accomplishment in reaching this high point. We hiked the entire loop, but wished we had turned back at this point and gone back to the trailhead the way we came because the hike was less interesting going down the Butcher Creek drainage. Still, hiking the entire loop was a good accomplishment. Return the way you came or head over and down to Butcher Creek.

If you decide to do the entire loop, switchback down the other side into Pack Basin and hike down. You will come to a creek, a fork of Mill Creek that drains Pack Basin. The trail levels as it goes into spruce-fir forest. Hike down the west-facing slope. You'll have a good view of Lookout Peak. Hike down some more and around to the west; switchback into aspen grove. The switchbacks go on and on from here; you'll come to Butcher Creek, then hike down to a level place in the forest, Epees Park.

At a signed fork go right (west) on the waterline section of the Deep Creek Trail going toward Mill Creek. Follow the south-facing slope, then bend into Mill Creek and cross a bridge. Go downhill at the fork with the sign you saw at the beginning of your hike. You'll arrive back at the trailhead and parking.

Options: Make this loop hike into an out-and-back day hike by hiking in as far as you like from the trailhead for the Deep Creek Trail, then returning the way you came.

If staying in Telluride, you can hike the loop from the Cornet Creek Trailhead at the top of Aspen Street in Telluride. Hike up the Jud Wiebe Trail (Trail 432) to Epees Park and then hike the loop opposite of the way it is described here. It is a steeper but shorter hike up to the high point on the ridge this way. Or have someone drop you off at the trailhead for the Deep Creek Trail, hike the loop, then take the Jud Wiebe Trail down into town.

This is also a good two- or three-day backpack trip.

Camping and services: Good camping spots can be found in some of the meadows and in the Mill Creek and Pack Basins. Be sure to camp at least 200 feet away from the creek.

For more information: Uncompahgre National Forest, Norwood Ranger District.

38 East Fork Bear Creek

Highlights:	Views; waterfall; cliffs.
Location:	South of Telluride.
Type of hike:	Out-and-back day hike.
Total distance:	4.2 miles.
Difficulty:	Easy.
Elevation gain:	930 feet.
Best months:	July–October.
Maps:	USGS Telluride quad; Trails Illustrated Map 141; Uncompahgre National Forest Map.

Finding the trailhead: In Telluride drive to Pine Street and turn south. Park at the end of the street, or go west a few streets and park in the lot for the River Corridor Trail, then walk back to Pine Street.

Parking & trailhead facilities: Minimal parking; no facilities.

Key points:
- 1.9 Wasatch Trail
- 2.1 Bear Creek

The hike: This short, easy hike goes up a jeep road to a junction with the Wasatch Trail, following the East Fork of Bear Creek. It's a hike you can easily do on a short visit to Telluride, with numerous options for extending it to a more strenuous trek.

Hiker along the Bear Creek Trail.

East Fork Bear Creek

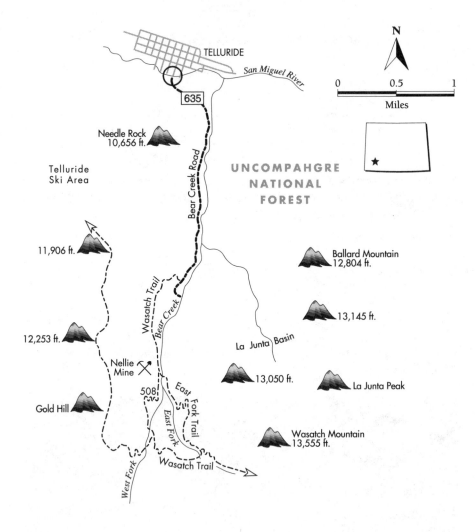

This entire area was the site of much mining activity in the 1800s. In *Sidelights on Colorado*, Al Look writes: "There are around 260 miles of tunnels in the old mines above Telluride from which gold, silver, lead and zinc have been dug since 1878 when the white man took tellurous rocks from the Ute Indians who didn't want them in the first place. In the two decades of feverish activity the area produced enough gold and silver to build three Army bombers." You will follow a road that was built for mule trains to carry ore from the Nellie Mine.

Begin your hike over the bridge at the end of Pine Street, where there is a gate and a large carved sign for Bear Creek Preserve. Walk the mild grade for about 2 miles to the junction with the Wasatch Trail above the road on the right. The road ends 0.2 mile farther at a fall, and a boulder. Continue to the end of the road, then return as you came.

Options: Extend this hike into a strenuous loop by taking the Wasatch Trail at mile 2 and following it to the Bridal Veil drainage and then down the road to the Idarado Mine and to Telluride, about 10 miles total.

You can also make a shorter loop up the Wasatch Trail into the East Fork drainage and back down the East Fork Trail, or take the Wasatch Trail and then follow a trail up onto Gold Hill and along a ridge back to the Telluride Ski Area.

All of the options above are strenuous, and when hiking them you will come upon many intersecting jeep roads and trails to old mines, so you'll want to take a topo map with you. Around the national forest are mining claims on private property. Never poke around private property or old mines; they are dangerous!

Camping and services: None.

For more information: Uncompahgre National Forest, Norwood Ranger District.

---

39 Lone Cone

Highlights:	Expansive views; wildflowers.
Location:	South of Norwood in the San Miguel Range.
Type of hike:	Up-and-down day hike.
Total distance:	4 miles.
Difficulty:	Strenuous.
Elevation gain:	2,100 feet.
Best months:	July–September.
Maps:	USGS Lone Cone quad; San Juan National Forest Map.

Special considerations: A four-wheel-drive vehicle is recommended. Loose rock talus requires sturdy boots.

Finding the trailhead: From Norwood go east on Colorado Highway 145 about 1.5 miles to 44.Z Road. Turn right and go south on the main road, straight toward Lone Cone Peak. At about 11 miles the road bears right (west). At 13.6 miles stay left at the fork, keeping on 44.Z Road. The road makes a few sharp bends; at 16 miles bear left at the T, onto 31.U Road and drive south. At 17.7 miles take the jeep road on the left (east). (If you get to a sign for Acorn Ranch, you went too far.)

The rocky summit of Lone Cone.

From the start of the jeep road, cross a cattle guard and watch for signs that read "No Trespassing" and "Stay on Trail." Please note this is public access through private property for the next 4 miles. Most passenger cars can get to the national forest boundary by this jeep road (Forest Road 534), provided it is dry. You will reach the boundary at mile 4 on the jeep road. If you have a two-wheel-drive vehicle, you may want to park here; if you have four-wheel-drive, take your first left and begin climbing. At 4.5 miles go left, staying on FR 534. Stay right at the next fork at 5 miles and continue another 0.8 mile to an open timber sale and meadows. You should be able to see the peak above you to the east. If your car can't make it this far, park where you can and hike along the road until you see Lone Cone Peak. There is no formal trailhead or trail.

Parking and trailhead facilities: None.

Key points:
 0.8   First talus
 1.0   Saddle
 2.0   Summit

The hike: This hike takes you up to the summit of Lone Cone Peak (12,613 feet), which rises like a lonely sentinel above the mesa country. More than half of this hike is over boulder fields and rock talus, which makes it tough and tricky for the ankles.

Begin your hike from wherever you parked and head for a small drainage, which comes down from the west side of the mountain. There are a number of jeep roads and timber sale roads below timberline, which don't

Lone Cone

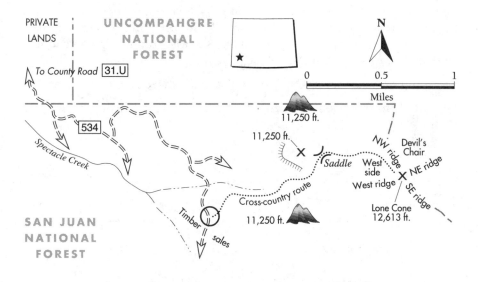

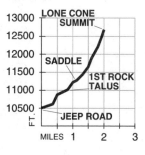

take you anywhere. You can follow these for a short distance, but be prepared to bushwhack some.

We found the best route is to head for the drainage that leads up past a bare rock ridge below the northwest side of the peak. At the base of this ridge is the first of many talus slopes. You can find your way along the forest edge in places, but eventually you have to head out across the rocks. When you reach a flat bench the best route is to head north toward a saddle, then from the saddle turn east to climb the west side of the peak.

There are a couple of steep sections where you may need to use your hands. As you climb, keep angling toward the northwest ridge, which provides the best route to the summit. Be careful in hiking the rocks because they can easily shift under you. This is not a technical climb, but you need to use caution because you could easily hurt yourself. A walking stick is helpful.

You'll come to a false summit and a short, flat section before you reach the actual summit from which there is a 360-degree view of the nearby San Miguel, San Juan, and La Plata Mountains as well as the entire plateau and canyon country of Colorado. Due south is Mesa Verde and, beyond that, you should be able to see Shiprock in New Mexico. To the southwest is Sleeping Ute Mountain, and to the west are the Abajo Mountains in Utah. In between, but mostly out of view, are the canyons of the Dolores River. To the north beyond Norwood is the long profile of the Uncompahgre Plateau, and to the northwest are the La Sal Mountains near Moab, Utah.

This peak is the westernmost high peak in Colorado, and is a landmark for much of the surrounding area. On the way down be sure to be careful of your footing.

Options: You could make this into a short backpack to the base of the peak. If you don't have a four-wheel-drive vehicle but can make it to the national forest boundary to park, it will add about 3.5 miles round trip and another 600 feet in elevation gain to the hike.

Camping and services: Camping in the many meadows; no services.

For more information: Uncompahgre National Forest, Norwood Ranger District.

40 Calico Trail

Highlights:	Views; wildflowers; tundra and wildlife; long trail with many options.
Location:	West of Rico (between Dolores and Telluride) in the Rico Mountains.
Type of hike:	Out-and-back day hikes at each end, or a long backpack.
Total distance:	4.6-mile day hike; 19.1-mile backpack.
Difficulty:	Moderate to strenuous.
Elevation gain (or loss):	1,050 feet (day hike); 4,300 feet (700 feet) for backpack.
Best months:	May–October (Priest Gulch), July–September (Calico).
Maps:	USGS Wallace Ranch, Clyde Lake, Rico, and Dolores Peak quads; San Juan National Forest Map.

Finding the trailhead: There are two trailheads for this long trail: the Calico and the Priest Gulch, as well as several other trails that provide access to the Calico Trail along its midsection. To reach the Priest Gulch (south) Trailhead, from which we did a short day hike, drive south from Rico 12 miles or northeast from Dolores about 23 miles on Colorado Highway 145 to Priest Gulch. There is a commercial campground on the south side of the road. Across the road from the campground on the west side of Priest Gulch, turn north next to a private residence onto a dirt road. The trailhead is a short distance beyond the residence. At this trailhead, the Calico Trail is signed as Trail 649.

To reach the Calico (north) Trailhead, take CO 145 north about 6 miles from Rico to Dunton Road, which is across from Clayton Campground. You can also reach this same point by driving south from Telluride and over Lizard Head on CO Hwy 145. Across from the campground, go west on Dunton Road (Forest Road 535) about 4 miles to the junction with Eagle Creek Road (FR 471), then turn left (south) on FR 471 for 0.8 mile. The

Calico Trail

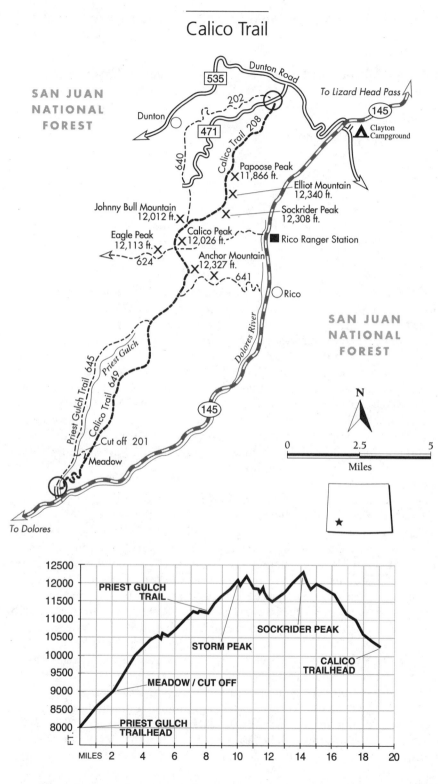

Winter Trail (Trail 202) goes off the road to the west, and just beyond it the Calico Trail (Trail 208) is marked by a Forest Service sign and goes southwest from the road.

Parking and trailhead facilities: Both trailheads have gravel parking areas and bulletin boards; the Calico Trailhead also has a restroom.

Key points:
2.3	First meadows and junction with Priest Gulch cut-off
3.4	Second meadows
8.4	Junction with Priest Gulch Trail
10.0	Storm Peak (12,095 feet)
11.6	Junction with Eagle Peak Trail
12.2	Junction with Johnny Bull Trail
13.0	Junction with Fall Creek Trail
14.2	Sockrider Peak (12,308 feet)
15.6	Papoose Peak (11,866 feet)
19.1	Calico Trailhead

The hike: Created by the Civilian Conservation Corps in the 1930s as a route for driving stock, the Calico Trail follows a long ridge, about a third of which is above timberline. This trail offers many options for day hikes or for a two-or three-day backpack. From the higher points along the ridge you will be treated to great views of the San Miguel Mountains to the north and the La Platas to the southeast. The Needle Mountains are also visible to the east in places, as is much of the Four Corners region to the south and west.

We hiked a portion of the Calico Trail from Priest Gulch for a quick out-and-back day hike while traveling from Telluride to Dolores. Unfortunately, road construction and weather have prevented us from hiking the higher portion of this trail from the north end. Therefore, we have included this as a short day hike and as a long hike based on descriptions provided by the Forest Service.

For the day hike begin from the parking area at Priest Gulch by going right (east), following the signs. The trail crosses Priest Gulch by way of a bridge, and starts up a red-dirt ridge. It switches back and forth as it goes away from the creek and climbs through a mixed ponderosa pine and aspen forest. At about 1.4 miles you will reach the top of the switchbacks and then you'll get a breather a little farther along as the trail levels and follows the broad top of the ridge. At about 2.3 miles is an even broader bench with a large meadow—a good turnaround point for a short day hike. From the meadow you can return as you came, or take the Priest Gulch cut-off (Trail 201) to the west for a return to the trailhead by way of Priest Gulch. If you continue on the Calico Trail, the next open meadow area with good views is another 1.1 miles and 1,000 feet higher.

The rest of the trail is supposed to be well worth hiking, too. If you continue on, you will climb steadily along the ridge through a mixture of forest and ridgetop meadows until you reach timberline at 9 miles. From that point the trail stays mostly above timberline as it crosses over or next to a succession of peaks, including Storm Peak at 12,095 feet, Anchor Mountain at 12,327 feet, Calico Peak at 12,026 feet, Sockrider Peak at 12,308 feet, Elliot Mountain at 12,340 feet, and Papoose Peak at 11,866 feet. The entire trail from the Priest Gulch Trailhead to the Calico Trailhead is about 19 miles.

The higher portions of the ridge are most accessible from the Calico Trailhead, beginning with Papoose Peak at 3.5 miles. The Forest Service writes about the northern portion of the trail: "The scenery along the upper Calico Trail is a 'must see.' To the north of the Calico Trail is 14,000-foot El Diente Peak. To the northeast are views of the high mountains around Trout Lake including Sheep Mountain and San Miguel Peak. To the east is Hermosa Peak and the Rico Mountains, with the Needle Mountains at some distance in the background."

Options: From the Priest Gulch Trailhead hike the Calico Trail north, connect with the Priest Gulch Trail (Trail 645) at about 8.4 miles, and hike it back to the Priest Gulch Trailhead. From the Calico Trailhead there is a 14-mile loop called the Calico National Recreation Trail, which is made up of a combination of the Calico, Winter, and Fall Creek Trails. Begin on the Calico Trail (Trail 208), hike to the base of Johnny Bull Mountain and the junction with the Fall Creek Trail (Trail 640), then hike north toward Dunton Hot Spring and connect with the Winter Trail (Trail 202), which takes you back to FR 471 and the Calico Trailhead across the road. There are also several other trail loops and options using trails that connect to the Calico Trail.

Camping and services: There are many potential campsites along this trail, but little water and no services.

For more information: San Juan National Forest, Dolores Ranger District.

41 Engineer Mountain Overlook

Highlights:	Views; wildflowers.
Location:	South of Silverton at Coal Bank Pass.
Type of hike:	Out-and-back day hike.
Total distance:	5 miles.
Difficulty:	Moderate.
Elevation gain:	1,250 feet.
Best months:	July–September.
Maps:	USGS Engineer Mountain quad; Trails Illustrated Map 140; San Juan National Forest Map.

Special considerations: Wear insect repellent.

Finding the trailhead: Drive 13.8 miles south from Silverton (or 36 miles north from Durango) to Coal Bank Pass on U.S. Highway 550 and look for

Engineer Mountain Overlook

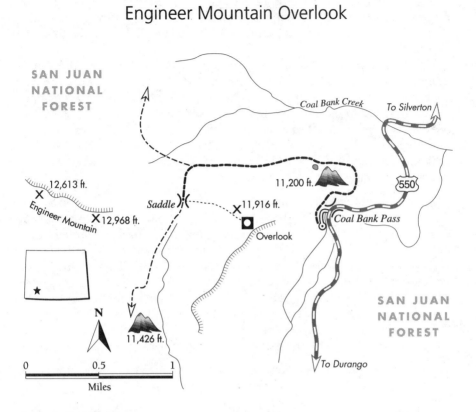

SAN JUAN NATIONAL FOREST

Coal Bank Creek

To Silverton

12,613 ft.

Engineer Mountain   X 12,968 ft.

Saddle

11,916 ft.

11,200 ft.

550

Coal Bank Pass

Overlook

N

11,426 ft.

0   0.5   1

Miles

SAN JUAN NATIONAL FOREST

To Durango

the sign for Pass Creek Trail on the right (west). Drive up the gravel road a short way to the turnaround, and park.

Parking and trailhead facilities: Parking available; no facilities.

Key points:
0.5   Pond
1.9   Saddle, junction with other trails
2.5   High point overlook

The hike: This hike takes you to the saddle at the base of Engineer Mountain and a high point overlooking Coal Bank Pass.

Begin on the west side of the turnaround. Hike north through chin-high wildflowers with larkspur and Queen Anne's lace predominating. Indian paintbrush, penstemon, and others are here, too.

The trail climbs east around the edge of a ridge and then bends westward through spruce-fir forest. Pass

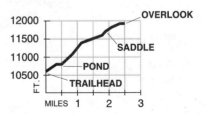

Engineer Mountain.

a small, stagnant pond, then a larger pond, and then climb out of the forest after 0.8 mile, onto the tundra.

As the trail descends, go left (south) and up toward Engineer Mountain. Stop at the saddle and enjoy the views, then walk east along the tundra up to a rounded knob. Continue across the top and to a cliff that overlooks Coal Bank Pass and the canyon of Lime Creek to the Needle Mountains to the east. After enjoying the view, go back the way you came.

Options: From the saddle at the base of the mountain climb Engineer Mountain, but follow the advice of Paul Pixler in his book, Hiking Trails of Southwestern Colorado, and leave early in the day. It is a difficult climb and we were not able to attempt it because we left too late in the day when thunderstorms threatened.

Camping and services: None.

For more information: San Juan National Forest, Columbine Ranger District West.

42 Highland Mary Lakes

Highlights:	Waterfalls; lakes; alpine tundra.
Location:	East of Silverton in the Weminuche Wilderness.
Type of hike:	Out-and-back day hike or backpack.
Total distance:	6.2 miles.
Difficulty:	Strenuous.
Elevation gain:	1,700 feet.
Best months:	July–September.
Maps:	USGS Howardsville quad; Trails Illustrated Map 140; San Juan National Forest Map.

Special considerations: Stream crossings on the four-wheel-drive road and hiking trail may be difficult during the early summer snowmelt.

Finding the trailhead: From the north end of Silverton, go northeast on Colorado Highway 110, which becomes County Road 2 after the pavement ends. At about 4 miles, and shortly after the road crosses the Animas River, turn right (south) onto Cunningham Gulch Road (CR 4) and follow it up the main valley for about 3.6 miles, staying on the main road at all intersections, until you come to where the valley climbs steeply and the road drops down to ford Cunningham Creek. This is the site of the old Highland Mary Mill, and it is a four-wheel-drive road beyond this point. If you have a passenger car, park here at what is the starting point for the trail description. If you have a four-wheel-drive vehicle, continue across Cunningham Creek, up the switchback into the upper valley, and in about 1 mile, after going

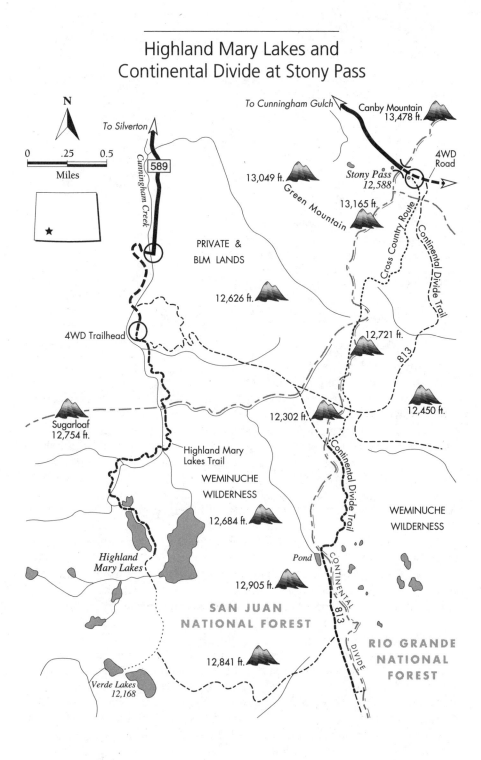

Highland Mary Lakes and
Continental Divide at Stony Pass

N

To Cunningham Gulch

To Silverton

Canby Mountain
13,478 ft.

Cunningham Creek

589

0   .25   0.5
Miles

Stony Pass
12,588

4WD
Road

13,049 ft.

Green Mountain

13,165 ft.

Cross Country Route

Continental Divide Trail

PRIVATE &
BLM LANDS

12,626 ft.

12,721 ft.

813

4WD Trailhead

12,450 ft.

Sugarloaf
12,754 ft.

12,302 ft.

Highland Mary
Lakes Trail

WEMINUCHE
WILDERNESS

Continental Divide Trail

WEMINUCHE
WILDERNESS

12,684 ft.

Highland
Mary Lakes

Pond

CONTINENTAL

12,905 ft.

SAN JUAN
NATIONAL FOREST

813

RIO GRANDE
NATIONAL
FOREST

DIVIDE

12,841 ft.

Verde Lakes
12,168

left at a fork and crossing the creek again, you will come to the end of the road and the signed trailhead.

Parking and trailhead facilities: Adequate parking at both trailheads, but no formal parking or facilities.

Key points:
- 0.8   Four-wheel-drive accessible trailhead
- 1.0   Fork with horse trail
- 1.7   Main stream crossing at forks
- 2.7   Lower two lakes
- 3.1   Largest of Highland Mary Lakes

The hike: This hike takes you up a series of steep climbs to successively higher sections of Cunningham Gulch, until you emerge into the broad, above-timberline basin that holds the Highland Mary Lakes. Each of the stairsteps in the valley is separated by falls and cascades. Hike them and you will be rewarded with wildflowers all along the way.

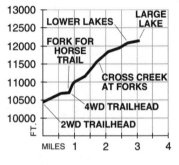

If you parked at the lower trailhead, begin your hike by crossing Cunningham Creek and then follow the jeep road as it switchbacks to gain the upper valley. You can cut off a little distance here by taking the old steeper route—the one time you are allowed to cut switchbacks! After you emerge into the upper valley, follow the jeep road at a fork down and across Cunningham Creek again and along the meadow to the next steep point in the valley, where it ends. A sign here marks the trailhead.

After the sign, the trail gradually becomes steeper, first passing a set of falls that have cut deeply into the rock, and then reaching a fork. The left fork is signed for horses and leads to the Continental Divide. Take the right fork, which leads to Highland Mary Lakes. From this point, the trail climbs steadily, alternately approaching then going away from the creek, with occasional glimpses of falls along the way. At 1.4 miles you will come to a meadow and cross a side creek, which comes down from the Continental Divide and defines the Weminuche Wilderness boundary (although the sign is some distance up the trail). With falls at its upper end, this meadow is a good destination for a short hike.

After the meadow, climb steeply again, and at 1.7 miles cross the two forks of Cunningham Creek that drain the lakes above. Although there are logs here, this could be a difficult stream crossing at high water. From here it is about a 1-mile climb to the first of the Highland Mary Lakes. Along this section, the valley quickly changes from forested subalpine to alpine, with much evidence of glacial action in the form of steep cliffs, talus slopes, and glacial polish or grooves in the bedrock. After crossing one side creek and the main creek two more times, you will arrive first at a small lake and then

One of the Highland Mary lakes.

at the lower end of the second largest lake. Another 0.4-mile walk along the east side of this lake brings you to a low divide where you can hike down to the largest lake.

Options: There are a number of options for exploring the smaller lakes in this alpine basin, particularly if you backpacked in and can spend some time; most can be reached with an easy hike across the tundra. One option is to continue south along the trail (which becomes indistinct in places) and over a saddle 0.7 mile to Verde Lakes. The view from this saddle is spectacular and well worth the extra distance, even for a day hike. From this vantage, you can look straight across to the Grenadiers, some of the most rugged peaks in Colorado. Another option is to continue past Verde Lakes on a trail that loops back east to the Continental Divide. From here, head north on the Continental Divide Trail to a horse trail, which drops down to join the Highland Mary Lakes trail near the four-wheel-drive trailhead. For more information on the Continental Divide portion of this hike, refer to Hike 43.

Camping and services: The best camping sites are above timberline, provided you have good weather. Please camp at least 200 feet from any of the lakes and streams.

For more information: San Juan National Forest, Animas Ranger District.

43 Continental Divide at Stony Pass

See map on page 157

Highlights:	Alpine tundra; wildflowers; views.
Location:	East of Silverton in the Weminuche Wilderness.
Type of hike:	Out-and-back day hike.
Total distance:	6.8 miles.
Difficulty:	Moderate.
Elevation gain (or loss):	690 feet (620 feet).
Best months:	July–September.
Maps:	USGS Howardsville and Storm King Peak quads; Trails Illustrated Map 140; San Juan or Rio Grande National Forest Map.

Special considerations: Check with the USDA Forest Service or San Juan County on snow conditions and status of Stony Pass Road in early summer or late fall.

Finding the trailhead: From the north end of Silverton, go northeast on Colorado Highway 110, which becomes County Road 2 after the pavement ends. At 4 miles, and shortly after the road crosses the Animas River, turn right (south) onto Cunningham Gulch Road (CR 4) and follow it up the main valley for about 1.8 miles to the fork for the Stony Pass Road (CR 2) on the left. Take Stony Pass Road as it switchbacks around into Stony Gulch and climbs to the top of Stony Pass. Park where you can at the top of the pass or just down the other side. The road to the pass is fairly rough, but most

The Grenadier Range from the Continental Divide.

passenger cars can make it. You can also reach Stony Pass from the other (east) side by continuing past Rio Grande Reservoir, but it is definitely a four-wheel-drive route from that direction.

Parking and trailhead facilities: Adequate parking; no facilities.

Key points:
0.2 Old cabin
0.9 Cross head of gully just below the Continental Divide
1.3 First high point
1.8 Saddle and Continental Divide Trail
2.7 Pond near Divide

The hike: This hike takes you into some classic Colorado alpine country—a hike along the rolling tundra of the Continental Divide with spectacular views of surrounding peaks in all directions. And if you hit this hike at its midsummer prime, the combination of bright green tundra, white snow, blue skies, and multicolored wildflowers is indescribable.

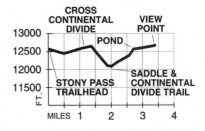

Begin your hike by starting down the east side of the pass along the road until you see an old cabin below. Hike down and past the cabin on the west side and look for a faint trail heading straight south.

Maps show the main Continental Divide Trail also at this location, but for this hike stay to the west and follow a slightly higher route. Follow the trail as it climbs and bends around to the southwest until you lose sight of the cabin behind you. For the next 0.5 mile you will climb up and over or contour around a series of small benches and low ridges that connect back to the higher divide to the west. You may lose the trail in the tundra in places along this section, but this old route is generally marked by large rock cairns, probably placed there by sheepherders. When in doubt, stay high, and eventually you will find the trail again as it goes around the head of a steep gully that drops off to the northeast—one of the tiny headwater streams of the famous Rio Grande. Just past the gully, the trail goes up to and over the Continental Divide to a broad meadow where it again becomes faint. This is an interesting spot, a little wet meadow on top of the divide that seems to fall away to drainages in several directions.

Continue south and aim west of the high point to pick up the trail again and follow it along a ridge that drops steeply to a very large saddle with a small hill in the middle. On either side (north and south) of the hill are two well used trails that cross over the divide. The first is the Continental Divide Trail coming from Stony Pass, and the second is the Divide Trail coming from the south. They meet to the west of the hill and the Divide, where they connect with a horse trail coming up from Cunningham Gulch. Sidestep this little detour in the Continental Divide Trail by traversing the east side of the hill and connecting with the trail on the south side. You are now on the formal Continental Divide Trail, as evidenced by the well-worn path.

161

From the saddle, begin climbing again, following the main trail. At 2.7 miles is a small, shallow pond; just beyond it you cross a low saddle. Views of the spectacular Grenadier Range are to the south and southwest. Go to a junction with the trail that leads west to Verde Lakes. Stay on the Continental Divide Trail a little farther, then climb east to gain a gentle high point along the divide, the destination for this hike. From here you have views down the headwaters valley of the Rio Grande and into the heart of the Weminuche Wilderness. To the south and southwest is the Grenadier Range, containing some of the most challenging climbs in Colorado. Enjoy the view and return as you came.

Options: On your return take the main Continental Divide Trail back to Stony Pass, and avoid the steep climb back up from the saddle. You can also make a side trip to Verde Lakes, or continue on as we did past Highland Mary Lakes to Cunningham Gulch, where you need to shuttle a car. You can also return back up to the divide via the horse trail. For more information on these options, refer to Hike 42.

Camping and services: There are camping opportunities along the divide and down into some of the side drainages; no services.

For more information: San Juan National Forest, Animas Ranger District.

---

44 Bristol Head

Highlights:	Overlooks the Rio Grande and the Weminuche Wilderness; wildlife.
Location:	West of Creede in the San Juan Mountains.
Type of hike:	Out-and-back day hike.
Total distance:	6.6 miles.
Difficulty:	Moderate.
Elevation gain:	1,200 feet.
Maps:	USGS Bristol Head quad; Trails Illustrated Map 139; Rio Grande National Forest Map.
Best months:	July–September.

Special considerations: This hike requires a long drive over a road that demands a four-wheel-drive vehicle for part of its length. In the spring or after wet weather, check with the Forest Service before driving to this hike.

Finding the trailhead: From Creede take Colorado Highway 149 toward Lake City 27 miles to the Bristol Head–Crystal Lake Road. This turnoff is located just past the North Clear Creek Falls scenic turnoff on the northeast side of the highway bridge. Turn right (east) onto the gravel road and, in a short distance, ford Big Spring Creek. This is a fairly deep crossing and you must have a high-clearance vehicle, or you should do this hike in late summer when the creek is low. Follow the road for 12 miles as it circles a large

Bristol Head

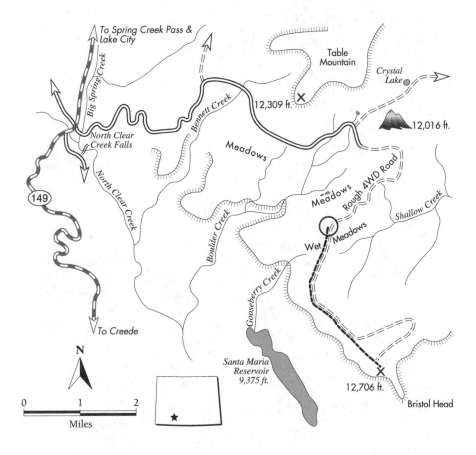

meadow area on the plateau. (Please note that most maps have this road marked incorrectly. It actually takes a longer route, going farther south and east rather than cutting across the meadow.)

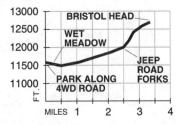

At 8.4 miles you will pass a jeep road turnoff to Crystal Lake—keep right. The road becomes increasingly rough. Park along the side of the road when you feel you must stop. At 12 miles, after the road traverses through willows, it enters a wet meadow. Stopping here provides for a good hike and will prevent damage to the meadow and the slopes below Bristol Head.

Parking and facilities: None.

Braving the cold water to see Zapata Falls.

Key points:

  2.5 Fork in jeep road
  3.3 Summit

The hike: This hike takes you across high meadows for an easy climb of the northwest side of Bristol Head, a prominent landmark that can be seen from much of the Rio Grande Valley above Creede.

Begin by hiking the road from wherever you parked. From where we parked at 12 miles we dropped down and crossed a gentle saddle between Gooseberry Creek and Shallow Creek drainages. For the next 2 miles it is a gentle stroll along the road across meadows. We saw a big herd of elk in this stretch and heard bugling in midsummer.

At 2.5 miles is a fork in the jeep road at the base of a steeper slope. The main jeep road continues east and switches back to the top. Go straight up the steeper jeep road and slope. Here we saw bighorn sheep grazing in the meadow; when they sensed our presence, they ran off to the cliffs.

After a short, steep climb of 0.3 mile you gain the gentler slopes of the broad summit. It is another 0.5 mile to the radio tower located at the summit.

It is surprising once you arrive to see that the south side of the mountain drops away almost 4,000 feet to the Rio Grande. On the west side the cliffs go down more than 3,000 feet to Santa Maria Reservoir. (Hold on to children and pets around the cliffs. And be careful yourself.) You are standing on the northwest rim of the ancient Creede caldera, a huge volcano that erupted and then collapsed. To the southeast and east is the large mountain mass of Snowshoe Mountain, around which the Rio Grande makes a sweeping bend. This is the central volcanic plug that pushed up after the collapse of the caldera, much like the dome observed after the eruption of Mount St. Helens in Washington, but on a much larger scale here.

You can also look west to the great bend of the Continental Divide encircling the headwaters of the Rio Grande. To the northwest are great views of Uncompahgre Peak as well as much of the Weminuche Wilderness.

Options: None.

Camping and services: Good camping along the jeep road in the meadows.

For more information: Rio Grande National Forest, Divide Ranger District.

45 Zapata Falls and South Zapata Creek

Highlights:	Interesting falls; rugged terrain in the Mount Blanca Massif; lake.
Location:	Northeast of Alamosa and south of the Great Sand Dunes in the Sangre de Cristo Wilderness.
Type of hike:	Out-and-back day hike; longer day hike or backpack.
Total distance:	0.6 mile; 9.4 miles.
Difficulty:	Easy to strenuous.
Elevation gain (loss):	200 feet; 2,790 feet.
Best months:	June–September.
Maps:	USGS Twin Peaks quad; Rio Grande National Forest Map.

Finding the trailhead: From the junction of U.S. Highway 160 and Colorado Highway 150 about 16 miles east of Alamosa, go north on CO 150 about 10 miles and look for a road and sign on the east (right) side of the highway for Zapata Falls Recreation Area. Turn right on this road and follow it about 3.5 miles to the Zapata Falls trailhead.

Parking and trailhead facilities: Picnic area, parking, and restrooms.

Key points:
0.3   Zapata Falls
0.9   Stream crossing
1.1   Cabin
2.1   California Gulch
2.4   North Fork of Zapata Creek
3.5   Upper stream crossing
4.1   Timberline
4.7   South Zapata Lake

The hike: This hike really is two separate hikes: a short, easy hike to view Zapata Falls and a long, strenuous day hike or backpack into the Sangre de Cristo Wilderness and South Zapata Lake.

Begin at the signed trailhead and follow an old jeep road 0.3 mile to the base of Zapata Falls. Although this trail is rocky and a little steep in places, there are benches along the way for resting, and family members of all ages should be able to make it. The falls, on the other hand, require a little extra effort to view. You must wade across the stream and then up through the stream in order to get to the hidden alcove where the falls have cut through the rock. Be prepared to bring good hiking sandals or to remove your shoes or boots and roll up your pant legs. The best time to do this hike is in late summer and fall after the snowmelt. For those who pursue the adventure to the alcove there is the reward of being close to the falls. Those who don't go to the alcove can sit and enjoy the stream and the sound of the water.

Zapata Falls and South Zapata Creek

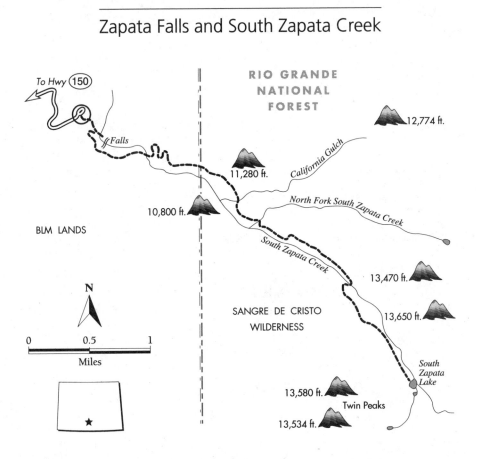

If you want to hike beyond the falls into the upper valley, backtrack a short distance down the trail and look for the place where the upper trail takes off and up a switchback to the west, away from the falls. Do not take any of the steep trails that people have made to try and get a look at the top of the falls.

After the switchback the trail follows a bench, which is an old glacial moraine from the South Zapata glacier, and then climbs through forest into the valley above the falls. At 0.9 mile cross South Zapata Creek and switchback to another bench where there is an old cabin. A couple more switchbacks bring you to your first view of the upper valley and the high peaks of the Mount Blanca Massif.

For the next reach the trail stays high on the south-facing slope and away from the creek. Along this section you will cross from Bureau of Land Management lands onto national forest lands and the Sangre de Cristo Wilderness. At 2.1 miles you will cross California Gulch and then come to the North Fork of South Zapata Creek. Some maps show a trail going up the North Fork, but we did not see it.

After the North Fork the trail begins a steep climb, and in places it
crosses talus slopes. At 3.5 miles cross
South Zapata Creek for the second
time, and then there is another steep
climb to reach timberline. Above timberline the valley rises more gently
and you will reach South Zapata Lake
at 4.7 miles. In places, the trail becomes indistinct for this last section
of the hike. —*Becky and Mandy Gennerman and David Schroeder*

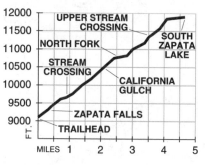

Options: Camp at South Zapata Lake and climb the Twin Peaks to the west from that base.

Camping and services: There are very few good campsites until you get all the way up near timberline. Camp at least 200 feet away from the lake and 100 feet away from the creek.

For more information: Rio Grande National Forest, Conejos Peak Ranger District; Bureau of Land Management, San Luis Resource Area.

46 Lower Medano Creek and the Great Star Dune

Highlights:	Interesting geology and hydrology; opportunities to explore the vast sand dunes.
Location:	Great Sand Dunes National Monument, northeast of Alamosa.
Type of hike:	Bushwhack.
Total distance:	9.8 miles.
Difficulty:	Strenuous.
Elevation gain (or loss):	700 feet (300 feet).
Best months:	May–October.
Maps:	USGS Great Sand Dunes National Monument map or Liberty and Zapata Ranch quads.

Special considerations: Bring water, sunscreen, good boots, and long pants.

Finding the trailhead: From U.S. Highway 160 east of Alamosa go north about 16 miles on Colorado Highway 150 to the Great Sand Dunes National Monument. Stop just after you cross into the park boundary and look over at the sand dunes. You will notice one large dune that stands out on the west (left) side of the main dune mass—this is the Great Star Dune. Record the image of this landmark to memory so that you can find it later on the hike.

Along the ridge to the Great Star Dune.

Continue past the entrance station and visitor center and turn left at the signs for the dunes picnic area and parking. Park in the large parking area.

Parking and trailhead facilities: Parking, restrooms, and a picnic area provided.

Key points:
- 0.9   Side channel of Medano Creek
- 1.6   Last of the cottonwoods
- 2.0   The Bush
- 2.2   Head toward the Star Dune
- 4.9   The Great Star Dune

The hike: This hike takes you downstream along the broad sand channel of Medano Creek and then into the wilderness of sand for a climb of the Great Star Dune, so named because of the star shape of the dune ridges when viewed from the air. There is no trail for this hike—you must rely on a few sparse vegetation landmarks—and the actual effort and distance will depend on sand conditions and your ability to navigate the dunes. That said, this hike can be great fun, with infinite options

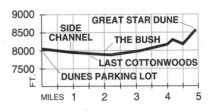

Lower Medano Creek and the Great Star Dune

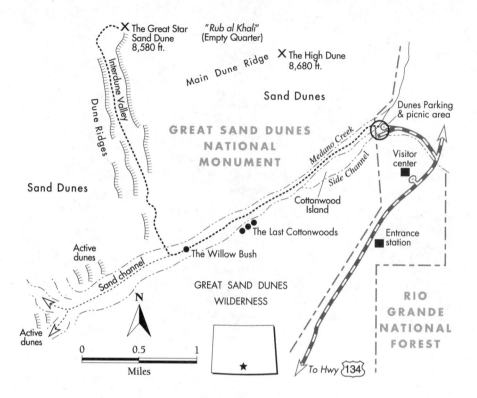

for exploration, including a search for the elusive and ever-changing terminus of Medano Creek.

Begin your hike at the northwest corner of the parking lot by walking out onto the broad channel of Medano Creek and head downstream (southwest). Depending on the time of year, the channel may be completely dry or flowing a hundred yards wide and a few inches deep. If there is a good flow, as is the case during the spring and early summer snowmelt, be sure to take time to observe the pulsating flow, a phenomenon unique to Medano Creek and a few of the other dune streams.

As you hike downstream, follow a line of cottonwoods on your left. This is actually an island formed by a side channel of Medano Creek and Mosca Creek, which began right where you left the parking lot. You may also come across an occasional plastic or metal pipe sticking up from the sand. These are monitoring wells used for research to understand and protect the unique hydrology of Medano Creek and some of the other features of the dunes. Please do not disturb them.

At 0.9 mile is where the side channel returns to the main creek bed, one of a few landmarks useful in judging distances. Two of the other landmarks

170

are the last group of cotttonwoods along the channel, 0.7 mile farther along, and "the Bush," a lonesome group of willows in the middle of the channel 0.4 mile past the cottonwoods.

The Bush is a very useful landmark for hiking the Great Star Dune. In fact, if you have kids along, you can play a game to test your sense of direction and kill time as you plod through the sand. Start by hiking for five minutes as you have been, looking around and generally following a straight course downstream. Now stop and look back at your tracks. Would you call them a straight line? (Perhaps one leg is shorter than the other.) Now, line up the Bush with a distant peak across the San Luis Valley, and begin hiking again for five minutes, this time keeping the two landmarks in perfect alignment in front of you. Now look back. You have just demonstrated how to navigate on a compass course using landmarks, an especially useful skill in a place like the dunes.

Continue downstream (this time in a straight line), past the Bush, and begin looking for the Star Dune to the north-northwest. Line yourself up with the long dune ridge connecting to the Star Dune, which happens at 0.2 mile past the Bush. Once you are lined up, head for the dunes. The best route to the Star Dune is up the interdune valley to the west of the dune ridge, instead of the ridge itself. If you want more of a challenge, and a new definition of "false summit," take the ridge route. No matter what route you take, you will end up backtracking in some places along the way—that is the nature of hiking in the dunes. As you hike along, you may come across more of the plastic monitoring wells, which will lead you up the valley. At 4 miles cross a saddle into a broader valley near the Star Dune. Continue a little farther until you are even with the Star Dune and then climb it by way of the west side or northwest ridge.

The view from the top of the Star Dune is well worth the effort. You now have a nearly complete view of the main dune mass, which we have dubbed the *Rub al Khali* ("Empty Quarter") for that famous sand pile in Saudi Arabia. You are also just high enough to have a view of most of the San Luis Valley and surrounding mountains. And to the south is your friend, the Bush, clearly visible almost 2 miles away. Return as you came, or plot a more interesting return route from this vantage point.

Options: One interesting option if you don't want to tackle the Star Dune, is to continue down Medano Creek past the Bush and search for the terminus of Medano Creek where it disappears into the sands. Medano Creek is important to the cycling of sand in the dune field. Each year, depending on weather and snowpack, Medano Creek swells with snowmelt and begins eroding and carrying sand far down its channel, depositing it in a different location to the southwest of the main dunes as the creek loses water and disappears. And each year after the snow melts, the winds dry the wet sand and blow it back toward the dunes. Depending on when you hike, you can observe either the stream eroding sand and new channels on this lower end, or the tiny dunes beginning to form and migrate back upstream.

Camping and services: You must obtain a backcountry permit at the visitor center for camping in the dunes. There is also a campground north along the main park road.

For more information: National Park Service, Great Sand Dunes National Monument.

47 Sand Creek Lakes

Highlights:	Spectacular views of the Sangre de Cristo Range; many opportunities for fishing.
Location:	South of Westcliffe in the Sangre de Cristo Wilderness.
Type of hike:	Out-and-back day hike or backpack.
Total distance:	12.6 miles.
Difficulty:	Strenuous.
Elevation Gain (loss):	2,350 feet (540 feet).
Best months:	July–September.
Maps:	USGS Crestone Peak and Beck Mountain quads; San Isabel and Rio Grande National Forest Maps.

Finding the trailhead: From Westcliffe go south on Colorado Highway 69 for 5 miles to Colfax Road (County Road 119). Turn right (south). Follow the Music Pass signs, driving 11 miles to where Colfax Road turns into

Upper Sand Creek Lake. RYAN STARR PHOTO

a four-wheel-drive road. If you have a passenger vehicle, park at the base of the four-wheel-drive road and hike to the trailhead; if you have a four-wheel-drive vehicle, head up the road 2.6 miles to the trailhead. Music Pass Trailhead is located on the west side of the parking area.

Parking and trailhead facilities: There are plenty of places to park at the base of the four-wheel-drive road, and there are spaces to pull off and park along the road itself. At the trailhead there is a large open area to park. There is no running water at the trailhead, and no facilities.

Key points:
  2.6   Four-wheel-drive trailhead
  3.7   Music Pass
  4.9   Sand Creek crossing
  5.2   Trail to Lower Sand Creek Lake
  6.3   Upper Sand Creek Lake

The hike: The hike, if starting from the base of the four-wheel-drive road, is a fairly steep and sustained rolling climb to the trailhead—total distance is 2.6 miles. It is fairly rough, but easily walkable all the way along the road. Once the trailhead is reached, the road continues to climb up to Music Pass, but a chain restricts vehicles past this point.

Follow Music Pass Trail (Trail 743) upward through woods to reach a clearing at about 11,000 feet. The clearing extends up to the top of Music Pass at 11,400 feet and down the other side to 11,000 feet. There are spectacular views from the pass of some of the rugged glacially carved mountains that make up the Sangre de Cristo Range. Milwaukee Peak, Music Mountain, and Tijeras Peak are visible from here.

On the other side of the pass, the trail makes its way back down into the woods where there are springs running down the hillside. These are ideal places to purify and collect drinking water. The trail continues downslope to an open mountain meadow, and the junction with Trail 877. Stay on Trail 743, heading northwest toward the Sand Creek Lakes.

Cross Sand Creek—trees and rocks across the river should make it relatively easy. The trail then dives back into the woods, still trending to the northwest (it may become muddy in areas, and horse traffic has made it pretty sloppy and rough). At 0.3 mile from the river crossing, Trail 862 intersects Trail 743 and heads southwest to Lower Sand Creek Lake; it is roughly 0.6 mile to the lake.

In order to reach the upper lake, stay on Trail 743 as it climbs through switchbacks and crosses Sand Creek again. This part of the creek is draining directly from Upper Sand Creek Lake. The lake seems to appear out of nowhere once you ascend the glacial moraine. Upper Lake is about 11,745 feet above sea level, and the glacial moraine acts as a natural dam for it.— *Ryan E. Starr and Casey M. Forth.*

Options: As a side trip it is worth the effort to climb up the north side of Milwaukee Peak—steep, fairly strenuous, and dangerous in some areas. Use extreme caution across loose rock fields and watch for loose footholds and

Sand Creek Lakes

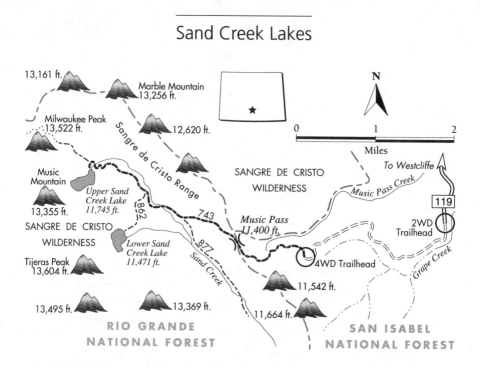

wet foliage on steeper slopes. The highest point is to the north of Milwaukee Peak and is the boundary of Custer and Saguache Counties. Straight-line distance from the lake to the county line is about 1 mile, but the hike can be much longer because it is necessary to make cutbacks due to the pitch of the slope. Approach the summit with caution because it is a steep drop on the opposing side. There is a fantastic southeastern view back down the valley and up to Music Pass, and across the county line looking northwest to the South Colony Lakes, Broken Hand Peak, Crestone Needle, and Humbolt Peak. The weather can change in a hurry at this elevation, so take some extra clothes (waterproof), food, and water.

Camping and services: Please camp at least 200 feet away from the lake. The majority of camping sites are on the north side of the lake, but some are on the east. The sites on the east side of the lake are up on the moraine and tend to catch more wind because of the limited tree cover.

For more information: Rio Grande National Forest, Saguache Ranger District; San Isabel National Forest, San Carlos Ranger District.

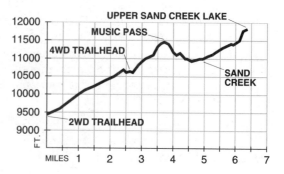

48 Greenhorn Mountain

Highlights: Views; tundra; wildflowers.
Location: Southwest of Pueblo in the Wet Mountains or Cuerna Verde Range.
Type of hike: Up-and-down day hike.
Total distance: 6 miles.
Difficulty: Moderate.
Elevation gain (or loss): 930 feet (330 feet).
Best months: July–September.
Maps: USGS San Isabel and Bandito Cone quads; San Isabel National Forest Map.

Finding the trailhead: From Pueblo drive southwest on Colorado Highway 78 through Valley View, as it turns south, then as it becomes a dirt road and goes west to CO 165. Go (right) north on CO 165 for 3.5 miles, passing Bishops Castle, to the road to Ophir Creek Campground (Forest Road 360). Go straight on this road, then left at the fork in 8.2 miles on FR 369. Follow this road southeast to the road's end and the trailhead, which is 16.5 miles from the fork. You can also take CO 165 northwest from the town of Rye to the road to Ophir Creek Campground.

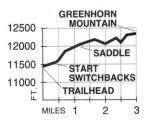

Parking and trailhead facilities: Parking; no facilities.

On the trail up Greenhorn Mountain.

Greenhorn Mountain

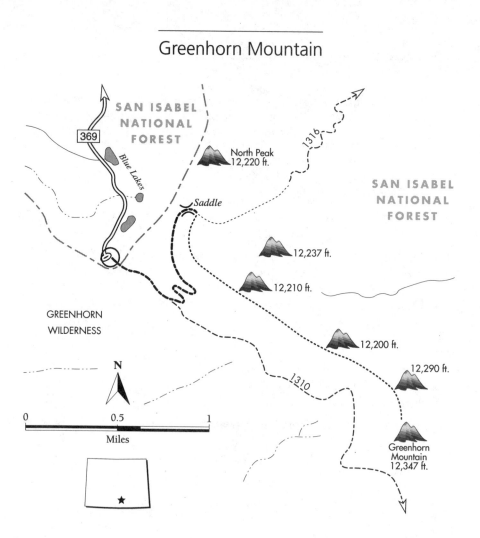

Key points:
- 0.4 Start switchbacks
- 1.2 Saddle
- 3.0 Summit of Greenhorn Mountain

The hike: A long drive and a fairly short hike take you to the summit of Greenhorn Mountain in the Greenhorn Wilderness for views of the eastern plains and the mountains and valleys around Spanish Peaks to the south.

Begin your hike by heading southeast from the parking lot on Trail 1310, an old jeep road. At 0.4 mile the trail to Greenhorn Mountain (Trail 1316) takes off to switchback up the south-facing slope through thick wildflowers, and then bends north along the west-facing slope with views of the Blue Lakes.

Climb onto the saddle just south of North Peak. The trail disappears on the tundra, but turn and follow the ridge south and southwest to the summit of

176

Greenhorn Mountain (12,347 feet). It's easy walking on the tundra. You will come to two false summits along the ridge, each separated by a saddle. Greenhorn Mountain is the farthest and highest point south on the ridge.

The Wet Mountains are a continuation of the same geologic structure that forms the Front Range—Greenhorn Mountain is an anticline at the south end. From the summit you can see the Sangre de Cristo Range to the west beyond the Wet Mountain Valley; the town of Rye and the plains to the east; and to the south the Culebra Range with the Spanish Peaks extending out into the plains. These peaks, and Greenhorn Mountain, were important landmarks that guided people into the San Luis Valley via La Veta Pass for hundreds, maybe thousands, of years.

Enjoy your accomplishment and the views, then hike down as you came up.

Options: For more of a climb, drive to the town of Rye and to Cuerna Verde Park on its west end. Take the Greenhorn Trail (Trail 1316) to the saddle just south of North Peak. Then hike south to Greenhorn Mountain.

Camping and services: Camping is good on the saddle above timberline; no services.

For more information: San Isabel National Forest, San Carlos Ranger District.

The Western Plateaus and Canyons

Western Plateaus and Canyons

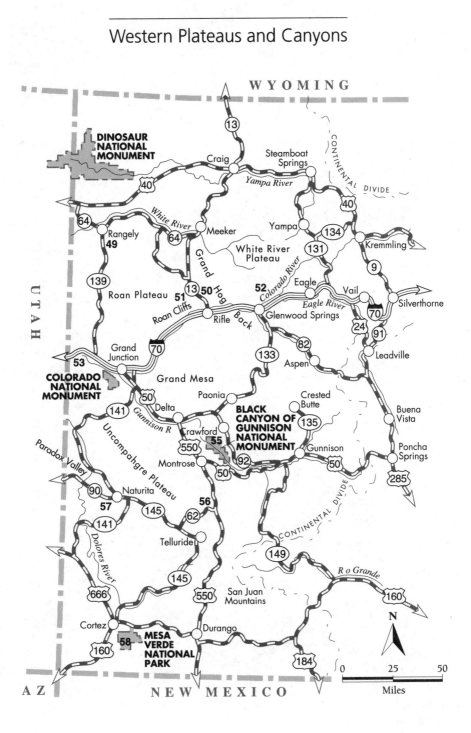

WYOMING

DINOSAUR NATIONAL MONUMENT

13

Craig

Steamboat Springs

Yampa River

CONTINENTAL DIVIDE

40

40

64

Rangely
49

White River

64

Meeker

Yampa

134

131

Kremmling

White River Plateau

9

139

Roan Plateau

13 50

51

Colorado River

Eagle

Vail

70

Silverthorne

Grand Hog Back

Roan Cliffs

Rifle

52

Eagle River

Glenwood Springs

24

91

Grand Junction

70

133

Aspen

82

Leadville

53

COLORADO NATIONAL MONUMENT

Grand Mesa

Paonia

BLACK CANYON OF GUNNISON NATIONAL MONUMENT

Crested Butte

Buena Vista

50

Delta

135

141

Gunnison R

Crawford

55

Poncha Springs

Paradox Valley

Uncompahgre Plateau

550

Montrose

92

Gunnison

50

285

90

Naturita

50

57

145

62

56

141

Telluride

149

CONTINENTAL DIVIDE

Dolores River

145

R o Grande

160

N

666

550

San Juan Mountains

Cortez

160

58

MESA VERDE NATIONAL PARK

Durango

184

0   25   50
Miles

A Z

NEW MEXICO

UTAH

Robin at the petroglyphs in East Fourmile Draw.

49 East Fourmile Draw

Highlights:	Fremont Culture rock art; low elevation canyon; solitude; wild horses.
Location:	South of Rangely in the Canyon Pintado Area.
Type of hike:	Out-and-back or loop day hike.
Total distance:	2 miles.
Difficulty:	Easy.
Elevation gain (or loss):	Minimal.
Best months:	April–May; September–November.
Maps:	USGS Philadelphia Creek and Water Canyon quads.

Special considerations: Take lots of water with you. Take only pictures home, and leave no fingerprints on the rock art panels.

Finding the trailhead: From the intersection of Colorado Highways 64 and 139 just east of Rangely, go south on CO 139 for 10.5 miles. Look for East Fourmile Canyon on the left (east) and a gate and jeep road just after you cross the draw.

Parking and trailhead facilities: Limited parking in the turnoff; no facilities.

Key points:
- 0.2 First panel of rock art
- 0.3 Cross side draw; second panel of rock art
- 0.5 Third panel of rock art
- 1.0 Junction of forks of East Fourmile Draw

The hike: Begin your hike by following the jeep road beyond the gate (be sure the gate is closed behind you). In about 100 yards look for a trail heading north down and across East Fourmile Draw. Immediately after climbing out of the draw, look for a panel of rock art up on a ledge along the cliffs to the north. As you take your time looking at the panels, which are primarily of Fremont culture, understand that the Escalante expedition was led into this area long before you by the Ute Indians. Members of the expedition named this Canon Pintado, "Painted Canyon." Please do not touch the rock because the oil from your fingers destroys the art. Of course, you would not vandalize the art in any other way such as chalking or chipping the rock. Notice the petrified logs embedded in the overhangs.

This and other rock art sites near Rangely are Fremont or Ute art or both. The Fremont culture dates from around A.D. 650 to 1150; the Ute culture from about A.D. 1200 to 1881. According to a self-guided tour brochure from the Rangely museum: "The Fremont people built villages, farmed the valley areas and on high points located watchtowers. In hidden places on the cliffs are still found cisterns and granaries where they stored corn and seeds. Petroglyphs of corn stalks are at a number of these sites. Later the Utes

East Fourmile Draw

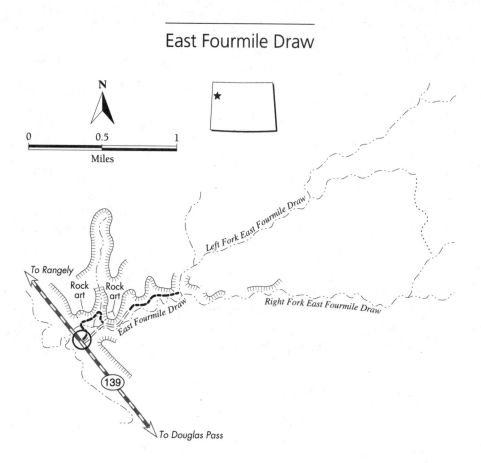

hunted the area and used the valley until they were moved to a reservation in 1881."

Head toward the cliff face directly east and cross the first side draw that comes in from the north. Along the cliff is another panel, this one facing the trail near the entry of the side draw. Some pioneer cabin ruins are about 100 yards farther east along the cliff. Continue around the bend in the cliff and you will see a stunning Fremont panel that faces the direction you are going.

The Rangely museum brochure offers a glossary of rock art terms: anthropomorphic for humanlike forms; meanders for wavy, abstract figures; metates, grinding stone grooves; petroglyphs, pecked or incised art; pictographs, for painted rock art; and problematics, for abstract figures. The rock art was created, it is believed, for various reasons, including religious purposes and to mark great events. Some may simply be doodles.

After viewing this panel, continue along the north side of the draw until you reach the junction of the Left and Right Forks of Fourmile Draw at about 1 mile.

Options: Explore either canyon, going as far as you like, then return as you came. There are wild horse and game trails to follow.

At 2 miles up the Right Fork you'll come to a side canyon from the north; there is a good route where you can bushwhack up that side canyon, up and over the divide, and down a side canyon to the Left Fork, then follow it back to the junction of the forks again.

You can also make a short hike up the first draw from the north that you crossed to reach the second panel of rock art, then return the way you came.

Camping and services: You may camp anywhere you like in the upper canyon above the forks; no services.

For more information: Bureau of Land Management, White River Resource Area; Rangely Museum.

---

50 Rifle Arch

Highlights:	Unusual arch; views; wildlife.
Location:	North of Rifle at the base of the Grand Hogback.
Type of hike:	Out-and-back day hike.
Total distance:	3 miles.
Difficulty:	Easy.
Elevation gain (or loss):	470 feet (140 feet).
Best months:	April–May; October–November.
Maps:	USGS Rifle and Horse Mountain quads.

Finding the trailhead: From the intersection of Colorado Highways 13 and 25 about 2 miles north of Rifle, continue north on CO 13 another 3.7 miles. Look for a small parking area and Bureau of Land Management trailhead sign on the right (northeast) side of the highway.

Parking and trailhead facilities: Limited parking; no facilities.

Key points:
- 0.4 Bench
- 0.9 Jeep road/gulch
- 1.1 Leave jeep road
- 1.5 End of trail below arch

The hike: Begin by crossing a flat meadow and then climbing the low bluff next to a small drainage. Cross through piñon-juniper forest to a bench. The trail traverses the bench and at some open areas you will get your first glimpses of Rifle Arch, which is near the base of the steep rock face of the Grand Hogback just to the north of the small canyon.

Rifle Arch

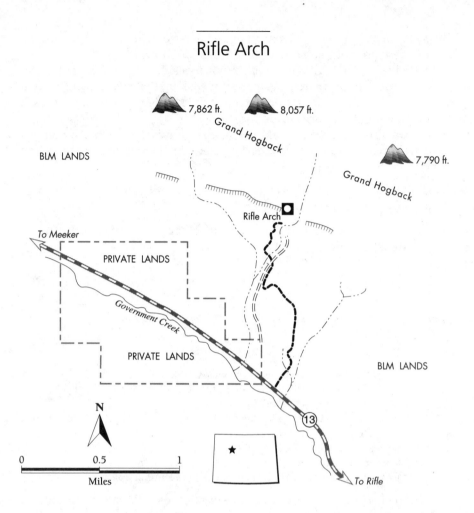

7,862 ft.

8,057 ft.

Grand Hogback

7,790 ft.

Grand Hogback

BLM LANDS

Rifle Arch

To Meeker

PRIVATE LANDS

Government Creek

PRIVATE LANDS

BLM LANDS

N

0   0.5   1
Miles

13

To Rifle

★

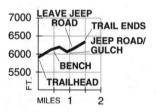

7000
6500
6000
5500
FT.

LEAVE JEEP ROAD

TRAIL ENDS

JEEP ROAD/ GULCH

BENCH

TRAILHEAD

MILES   1   2

Rifle Arch.

The open areas on the bench above you were created by chaining, which is dragging a large chain between two bulldozers to remove the junipers and open the area for cattle grazing. Although this method seems destructive, there is some evidence that this area was much more open before the white man came with his cattle. The grazing causes the juniper to grow in. The Indians may have set fires to keep the open meadow areas for hunting.

After crossing the bench, you will intersect a road, which you should follow down and into a gulch. Follow the jeep road and the gulch up a short distance and you will see a sign for the trail heading up a slope to your left. It is a short climb of 0.4 mile to where the trail ends below the arch.

We climbed up into the arch, but it was pretty steep, and we don't recommend it. On your way back, do not follow the jeep road down into private land.

Options: For a longer exploration, take either of the small drainages that fork near where you left the jeep road. We took the right (east) drainage, which deadended at a cliff and small waterfall. We did not explore the left (west) drainage.

Camping and services: None.

For more information: Bureau of Land Management, Glenwood Springs Resource Area.

51 East Fork Parachute Creek

Highlights: Falls; wildlife; views; high plateau.
Location: Northwest of Rifle on the Roan Plateau in the Naval Oil Shale Reserve.
Type of hike: Bushwhack.
Total distance: 5.2 miles.
Difficulty: Strenuous.
Elevation gain (or loss): (1,100 feet).
Best months: June–October.
Maps: USGS Anvil Points and Forked Gulch quads.

Special considerations: Four-wheel-drive vehicle is recommended, but you can get close to the start of the hike with a passenger car. Check the JQS Trail conditions before driving up to the top. Wear long pants.

Finding the trailhead: From the north end of Rifle, take Colorado Highway 13 north about 3.5 miles and turn west on 242 Road (JQS Trail). Cross Government Creek and climb to the base of the Roan Cliffs to the west. Continue up, staying on the main road at all forks. You will go through two gates and then switchback up the cliffs to the top of the Roan Plateau (not for the faint-hearted). Don't go if conditions are wet. After you reach the top of the plateau at 11.8 miles, there's a fork in the road; go left on Anvil Points Road and follow it as it rolls up and down close to the edge of the Roan Cliffs. It's definitely worth stopping to take in the view on the way: You are nearly 4,000 feet above the Colorado River! At 18 miles (from the highway)

Canyon of East Fork Parachute Creek below the falls.

East Fork Parachute Creek

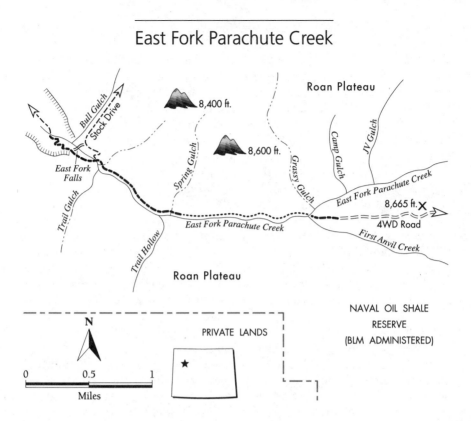

go right on Road 8028. This is a four-wheel-drive road, but most cars can make it partway. Continue on this road, which goes for about 2.3 miles and loses about 900 feet in elevation as it follows the ridgetop between East Fork Parachute and First Anvil Creeks. The last part of the road is very steep. Park where you feel comfortable stopping.

Parking and trailhead facilities: Parking along road only, and limited; no facilities.

Key points:

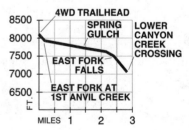

0.2	Junction of East Fork Parachute and First Anvil Creeks
1.4	Spring Gulch
2.2	Stock driving trail; creek crossing
2.4	View of East Fork Falls and canyon
2.6	Crossing of East Fork Parachute Creek below falls

The hike: This hike takes you along a mid-elevation canyon in an area seldom visited by hikers and ends where the canyon makes a spectacular drop at East Fork Falls. It is an adventure, from the drive to the last pitch back to your car.

Begin by following the jeep road from where you parked to its end and then down a steep trail to the confluence of the East Fork Parachute Creek and First Anvil Creeks. There is a little sandstone ledge here and you will have to search for a way down. An old road actually crossed First Anvil Creek and then followed the south side of the East Fork; however, it was blocked by so much downed timber that the more open slope of the north side of the East Fork is an easier route. But there is no trail. You must bushwhack from here for at least the next mile, and you will be tugged on by wild roses and, as Rudyard Kipling would say, "wait-a-bit thornbushes."

Cross the East Fork and find your way up and around the sandstone ledge. When in doubt for about the first half mile, stay high to avoid ledges and undercut banks. After that the route is easier and you can stay close to the creek.

By the time you get to Spring Gulch at 1.4 miles from the end of the jeep road, you should pick up a well-worn trail. At 2.2 miles, just after crossing another side drainage, you'll come to a gate and a jeep road, which is actually a stock drive for moving cattle up to the plateau from the lower canyon, and vice versa. Cross the East Fork here and continue along the south side of the creek.

We saw a young horse here that had slipped off the cliff above the creek and fallen to its death. It may have been a wild horse from the herd that normally ranges to the northwest along the Cathedral Bluffs. Just after that we came across a cinnamon-colored black bear, which crossed our path—no doubt on its way to the dead horse. As we said, this hike is an adventure.

Hike another 0.2 mile and you will come suddenly upon a spectacular view: East Fork Canyon. At the head of it is East Fork Falls, which will spray you. To view the falls, hike a short distance down the steep stock trail and look back. For the best views hike all the way down to the bottom of the canyon to where the trail crosses the creek, a distance of 0.4 mile from the top of the falls.

As you backtrack to your vehicle, realize that you are hiking over as much oil as is in a good Saudi Arabian oil field. This is part of what is called the Piceance Basin.

Options: From below the falls, continue about another mile before you get to private property owned by one of the oil companies.

Another option for a short hike is to hike south about 1 mile from Anvil Points Road back at mile 16.3 from CO 13. This is another bushwhack but an easy hike through mostly meadow and sagebrush to East Anvil Point for a great view.

Camping and services: Camping is pleasant on one of the grassy bluffs of the plateau near the Roan Cliffs; no services.

For more information: Bureau of Land Management, Glenwood Resource Area.

52 Hanging Lake

Highlights:	Beautiful river; waterfalls; and hanging lake. Accessible in winter.
Location:	In Glenwood Canyon, east of Glenwood Springs.
Type of hike:	Out-and-back day hike.
Total distance:	2.4 miles.
Difficulty:	Moderate.
Elevation gain (or loss):	1,100 feet
Best months:	June–September; February–March.
Maps:	USGS Glenwood Springs quad; Trails Illustrated Map 123; White River National Forest Map.

Special considerations: Wear sturdy boots if you are hiking in winter.

Finding the trailhead: Drive east into Glenwood Canyon on Interstate 70 for about 9 miles to Exit 125 or drive 19.3 miles west into the canyon from Gypsum to the exit for Grizzly Creek (Exit 121) then return east to Exit 125. Follow the signs to Hanging Lake Trailhead.

Parking and trailhead facilities: Parking is provided. There is a bulletin board and restrooms.

Key points:
- 0.3 Dead Horse Creek
- 0.5 Junction with Dead Horse Trail
- 1.2 Hanging Lake

The hike: This trail takes you to a lake perched on a terrace of its own making high in Dead Horse Canyon, a side canyon jutting north from Glenwood Canyon near Glenwood Springs. In the winter your hike will take you to a wondrous display of ice formations. Summer finds the canyon lush and inviting. And there are always the views from the top.

Begin hiking from the trailhead at the west end of the parking lot, heading northwest. This trail was built by the Civilian Conservation Corps in the late 1930s. During winter it is a well-tramped snow trail, winding its way along Dead Horse Creek, which you will cross several times via well-built bridges. Pass a sheltered resting spot as you go and through stands of oakbrush, alder, blue spruce, and Douglas-fir. Steep at first, the path levels out somewhat, then challenges with a last treacherous pitch to the terrace—with the help of a handrail.

Hanging Lake puts on a beautiful display of ice formations every winter, but the setting is at once peaceful and spectacular any time of year. Ringed by limestone cliffs to the north, waterfalls tumble to freeze on clumps of moss like frost freezing on a skier's mustache. To the south the limestone terraces end abruptly at the edge of a cliff. Beyond is a view of the canyon and its reddish gold walls.

Hiker at Spouting Rock in winter.

Hanging Lake

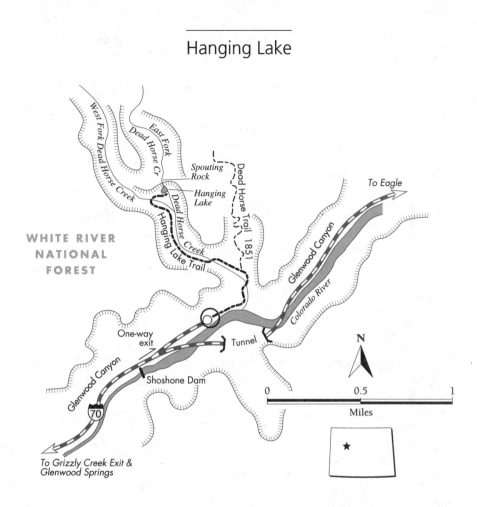

A boardwalk surrounds the southern edge of the lake. A faint trail leads to the locally famous Spouting Rock, where water pours from the cliff, creating huge mounds of blue ice below. Deep in the throes of winter, the waterfall becomes one huge icicle. Until then, you can walk behind the roaring stream and look out through the spray. Icicles line the cavern behind the waterfall and decorate the rock face.

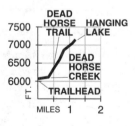

The unique features and ice formations of Hanging Lake and Spouting Rock are part of the geology of the White River Plateau into which Dead Horse Canyon and the larger Glenwood Canyon have been carved. The lake and the spouting waterfall are actually products of the same geologic process: the dissolution and later deposition of minerals from limestone.

Miners knew the lake and wanted to keep it to themselves. Someone supposedly said, "We may not have found any gold up there, but we sure found an emerald."

Enjoy the beauty of Hanging Lake, then head on down as you came.

Options: During warm months, hike up Dead Horse Trail, which leaves the Hanging Lake Trail at mile 0.5 and goes northeast to Dead Horse Road (Forest Road 622). This jeep road goes north to meet Coffee Pot Road (FR 600) just west of Coffee Pot Campground. You'll need to shuttle vehicles.

You can also make a loop by hiking the Tie Gulch Trail (Trail 1853), which takes off from the Dead Horse Trail just south of the jeep road. It goes east and loops back to I-70 at the East End Trailhead by way of Burnt Tree Ridge. Again a car shuttle is necessary.

Camping and services: None.

For more information: White River National Forest, Eagle Ranger District.

53 McDonald Canyon

Highlights:	Rock art; sandstone canyon; good introduction to canyon hiking.
Location:	West of Grand Junction near the Utah border.
Type of hike:	Out-and-back day hike.
Total distance:	3.6 miles.
Difficulty:	Easy.
Elevation gain (or loss):	(120 feet).
Best months:	April–May; October–November.
Maps:	USGS Bitter Creek Well (Utah-Colorado) quad.

Special considerations: May need high-clearance vehicle. Take water.

Finding the trailhead: Take Interstate 70 west from Grand Junction to the Rabbit Valley exit, which is about 2 miles before the Utah border. Go south on the gravel road, which becomes a dirt road. At 0.3 mile stay right at the first fork, then go left at the fork at 1 mile at a sign to a campground. Cross the creek and stay along it at all intersections. At 1.5 miles the road follows the creek bed through a short canyon section—this is the roughest part. After emerging from the canyon, continue straight across the broad, open valley. At 2.9 miles is a round rock that looks like Jabba the Hutt. Look for and take another jeep road going off to the left (east) and down to where it meets McDonald Canyon. The road deadends at the trailhead.

Pictograph panel in McDonald Canyon.

Parking and trailhead facilities: Parking; no facilities.

Key points:
    0.5   Side canyon and drop-off
    0.8   Big bend; canyon widens
    1.1   Second side canyon
    1.8   Canyon mouth and railroad

The hike: This is an excellent family hike and a good introduction to canyon and desert hiking. You will follow the creek bed along most of this hike. In fact, you should avoid making trails across the sensitive soils and meadows. There are also at least four sets of rock art, which add to the adventure of this hike. My dad and I wrote some riddles to help you find them:

The First.
Turtle, lizard, and sandhill crane,
hidden in shade, but basking in sun.
They welcome you to this adventure of fun.

The Second.
From the toppled rocks that help you down,
look across the canyon to where
a deer and a man are found.

The Third.
For a circle spiral pecked in rock,
look carefully back where the water drops.

McDonald Canyon

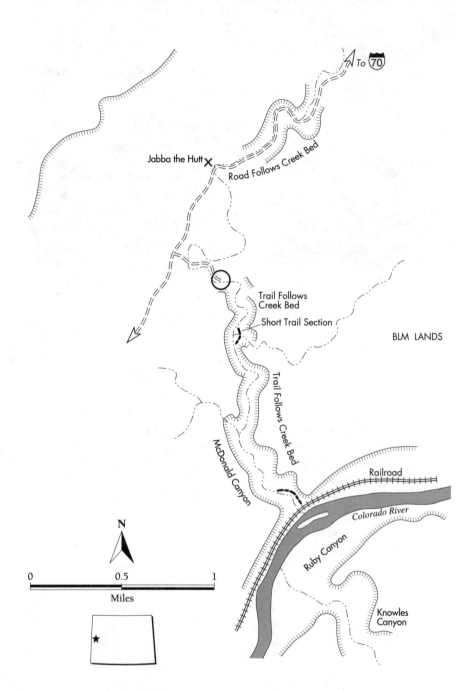

To (70)

Jabba the Hutt X

Road Follows Creek Bed

Trail Follows Creek Bed

Short Trail Section

BLM LANDS

Trail Follows Creek Bed

McDonald Canyon

Railroad

Colorado River

Ruby Canyon

Knowles Canyon

N

0   0.5   1
Miles

The Last.
To help you find the very last,
think of cool shade in the morning,
and echoes of the past.

There is probably other rock art in this canyon, but these are the easier ones to find. Please do not touch any of the artwork. The oil from your fingers will destroy it. There are also lots of lizards along this hike.

Start hiking down the creek bed; in 0.5 mile is a little side canyon and a short drop where the creek has cut a slot in the sandstone and you will have to climb around some rocks to get around this. Below this the canyon widens and the cliffs above it become higher. At 1.1 miles you'll come across another side canyon, this time from the west. Continue to the mouth of the canyon at the Colorado River (you will come across the Denver & Rio Grande Western railroad tracks, part of the Amtrak route). If you are lucky, you may get to wave at a passing train. Please note that the railroad right-of-way is private property. This is Ruby Canyon and directly across the Colorado is Knowles Canyon, part of the Black Ridge Canyon Wilderness Study Area.

Return as you came.—*Robin Boddie.*

Camping and services: There's no camping in McDonald Canyon, but there are campsites at Jabba the Hutt and other places along the road.

For more information: Bureau of Land Management, Grand Junction Resource Area.

54 Adobe Badlands

Highlights:	Rugged shale badlands.
Location:	North of Delta at the base of Grand Mesa.
Type of hike:	Bushwhack.
Total distance:	4.8 miles.
Difficulty:	Moderate.
Elevation gain (loss):	90 feet (800 feet).
Best months:	May–June; September–November.
Maps:	USGS North Delta quad; Grand Mesa National Forest Map.

Special considerations: We got to the trailhead in a passenger car, but it was a little rough. You definitely don't want to drive it when it's wet. Take water.

Finding the trailhead: Take U.S. Highway 50 north from Delta across the Gunnison River and look for the sign to the airport. Turn right and then immediately turn left onto 15.75 Road. Go north 1.2 miles and take a left onto 15.60 Road, which bends west around the airport and then continues

Adobe Badlands

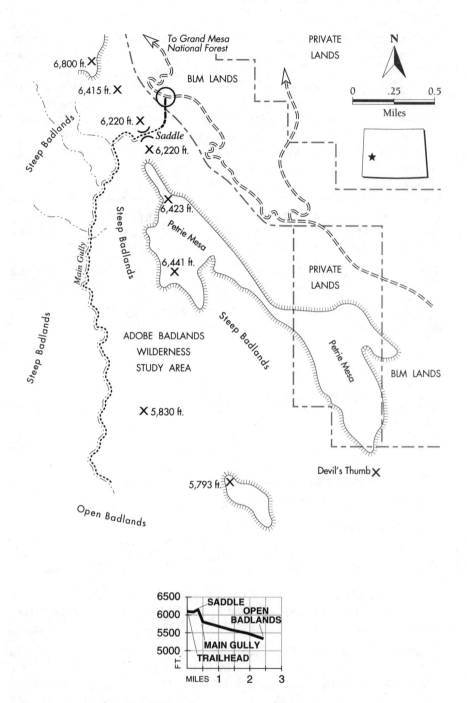

To Grand Mesa National Forest

PRIVATE LANDS

BLM LANDS

6,800 ft. X

6,415 ft. X

Steep Badlands

6,220 ft. X

Saddle
X 6,220 ft.

Steep Badlands

6,423 ft. X

Petrie Mesa

Main Gully

Steep Badlands

6,441 ft. X

Steep Badlands

PRIVATE LANDS

Petrie Mesa

ADOBE BADLANDS WILDERNESS STUDY AREA

BLM LANDS

Steep Badlands

X 5,830 ft.

Devil's Thumb X

5,793 ft. X

Open Badlands

N

0   .25   0.5
Miles

6500
6000
5500
5000
FT.

SADDLE
OPEN BADLANDS
MAIN GULLY
TRAILHEAD

MILES 1   2   3

Adobe Badlands.

north. At 2.9 miles the gravel road bends left to a landfill; continue straight on the dirt road. At 6.4 miles stay left at the fork. Continue around some steep bends. At 7.8 miles you will come to a little flat bench or saddle, just before the road starts to switchback steeply up the slope again. Park here.

Parking and facilities: Park off the road; no facilities.

Key points:
    0.2   Leave jeep road and head west for a low saddle (no trail)
    0.3   Top of saddle with rock wall; drop into gully
    0.5   Bottom of main gully
    2.4   Emerge into open badlands

The hike: This is an adventure through an area of stark beauty, made up almost entirely of eroding clay soils derived from the Mancos Shale Formation. Some people find this to be an unappealing moonscape, whereas others are fascinated by the myriad turns in the small canyons and gullies, or the feeling of isolation. Hidden in these canyons are many surprises.

From the parking pull-off, cross the county road and head south along a faint jeep road into a small grassy basin. Ahead to the south is Petrie Mesa, and to the west over a low ridge is the entry point to the badlands. Follow the jeep road south for 0.2 mile. Just before the road ends, look for the lowest saddle in the ridge to your right (west) and climb to it. A row of rocks here is presumably to discourage driving or cows or both.

The route into the badlands is immediately below you down a steep gully. Follow this gully down 0.3 mile until you reach the main canyon or gully.

From here you can explore as far as you want down the main canyon. At 2.4 miles you will emerge into the open badlands. Return as you came.

Options: Make a loop by climbing one of the ridges to the west and following it back north to the upper ridges so that you come out above the saddle or where you parked. For this option you must be careful to select a ridge or gully route that does not end on a steep slope. If you choose to continue farther down the canyon, be sure and note the gully you came down so that you can find your way back.

Camping and services: No good camping spots; no services.

For more information: Bureau of Land Management, Grand Junction Resource Area.

55 Exclamation Point

Highlights:	Spectacular views of Black Canyon of the Gunnison, piñon-juniper; access to wilderness.
Location:	South of Crawford on the north rim of the Black Canyon of the Gunnison.
Type of hike:	Out-and-back day hike.
Total distance:	4 miles.
Difficulty:	Easy.
Elevation gain (or loss):	Minimal, if you're careful (1,900 feet if you're not).
Best months:	May–October.
Maps:	USGS Grizzly Ridge quad; Trails Illustrated Map 245; National Park brochure.

Special considerations: Please note that the North Rim is closed in winter.

Finding the trailhead: From the town of Crawford, go west on 38.5 Drive, which will bend south and make a couple of jogs to intersect Amber Road. Stay on 38.5 Drive, following the signs to Black Canyon Road and to the North Rim. After entering the national monument turn right (west) at the signs for the campground and ranger station.

Parking and trailhead facilities: Park at the ranger station. Restrooms and information provided.

Key points:
    1.0   Gully going into the canyon
    2.0   Exclamation Point

The hike: This trek takes you along the less-visited North Rim of the Black Canyon of the Gunnison to a point where you have a view of one of the most awesome gorges in the world.

Exclamation Point

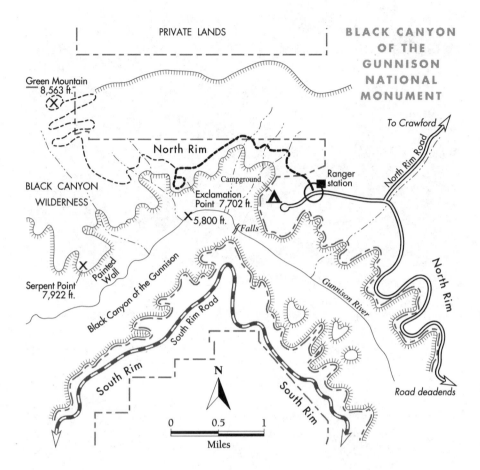

Begin next to the ranger station and go through a meadow with sagebrush, grass, and wildflowers, then down a gentle slope, which belies the dizzying drop-offs ahead. The trail then drops down to round two gulches, which fall off steeply to the Gunnison River below. The second of these is one of the access points for hiking to the bottom of the canyon, which is possible with much scrambling, but is not a technical climb. This side hike should not be attempted without preparation and contacting the park rangers. A permit is required for hiking into the inner canyon. After the second gully, the trail climbs a little into the piñon-juniper forest and comes to a trail junction.

Go left (south) and follow the trail. In a short distance you'll come to another fork. If you want to "get right to the point" take the left fork; if you want the more interesting and exciting route, go right. Either way, you will get there on a loop, which returns to this junction.

The Black Canyon from Exclamation Point.

At Exclamation Point is one of the best views in the park, because you are lined up with a long view of Black Canyon to the southeast. This is one of those places where you want to hang on to your kids. You are almost 1,900 feet straight up from the Gunnison River. South across the canyon is Chasm View; southwest is the famous painted wall.

Options: For a longer hike continue on the main trail another 2.5 miles to the top of Green Mountain, which provides some more expansive views of the entire area and the canyon to the west. You can also bushwhack along the North Rim to Serpent Point or points west, but you must obtain a backcountry permit from the ranger station.

Camping and services: Camping is not recommended along this short trail, but you may camp in the wilderness with a permit. Rangers are available.

For more information: Black Canyon of the Gunnison National Monument.

56 Dallas Creek at Ridgway State Park

Highlights:	Riparian and piñon-juniper habitats; views; opportunity to see kokanee salmon. Good family hike; wheelchair accessible.
Location:	North of Ridgway in Ridgway State Park.
Type of hike:	Loop day hike.
Total distance:	1 mile.
Difficulty:	Easy.
Elevation gain (or loss):	Minimal.
Best months:	May–October.
Maps:	Ridgway State Park map.

Finding the trailhead: Drive north from Ridgway on Colorado Highway 550 for 4 miles and turn in at the south entrance to Ridgway State Park. Pay an entrance fee at the self-serve station, drive to the south end of the road, and park at the picnic area.

Parking and trailhead facilities: Parking, picnic area, water, and restrooms are available.

Key points:
0.1 Turn south along Dallas Creek

The hike: This hike in one of Colorado's newer state parks takes you through riparian habitat then up and around through piñon-juniper and oakbrush

Mount Sneffels from Dallas Creek Trail.

Dallas Creek at Ridgway State Park

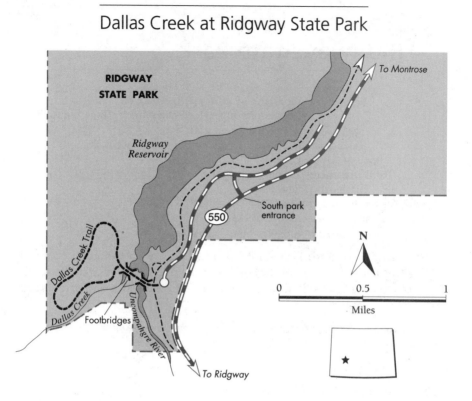

(Gambel's oak) and back to your starting point. At this writing, Ridgway State Park had about 7 miles of trails, but they were planning to extend their trail system as they acquire additional land. By the time you get there, you may well be able to extend this loop hike to enjoy more of this beautiful park.

Begin by crossing the bridges and turning south on the west bank of Dallas Creek. You will walk through riparian habitat with narrow-leaf cottonwood, oakbrush, and vines. Head uphill and take a moment to look south and enjoy the views of the Uncompahgre Plateau, as well as Mount Sneffels and the surrounding mountains.

The trail bends north as you walk through piñon-juniper forest and oakbrush. Soon you will loop back to the bridges where you began your hike. As you head back to your car, look for kokanee salmon, which run here in the fall.

This site used to be the town of Dallas in the 1880s. Fire and the railroad decided the fate of the town; the railroad chose Ridgway as its headquarters in 1890.

Options: Take a 0.6-mile nature trail—a loop—from the visitor center. Drive north on CO 550 to the Dutch Charlie gate and follow the signs to the center. There are other trail options as well.

Camping and services: Camping is available in the park at designated sites. Information is available at the visitor center.

For more information: Ridgway State Park.

57 Dry Creek Anticline

Highlights: Interesting geology; canyon hiking; good echoes.
Location: West of Naturita at the southeast end of the Paradox Valley.
Type of hike: Out-and-back day hike or backpack.
Total distance: 6 miles.
Difficulty: Moderate.
Elevation gain (or loss): 400 feet (850 feet).
Best months: April–May; September–November.
Maps: USGS Naturita NW quad.

Special considerations: Rough road, but most passenger cars can make it. Don't go when it's wet. Take water.

Finding the trailhead: From Naturita go northwest on Colorado Highway 141 about 2 miles to the junction with CO 90. Go south on CO 90, which bends around back to the west into the Paradox Valley. At 4.4 miles look for a jeep road to the left (southwest)—this is located between mile markers 30 and 29, just past a small road cut. Follow this jeep road, which is a little rough but passable for most cars, going right at a fork at 0.5 mile. Follow the road next to the natural gas pipeline another 0.5 mile straight across the flat grass park. Just past pipeline marker 32 and before the jeep road climbs, go left (southeast) at a fork. Follow this road to the end of the grass area, and park. You will be near an old stock pond and a junction with another jeep road. Beyond this point, the road gets very rugged and should not be attempted.

Parking & trailhead facilities: Park off the road; no facilities.

Key points:
0.5 First saddle
1.0 Second saddle
2.0 Dry Creek
3.0 Center of Dry Creek anticline

The hike: This hike takes you to an interesting geologic feature: a paradox.

Start from where you parked. Follow the jeep road down and across a drainage and begin a short but steep climb to the first saddle. At this saddle you are standing at the edge of a small basin created by a water gap in the Dakota Sandstone hogback. As you look across the basin, you will see another saddle 0.5 mile away. Look for a steep jeep road, which has been cut

Dry Creek Anticline

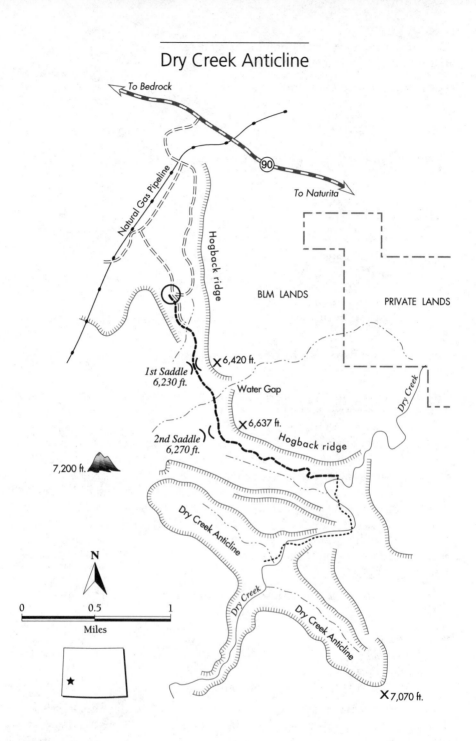

To Bedrock

Natural Gas Pipeline

90

To Naturita

Hogback ridge

BLM LANDS

PRIVATE LANDS

✗ 6,420 ft.

1st Saddle
6,230 ft.

Water Gap

Dry Creek

✗ 6,637 ft.

2nd Saddle
6,270 ft.

Hogback ridge

7,200 ft.

Dry Creek Anticline

N

Dry Creek

0   0.5   1

Miles

Dry Creek Anticline

★

✗ 7,070 ft.

to the left (east of the low point in the saddle). This is the route you want to aim for and not the low point in the saddle. Continue into the basin to where the jeep road forks and there is a small metal structure made of pipe. Go left here, cross a little meadow, and go across a drainage. From here it is another short but steep climb to the second saddle, the high point of this hike.

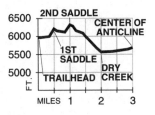

Hike down this old, steep, and eroding jeep road 1 mile to Dry Creek, which you can see below. As you descend you'll get some great views of the San Juan Mountains far to the southeast. If the road deadends, you went the wrong way and you must climb up and above the rocks to your left to intersect the correct trail.

Cross Dry Creek and follow game trails and remnants of an old jeep road upstream. After the very first rock cut you will pass by a layer of smooth, red sandstone between the two hogback formations. This is Entrada Sandstone, which forms the arches in nearby Arches National Park.

Continue through the main hogback and into the Dry Creek anticline. Hike into the center. As you look to both ends of this 2-mile-long hole in the mountain, notice that the same rock formations form the cliffs on either side. You are in the very center of a small anticline, which is a dome in the sedimentary rocks that has been eroded by the creek. It is unique to find such a symmetrical structure as this.

We didn't have a camera on this hike, so we've provided an illustration. Enjoy this anomaly, and after bouncing a few echoes off the rock, return as you came. Please note that Dry Creek flows out onto private land, so you can't hike along it.

Options: Extend this into a longer day hike or backpack by continuing up the drainage. At about 7.5 miles you'll come to the junction of the west and main forks of Dry Creek.

Camping and services: Camp where you want, but keep at least 200 feet away from the stream; no services.

For more information: Bureau of Land Management, Montrose District Office.

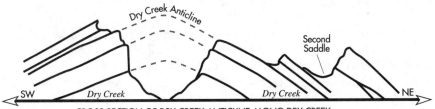

CROSS SECTION OF DRY CREEK ANTICLINE ALONG DRY CREEK

58 Petroglyph Point

Highlights:	Petroglyphs; chance to experience area below the canyon rim; views of canyon and beyond.
Location:	Mesa Verde National Park near Cortez.
Type of hike:	Loop day hike.
Total distance:	2.8 miles.
Difficulty:	Easy.
Elevation gain (loss):	330 feet (330 feet).
Maps:	Mesa Verde National Park trail map, available at the park.
Best months:	May–June and September–October.

Special considerations: Register at the park museum; check on seasonal and evening gate closure times. No water available; take plenty.

Finding the trailhead: From the entrance to Mesa Verde National Park, follow the main park road to Far View Visitor Center. If you are planning to take a guided tour to any of the big ruins such as Cliff Palace or Balcony House in addition to hiking, you need to stop here and purchase a tour reservation. Otherwise, continue past Far View on the main road and follow the signs to the park museum. The total driving distance from the park entrance is about 21 miles. Park where you can at one of the museum lots and walk to the museum to begin your hike. You must register at the museum or the park ranger station before beginning your hike. The trail begins on the south side of the museum as a paved path to the Spruce Tree House Ruins.

Key points:
0.1	Fork for loop to Spruce Tree House, or start of Petroglyph Point Trail
0.3	Junction with Spruce Canyon Trail
1.6	Petroglyphs
1.7	Top of mesa and return trail along mesa and canyon rim
2.8	Museum

The hike: This is a wonderful hike for families with kids old enough to hike a few miles, and for those who want to stretch their legs and escape the crowds that congregate at the main ruins of Mesa Verde. Because of the popularity of this national park, you can expect to see others on the trail during most times when it is open. The National Park Service has made this a one-way trail in order to control access to the Spruce Tree Ruins and to enhance the enjoyment for everyone—please plan to complete the entire 2.8-mile loop in the direction described below.

Begin at the museum by going down the paved path for Spruce Tree House. Follow the signs and take the trail for the Petroglyph Point Trail at the fork. You can also take the loop to visit the Spruce Tree House and you will arrive back at this same point. Shortly, you'll come to a fork in this trail; go left and uphill toward Petroglyph Point.

Petroglyph Point

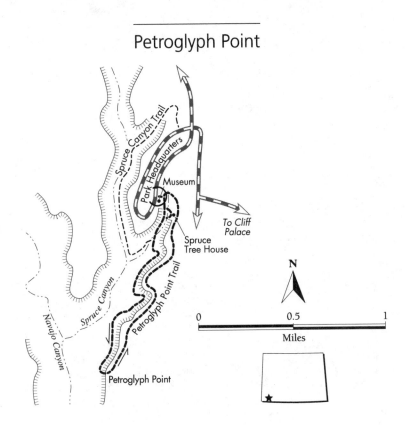

Immediately you will walk below the edge of the plateau and enter the world the Anasazi knew below the mesa top: quiet and varied, with beautiful views of Spruce and Navajo Canyons. Climb through a crack between a boulder and the canyon wall, reach an alcove, and scramble over some small boulders. Enjoy the views and the sound of the wind and birds as you walk. See the piñon pine, juniper, and ponderosa pine.

Soon you will come upon the reason for your trek away from the crowds: petroglyphs. These tell a story. Read them from right to left and see if you can understand the story of this person who existed so far away from you in space and time. After you finish "reading," make the short climb to the rim of the plateau—a different world. Now you'll hike an easy, clear trail along the canyon rim through piñon and juniper, back to the museum. Perhaps you'll want to rest a moment and look over the canyons before coming back to the present.

Options: Make the petroglyph loop and then go back to the junction with the Spruce Canyon Trail; take it southwest then north to the picnic area and parking lot, and then back to the museum, which is about another 2 miles.

Camping and services: None.

For more information: Mesa Verde National Park.

The Eastern Plains and Foothills

The Eastern Plains and Foothills

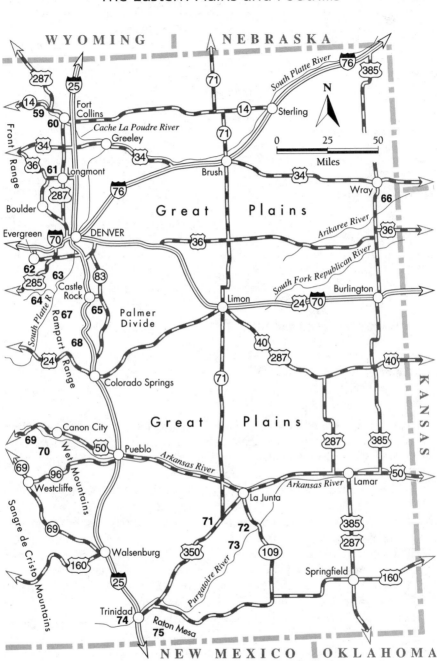

59 Kreutzer Trail, Mount McConnel

Highlights:	Views of the Mummy Range and Poudre Canyon; forest walk.
Location:	Northwest of Fort Collins in Poudre Canyon.
Type of hike:	Loop day hike.
Total distance:	4 miles.
Difficulty:	Moderate.
Elevation gain (or loss):	850 feet.
Best months:	June–September.
Maps:	USGS Big Narrows quad; Trails Illustrated Map 101; Roosevelt National Forest Map.

Special considerations: Steep and rocky in places. Wear good boots; take water.

Finding the trailhead: To reach the Mount McConnel Trailhead, go west about 23.5 miles from Fort Collins up Poudre Canyon on Colorado Highway 14. After the Narrows, turn south into the Mountain Park Campground. Bear right after you cross the Cache la Poudre River, and park at the picnic area and trailhead parking lot.

Parking and trailhead facilities: Parking; restrooms at the campground.

Key points:
- 0.9 Mount McConnel Trail
- 1.3 Second junction with Mount McConnel Trail
- 2.0 Back at bridge near trailhead

The hike: This hike takes you into the Cache la Poudre Wilderness and on the interpretive Kreutzer Trail (Trail 936—a nice hike for families). From the high point of the Kreutzer Trail you have the option to take the Mount McConnel Trail (Trail 801) to the summit of the mountain.

Begin your hike on the south side of the parking lot and head up and across the campground road. Start up the Kreutzer Trail. Most maps don't show this trail, or if they do they don't show the switchbacks, but there are several as you climb the north side of the mountain through Douglas-fir forest. At 0.9 mile is a trail intersection with the Mount McConnel Trail. Continue on the Kreutzer Trail as it traverses the northeast side of the mountain and around some interesting rock ridges. Enjoy the beautiful views of the Poudre Canyon and Cache la Poudre River below.

The trail eventually switchbacks down and then returns back closer to the river at the base of the mountain. It comes back to the road right at the bridge. Walk back along the road to your parking spot.

Options: To climb to the top of Mount McConnel, take the first fork off the Kreutzer Trail. From this trail junction it's about another mile to the top of Mount McConnel with a gain of 500 feet in elevation; you can loop back down and meet the Kreutzer Trail again. The trail continues to switchback.

Kreutzer Trail, Mount McConnel

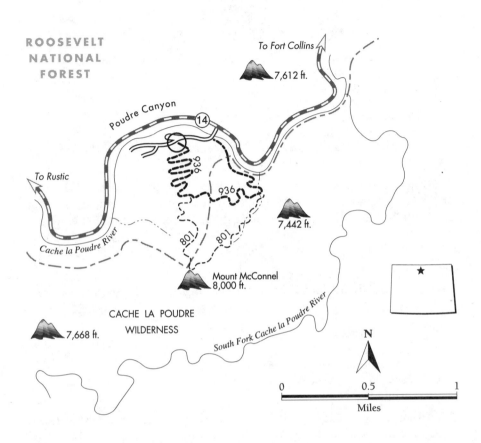

You'll come to a false summit with views of Poudre Canyon to the west before you make the final climb to the true summit at 8,000 feet, from which you can see the Mummy Range. The top of the peak forms a divide between the Cache la Poudre River and the South Fork, which goes through a wild canyon.

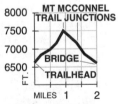

Camping and services: Camping is available at the Mountain Park Campground near the trailhead; no services.

For more information: Roosevelt National Forest, Estes-Poudre Ranger District.

60 Horsetooth Rock

Highlights:	Interesting geology; great views; wildflowers; pretty meadows.
Location:	West of Fort Collins in the northern foothills.
Type of hike:	Loop day hike.
Total distance:	6 miles.
Difficulty:	Moderate.
Elevation gain (or loss):	1,500 feet.
Best months:	May–September.
Maps:	Horsetooth Mountain Park map, available at the trailhead.

Finding the trailhead: From Interstate 25 go west on Harmony Road at Exit 265. Drive 6.6 miles to Taft Hill and turn right. In 0.5 mile turn left on 38E 2100 W. After 2 miles, at the top of the dam, turn left (south) and follow the signs to Horsetooth Mountain Park. Go around the southern tip of Horsetooth Reservoir to the parking lot, which is on the right side of the road.

Parking & trailhead facilities: Large parking lot; maps and restrooms.

Key points:
1.0	Soderberg Trail meets Horsetooth Rock Trail
2.5	Horsetooth Rock
4.0	Wathen Trail meets Spring Creek Trail
4.6	Junction with Soderberg Trail
6.1	Return to trailhead

The hike: A hike to Horsetooth Rock is a journey to one of the most recognized landmarks in northern Colorado. You will also pass other rock formations, pretty meadows, and, if you want to take a little side trip, a waterfall. Great views of the eastern plains and the high peaks of Rocky Mountain National Park will reward your efforts to reach the rock.

Begin your hike at the north end of the parking lot on the Soderberg Trail, which was named for the family who sold the park land to Larimer County. Go left at the fork with the Horsetooth Falls Trail. You'll begin your climb immediately up a south-facing slope where wildflowers are plentiful in spring. At the end of the first switchbacks is another fork in the trail; go left (west) to follow the Horsetooth Rock Trail. Climb into ponderosa forest. The trail splits: You can take either trail, because they join again. After hiking through some interesting rocks, you will arrive beneath Horsetooth Rock. Go left on a short spur trail that takes you to the base of Horsetooth Rock.

You can climb carefully to the top of the rock at the north or south end. Up top, swallows dive close to your head. Have a seat—carefully—and enjoy your reward: a great view of Front Range mountains, the tallest of which

Horsetooth Rock

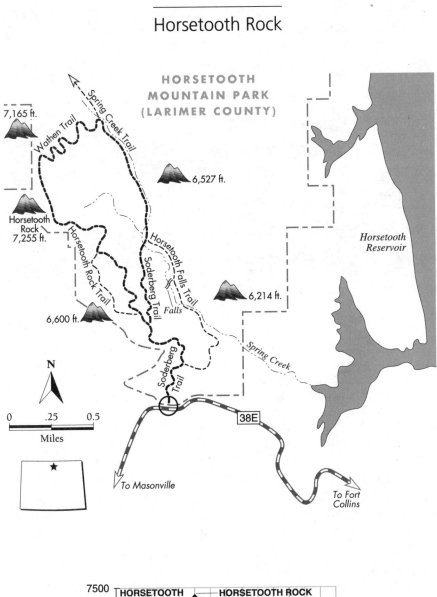

HORSETOOTH MOUNTAIN PARK (LARIMER COUNTY)

7,165 ft.

Spring Creek Trail

Wathen Trail

6,527 ft.

Horsetooth Rock 7,255 ft.

Horsetooth Rock Trail

Horsetooth Falls Trail

Soderberg Trail

Falls

6,600 ft.

6,214 ft.

Horsetooth Reservoir

Spring Creek

N

0   .25   0.5
Miles

38E

To Masonville

To Fort Collins

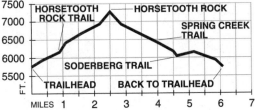

Up on Horsetooth Rock.

are Long's Peak, Mount Meeker, and Storm Peak in Rocky Mountain National Park, and a nice view of the eastern plains and the city of Fort Collins.

When you're ready leave, hike back down to the base of the rock and go left (north). At the first fork take the Wathen Trail downhill to the east. (This trail was named for one of the pioneer families of the area. A trail for another pioneer family, the Herringtons, is in a different part of the park.) It's easy walking through forest and meadow until you come to the Spring Creek Trail. Cross the creek and continue downstream to the junction with Horsetooth Rock Trail, then return to the trailhead on the Soderberg Trail.

Options: By adding another 0.5 mile you can hike down the Horsetooth Falls Trail from Spring Creek Trail to see the small falls, then continue to the Soderberg Trail and back to the trailhead. There are many other trails to explore in Horsetooth Mountain Park as well.

Camping and services: None.

For more information: Larimer County Parks and Open Lands Department.

61 Rabbit Mountain

Highlights:	Interesting natural and human history; great views of the mountains and plains.
Total distance:	3.9 miles.
Type of hike:	Loop day hike.
Difficulty:	Moderate.
Elevation gain (loss):	350 feet.
Best months:	April-November.
Maps:	USGS Hygiene quad; Boulder County Parks and Open Space brochure available at the trailhead.

Special considerations: Take water; watch for rattlesnakes from mid-March to October.

Finding the trailhead: Go east from the intersection of U.S. Highway 36 and Colorado Highway 66 just east of Lyons for about 1 mile on CO 66. Or go west from the city limits of Longmont for about 3 miles on CO 66. Turn north on North 53rd Street and drive for 2.7 miles. The trailhead is on the right.

Parking and trailhead facilities: Plenty of parking. Restrooms and information provided.

View into the Little Thompson Valley from Rabbit Mountain.

Rabbit Mountain

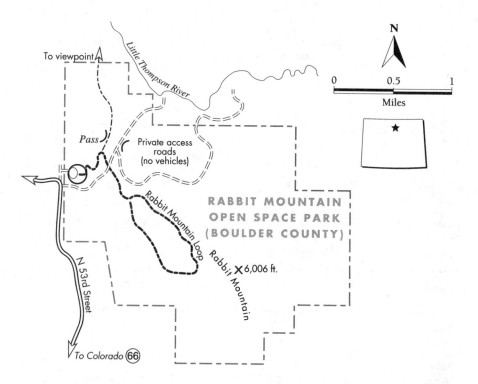

Key points:

- 0.6   Saddle
- 1.2   Start of loop
- 2.7   Back at start of loop
- 3.9   Back at trailhead

The hike: You will hike a loop on the slopes of Rabbit Mountain, an area rich in natural and human history, but will not attain its summit at 6,006 feet, which is southeast of where you begin.

Set out by following the signs and walking uphill from the restrooms at the east end of the parking lot. Pick up the informative Boulder County Parks and Open Space brochure for your trip, which includes a map.

In the first stretch hike up a dry, south-facing slope, achieving the lion's share of the elevation gain. At the top (at 0.6 mile) is a saddle through which the gravel road crosses and a trail intersects. The trail straight ahead leads to an overlook of the Little Thompson River. Take the trail to the right, cross the road, and follow the ridge at the northwest end of Rabbit Mountain.

You will come to the loop hike at 1.2 miles. When the trail forks go either right or left. Cruise along at a comfortable pace and enjoy yourself; it's easy walking on this trail. Your elevation gain will become more moderate. If you plan to hike the entire loop (1.5 miles), either trail is fine to follow. If you don't plan to get all the way around, take the right-hand trail, which leads around to the south-facing slope and to some spectacular views.

Rabbit Mountain is a unique place—an anticline or dome in sedimentary rock, which was created when the Rockies were uplifted, and the summit of which is a hogback, a hard ridge that was left after the erosion of the hilltop. This hogback is located considerably east of the other hogbacks of the foothills due to the activity of faults in the area. Dowe Flats, which you drove through to the trailhead, is a syncline or depression between Rabbit Mountain and the main foothills uplift to the west (detailed information is provided in the brochure). Also, due to slippage in the faults there are seven natural springs on Rabbit Mountain.

Notice the transition zone vegetation on your way: mountain mahogany, ponderosa pine, grasses.

Perhaps Native Americans valued Rabbit Mountain for the springs. Or maybe they chose Rabbit Mountain as a favorite place for the shelter it provided in the winter, for the variety of plants and game to feast upon, or for views of the mountains and the plains. Probably their reasons included more than one of these.

As you glimpse Longs Peak and Mount Meeker to the west, you may understand how the Arapaho Indians derived spiritual orientation from them. Was that their main reason for inhabiting Rabbit Mountain? Or was it the warm south-facing slopes?

As you make your way around the loop and back to your car, you may want to ponder some of these questions and perhaps even wonder if you could exist here for a time.

Options: None.

Camping and services: None.

For more information: Boulder County Parks and Open Space Department.

62 The Brother and Three Sisters

Highlights:	Rock formations; wildflowers; views; good family hike with options for shorter or longer hikes.
Location:	Southwest of Evergreen.
Type of hike:	Loop day hike.
Total distance:	2.0 miles.
Difficulty:	Easy.
Elevation gain:	300 feet.
Best months:	June–October.
Maps:	USGS Evergreen quad; Alderfer/Three Sisters Park Map.

Finding the trailhead: From the intersection of Colorado Highway 73 and Bear Creek Road in downtown Evergreen, go south 0.6 mile on CO 73 and turn right (west) on Buffalo Park Road. Follow this road past Evergreen High School and through a subdivision for 1.2 miles to a trailhead located on the right (north) side of the road in the Alderfer/Three Sisters Open Space Park.

Parking and trailhead facilities: Parking lot, restroom, and picnic area.

Key points:
- 0.6 The Three Sisters
- 1.4 The Brother
- 2.0 Back to trailhead

Hikers of all ages enjoy the Brother and Three Sisters hike.

The Brother and Three Sisters

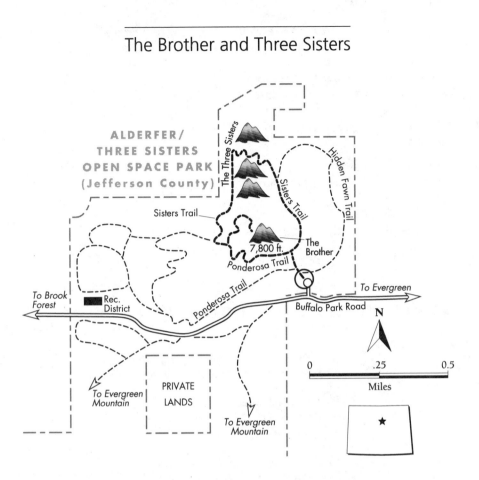

ALDERFER/
THREE SISTERS
OPEN SPACE PARK
(Jefferson County)

The Three Sisters

Sisters Trail

Sisters Trail

Hidden Fawn Trail

7,800 ft.

The Brother

Ponderosa Trail

Ponderosa Trail

To Brook Forest

Rec. District

Buffalo Park Road

To Evergreen

N

To Evergreen Mountain

PRIVATE LANDS

To Evergreen Mountain

0   .25   0.5

Miles

★

The hike: This hike takes you up to and around rock outcroppings that have been landmarks in the Evergreen area for all who have lived here. It's a really good area for families to hike because there are many options for loop hikes, and you can be flexible and adapt your hike to what everyone in your group will enjoy.

As you hike the trails here, avoid the temptation to cut over and climb the rocks, because this will create new trails and cause erosion. Stay on the designated trails; there are plenty of rocks at the top. You will see lots of wildflowers such as chiming bells and potentilla.

Begin by going north from the parking area, past the first junction with the Ponderosa Trail, and to a fork in 0.1 mile. Go right at the fork and then left at the next fork in 0.3 mile. Follow this, the Sisters Trail, past the rock outcropping known as the Three Sisters; the outcroppings are made of Precambrian metamorphic rock.

On the west side of this outcropping, the trail heads southwest and joins the Ponderosa Trail. Go left and then in a short distance go left again to get to the Brother, another rock outcropping. This is a good place to enjoy lunch or a snack while you take in the views of the entire Evergreen area and of Mount Evans to the west. Keep young children away from the edge; there are some big drop-offs.

When you are ready to descend, go back to the Ponderosa Trail and follow it east for 0.3 mile and back to the parking area.

For a longer loop hike, take the Ponderosa Trail right (west) after you descend from the Brother and follow it south and then east to the parking area.

Options: There are numerous other options from this and other trailheads in the park, which are indicated on the park brochure.

Camping and services: None.

For more information: Jefferson County Open Space.

---

63 Deer Creek Canyon Park

> **Highlights:** Diverse ecosystems; history; views.
> **Location:** Southwest of Chatfield Reservoir in Jefferson County near Denver.
> **Type of hike:** Loop day hike.
> **Total distance:** 3.7 miles.
> **Difficulty:** Moderate.
> **Elevation gain:** 500 feet.
> **Best months:** May–June; September–October.
> **Maps:** Jefferson County Open Space Park Map for Deer Creek Canyon Park.

Finding the trailhead: Take Colorado Highway 470 (C-470) to South Kipling Street, then go south to West Ute Avenue for about 1 mile to Deer Creek Canyon. Turn left and go about 2 miles to Grizzly Road. Turn left and drive 0.3 mile to the park. Turn in at Deer Creek Canyon Park.

Parking and trailhead facilities: Parking is provided. Facilities include phones, restrooms, picnic shelters, and drinking water.

Key points:
   1.6   High point
   2.2   Plymouth Creek Trail
   3.7   Back to the trailhead

The hike: This hike takes you on a loop through diverse foothill ecosystems where you will have the opportunity to see wildlife and catch some pretty views.

Begin at the parking area on Meadowlark Trail, which is only open to hikers. Walk to the west, skirting Rattlesnake Gulch, then hike up a couple

Deer Creek Canyon Park

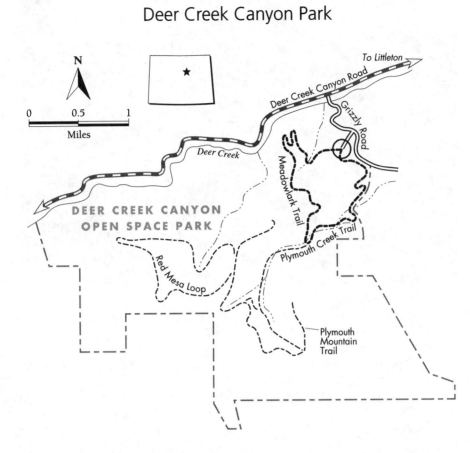

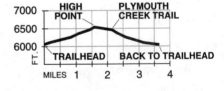

of switchbacks to a scenic view. From here go south to join up with the Plymouth Creek Trail, which is open to hikers, mountain bikers, and horse riders.

Because Colorado trails are receiving more and more use by different kinds of users—and Jefferson County Open Space Parks have felt this keenly—trail users must be courteous to each other. For example, hikers are obliged to yield to horses, mountain bikers are required to yield to both hikers and horsemen, and horsemen always have the right of way. In addition, a trail user going up a trail generally has the right-of-way over a user coming down the trail, simply because it's harder to go up and more difficult to get going again once you stop.

Look for changes in slope, rock type, and vegetation as you climb into the small canyon of Plymouth Creek, which is dry most of the year. Oakbrush, mountain mahogany, and juniper typify transition zone vegetation. As you

Deer Creek Canyon Park.

cross into the canyon with its Precambrian rocks, you will come into stands of Douglas-fir and ponderosa pine on the north-facing slope. On the south-facing slope are cactus and other vegetation suited to a drier slope, such as the juniper and mountain mahogany. Near the channel of the creek are narrow-leaf cottonwood, Rocky Mountain maple, willow, and chokecherry.

Take the Plymouth Creek Trail as far as you like, then return on it to your starting point, the trailhead.

Options: Head out from the trailhead south on the Plymouth Creek Trail, climb Plymouth Mountain for the views, then go west on the Plymouth Mountain Trail or Homesteader Trail to Red Mesa Loop. A hike of 2.5 miles to the west end of this loop takes you to another high point with views.

Camping and services: None.

For more information: Jefferson County Open Space.

64 Pine Valley Ranch

Highlights: Beautiful stream and riparian habitat; forest habitat; wildflowers; wildlife.
Location: Southwest of Conifer in the foothills.
Type of hike: Loop day hike.
Total distance: 2.9 miles.
Difficulty: Easy.
Elevation gain: Minimal.
Best months: May–October.
Maps: Pine Valley Ranch Park Map, available at the site; Trails Illustrated Map 105; Pike National Forest Map.

Finding the trailhead: Drive to Pine Junction on U.S. Highway 285. Take Colorado Highway 126 southeast for 5.8 miles. Go right on Crystal Lake Road (Pine Valley Ranch Road) past Crystal Lake Resort. Pine Valley Ranch is just ahead.

Parking and trailhead facilities: Parking, picnic areas, phones, restrooms, ranger assistance nearby.

Key points:
 0.4 Buck Gulch trail junction
 0.8 North Fork View Trail junction
 1.4 Turnaround point
 2.0 Take North Fork View Trail
 2.9 Trailhead

North Fork of the South Platte River.

Pine Valley Ranch

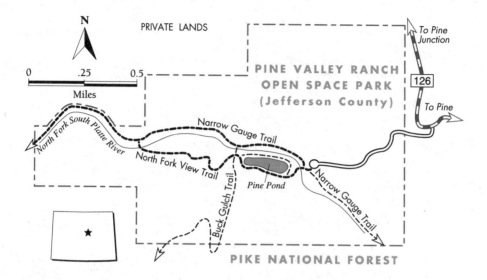

The hike: This loop takes you on a beautiful foothills hike along the North Fork of the South Platte River.

Begin hiking at the west end of the parking lot along the Narrow Gauge Trail—you will follow the river on the old railroad grade. Douglas-fir and ponderosa pine grace the drier slopes.

You will also pass a bridge, which you must cross to make your loop back. Keep going along the river to the west park boundary at 1.4 miles, where there is a view upstream into a more narrow canyon. The trail goes through meadows where wild geranium, and butter-and-eggs, among other wildflowers. Once you reach the fence at the boundary, retrace your steps 0.6 mile and cross the bridge on the North Fork View Trail into the meadow. Follow this trail back toward Pine Pond. You can go either direction around the pond on trails, which are wheelchair accessible. Look for ducks on the pond as you skirt it, then return to the trailhead.

Options: Include a trek up Buck Gulch to the park boundary and back for a longer hike.

Camping and services: None.

For more information: Jefferson County Open Space.

65 Castlewood Canyon

Highlights: Prairie, foothills, and canyon habitats.
Location: South of Franktown at Castlewood Canyon State Park.
Type of hike: Loop day hike.
Total distance: 2 miles.
Difficulty: Easy.
Elevation gain (or loss): 200 feet (200 feet).
Best months: May–June, September–October.
Maps: Castlewood Canyon State Park brochure.

Special considerations: State park entrance fee.

Finding the trailhead: From Franktown, at the intersection of Colorado Highways 86 and 83, go south on CO 83 about 5 miles to the Castlewood Canyon State Park entrance, located on the west side of the highway just after the bridge across Cherry Creek.

Parking and trailhead facilities: Ample parking; restrooms, picnic area, nearby visitor center, and wheelchair-accessible trails.

Key points:
0.9 Junction with Inner Canyon Trail

The hike: This hike takes you from the mesa top, with views of Pikes Peak to the southwest, down into Lake Gulch and returns by way of the pretty canyon of Cherry Creek. There are interesting rock formations, historic dam

Cherry Creek along the Inner Canyon Trail.

Castlewood Canyon

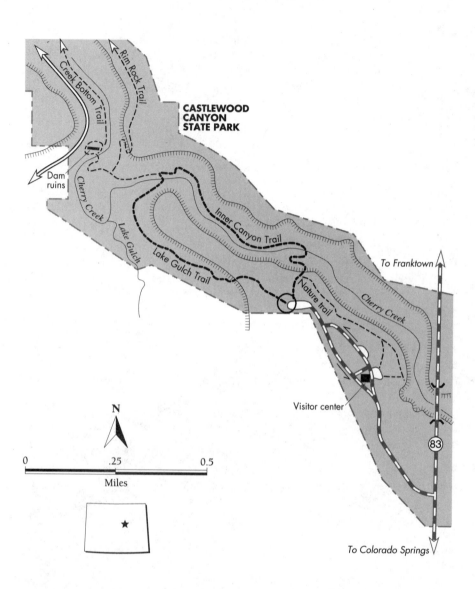

CASTLEWOOD
CANYON
STATE PARK

Creek Bottom Trail
Rim Rock Trail
Dam ruins
Cherry Creek
Lake Gulch
Lake Gulch Trail
Inner Canyon Trail
Nature trail
Cherry Creek
To Franktown
Visitor center
83
To Colorado Springs

N

0   .25   0.5
Miles

ruins, and a mixture of grassland, foothills shrub, ponderosa pine forest, and riparian habitats along the way.

Begin on the Lake Gulch Trail at the west end of the parking area by following the concrete path past the picnic sites to where it becomes a gravel and dirt trail. The first 0.1 mile of this route is wheelchair accessible. The trail drops down from the mesa rim and along the edge of the valley of Lake Gulch, with some nice views of Pikes Peak, then bends around to the east and into Cherry Creek Canyon. As you make this bend, you can see the ruins of the Castlewood Canyon Dam, which collapsed in 1933, killing two people. Behind the dam, in the valley of Lake Gulch, the old reservoir level is marked by terraces above the gully and by stains on the rocks in the canyon.

At 0.9 mile, just beyond a bridge over Cherry Creek, is the Inner Canyon Trail. Left (west) leads to the dam ruins, which makes an interesting side trip. Take the right fork, and head up Cherry Creek Canyon. The trail follows this canyon upstream 0.8 mile, where you will climb back to the mesa rim. Bear right along the concrete path to return to the parking area, or go left on the Canyon View Nature Trail for another interesting side hike.

Options: A side hike to the dam ruins is a good option. To hike there and back adds a total of 0.5 mile if you stop at a viewpoint, and about 1 mile if you make a complete loop up, over, and back down through the breach in the dam. Longer loops can be made by way of the Rim Rock and Creek Bottom Trails. The Canyon View Trail, which is wheelchair accessible, also is a nice side trip. All of these and other trails are easily followed and the distances are indicated in the park brochure.

Camping and services: Day use only, no camping; no services.

For more information: Castlewood Canyon State Park.

66 Beecher Island

Highlights:	Historic battle site; plains river; shortgrass prairie; breaks.
Location:	South of Wray at the Arikaree River.
Type of hike:	Loop day hike.
Total distance:	0.8 mile.
Difficulty:	Easy.
Elevation gain:	Minimal.
Best months:	April–May; September–October.
Maps:	Map posted at the site.

Finding the trailhead: From Wray go south on U.S. Highway 385 about 4.5 miles to where it curves to the west. Turn east and go about 1.3 miles on 30 Road, then south on JJ Road about 3 miles. Turn east on 27 Road and

Arikaree River at Beecher Island.

follow it as it bends south to become LL Road (follow the paved route at every intersection). Go south on LL Road about 6.2 miles to the Beecher Island Community Center, located on the right (west) just before the road crosses the Arikaree River. Turn in and park in the lot closest to the river.

Parking and trailhead facilities: Parking and restrooms are provided.

The hike: "In 1865 Roman Nose, Cheyenne chief, because he ate food prepared in a white man's iron skillets, had a premonition that he would die in his next battle, which took place at Beecher Island . . . the next day. He had no time to purge himself in necessary sacrifices and was killed in the battle."— *Sidelights,* by Al Look.

This hike at the historic Beecher Island battlesite goes along the Arikaree River and up to Roman Nose Ridge where there are views of the surrounding valley and the battle site, which was south of the river in what is now a large stand of cottonwoods.

Begin your hike by reading about the battle on the signs provided. Others have described the battle better than we can, but a brief account is that after the Sand Creek Massacre in 1864, the Cheyenne Indians were outraged and began raiding and killing settlers. The cavalry, under General Phil Sheridan tried to stop the raids. The general sent Major George Forsyth out to enlist local frontiersmen as scouts to fight against the Indians. On September 16, Forsyth, Lieutenant Fred Beecher, and the scouts made camp on the north bank of the Arikaree. The place where they camped was north of a sandy island in the river. The Indians decided to attack the scouts, which was not entirely a surprise to Forsyth, who had ordered the horses and mules secured. At daybreak the Cheyennes came, led by Roman Nose, and Forsyth

228

Beecher Island

and his scouts fled to the island. Both the Indians and the scouts fought bravely.

Look for the sign for the Roman Nose Trail, on the southwest side of the parking lot. Follow it as it heads through the cottonwoods along the north side of the Arikaree River. Continue along the river at a fork when the trail emerges from the cottonwoods and follow the posts that mark the route. The trail continues up the beautiful Arikaree River valley to a side gulch at a break in the bluffs. You can imagine Roman Nose leading his charge down this gully as you hike to the top of the bluff, called Roman Nose Ridge. From here you have some good views of the Arikaree River Valley and the prairie breaks, which it has eroded.

Follow the trail back down with the posts as your guide and to the trail junction and back to the parking lot.

In the 1920s the site was scheduled to become a state park, funded by the states of Colorado and Kansas, but unfortunately the Depression intervened. The site has been preserved and the trails developed by members of the Beecher Island Memorial Association. If you are there when the facilities are open, you might be able to talk with someone and purchase a book about the battle.

Camping and services: Available at the site.

For more information: Wray History Museum.

67 Devils Head

Highlights: Fire lookout tower; views; interesting geology.
Location: In the Rampart Range southwest of Sedalia.
Type of hike: Out-and-back day hike.
Total distance: 2.8 miles.
Difficulty: Moderate.
Elevation gain (or loss): 950 feet.
Best months: May–October.
Maps: USGS Devil's Head quad; Trails Illustrated Map 135; Pike National Forest Map.

Special considerations: Take plenty of water. A day use fee may be required.

Finding the trailhead: From U.S. Highway 85 (Santa Fe Drive) at Sedalia, turn west on Colorado Highway 67 and follow it, keeping right at the first fork. After 10 miles, go left (south) onto Rampart Range Road (Forest Road 300). Take this road for 9.2 miles and turn left (south) at the sign for the Devil's Head Fire Lookout and Campground. Follow that road past the campground to the trailhead. You can also reach this same point by driving Rampart Range Road north from Woodland Park, a distance of about 28 miles.

Parking and trailhead facilities: Parking lot; you can park along the road if the lot is full. Restroom.

Key points:
0.4 Switchbacks
1.3 Saddle
1.4 Devil's Head tower

The hike: This is a short but steep hike that goes to the top of Devil's Head Peak and up to a fire lookout tower, which is staffed from May through October. It is one of the few fire lookout towers still in use.

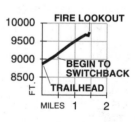

Begin by hiking south from the trailhead up a cool, quiet drainage through mixed forest past a spring that has been developed to supply the campground. At 0.4 mile the trail climbs out of the drainage and switches back around to the north and northeast side of the mountain past some interesting rock formations and occasional views.

The trail climbs and climbs, but there are a few rest stops along the way. At 1.3 miles you finally crest a small saddle after a spot with views to the north and reach a surprising little meadow nestled between the rocky ramparts of Devil's Head (the cabin here is for lookout staff). At the edge of the meadow the final climb is up stairs and hand-railed sections along the rock top of the peak. If the lookout tower is manned when you are there, you will

The stairs to the fire lookout.

Devils Head

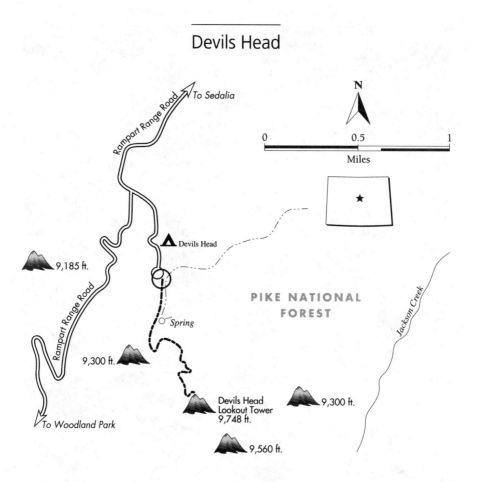

be allowed to go inside, and the person will be happy to answer questions about the history of the tower and how fires are spotted.

The reason this tower is still in use is that the rugged topography of this area and the increasing recreational use and encroaching development make the likelihood of fire greater. This need was proved by the recent 10,000-acre blaze near Buffalo Creek, part of which you can see from the tower. Besides the views of distant mountains, the plains, and Pikes Peak to the south, you can also see some interesting geology. As you look south notice how all of the foothills, with the exception of a few high points like Devil's Head and Pikes Peak, seem to top out at exactly the same level. This is an ancient erosion surface from the Eocene Epoch. Enjoy the views and return as you came.

Options: None.

Camping and services: There is a campground at the trailhead. Rangers provide information at the tower.

For more information: Pike National Forest, South Platte Ranger District.

68 New Santa Fe Trail

Highlights:	Views and vistas; railroad; history.
Location:	West of Interstate 25 from Palmer Lake to the U.S. Air Force Academy.
Type of hike:	Out-and-back day hike.
Total distance:	7 miles.
Difficulty:	Easy.
Elevation gain (or loss):	Minimal.
Best months:	May–June; September–October.
Maps:	Map posted at site.

Finding the trailhead: Go north on Interstate 25 to Exit 161 for Palmer Lake. Follow Colorado Highway 105 to the north end of the town of Palmer Lake. Go right on Spruce Mountain Road (CO 18) to County Line Road. (Driving south on I-25, turn off on Spruce Mountain Road [CO 18] at Exit 173. Follow it 9 miles south to County Line Road and the northern tip of Palmer Lake.) Go east on County Line Road, then turn right immediately at the sign into the parking area for the trail and a park on the east side of Palmer Lake.

Parking and trailhead facilities: Parking is plentiful. Picnic area; park; restrooms.

Key points:
    3.5   Monument trailhead

The hike: With this hike you will be "walking the line" that the Denver & Rio Grande, and the Atchison, Topeka and Santa Fe Railroads traveled between Denver and Colorado Springs.

Begin your hike south of the end of the parking lot at the trailhead sign. Walk by Palmer Lake with its graceful narrow-leaf cottonwoods, and the pretty park on the lake. The town of Palmer Lake was once a popular getaway by train for people in Denver.

The wheelchair-accessible gravel trail provides easy walking for all members of the family. This is one of the prettiest sections of this trail with views of the Rampart Range to the west and Pikes Peak to the south. You may see mule deer, rabbits, hawks, and other wildlife from the trail. To the east and northeast are sandstone cliffs with ponderosa pine and oakbrush. The most prominent sandstone formation is Elephant Rock.

The first section of the trail is fairly level and straight for the 3.5 miles to Monument. While we were walking, a train passed us by, headed south. Walk the trail as far as you like, then return to the trailhead.

Options: The entire length of the trail is about 14 miles. Hike the entire thing in sections on different days or in one day with a car shuttle. (The plan is to extend these trails to connect with the Colorado Springs trail system to the south and Douglas County trails to the north.)

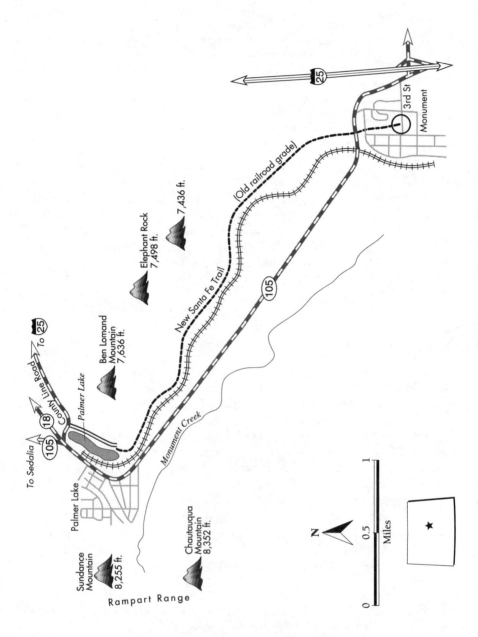

The 6.9-stretch of the trail going through the Air Force Academy is another particularly nice section. You could hike this entire stretch with a car shuttle between the north access point at North Gate Boulevard and I-25 and the south access point at which is north of the South Entrance to the Air Force Academy, west on Pine Drive, and south on a dirt road to the left.

Camping and services: None.

For more information: El Paso County Parks.

69 Horsetail Gulch

Highlights:	Rugged foothills canyon; interesting horsetail wetlands; wildlife.
Location:	West of Canon City along the Arkansas River Canyon.
Type of hike:	Out-and-back day hike.
Total distance:	4.6 miles.
Difficulty:	Moderate.
Elevation gain:	600 feet.
Best months:	April–May; September–November.
Maps:	USGS McIntyre Hills quad; San Isabel National Forest Map.

Special considerations: Day use fee required. There are bighorn sheep in this area. Please keep your distance from them, because they are stressed by human contact. This is mountain lion country: Don't hike at dusk or dawn and keep kids close by.

Finding the trailhead: From the junction of U.S. Highway 50 and Colorado Highway 115 in the center of Canon City, go west on US 50 past Royal Gorge and into the canyon of the Arkansas River 18.3 miles to the Five Points Recreation Site. Turn right (north) into the site and then immediately take a left and park in the parking lot.

Parking and trailhead facilities: Parking and restrooms are provided.

Key points:
- 0.7 Horsetail wetlands
- 0.9 Small falls
- 1.4 Side canyon
- 2.3 Pools

The hike: This hike leads to an unnamed side canyon of the Arkansas River, which we have dubbed Horsetail Gulch for some interesting wetlands filled with reeds called horsetails (this is the Bureau of Land Management McIntyre Hills Wilderness Study Area). You will bushwhack along the mostly dry creek bed of this rugged gulch.

Horsetail wetland.

Horsetail Gulch

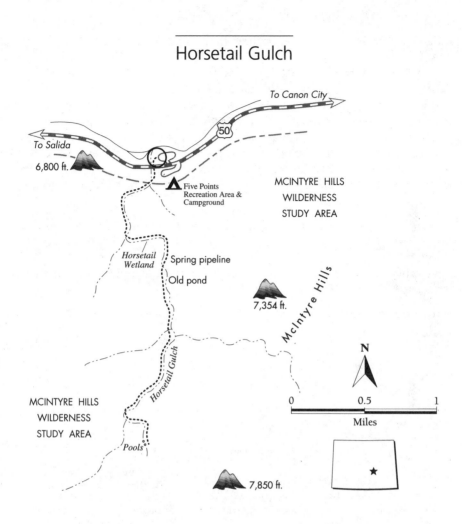

To Canon City

To Salida

6,800 ft.

[50]

Five Points
Recreation Area &
Campground

MCINTYRE HILLS
WILDERNESS
STUDY AREA

Horsetail
Wetland

Spring pipeline

Old pond

7,354 ft.

McIntyre Hills

MCINTYRE HILLS
WILDERNESS
STUDY AREA

Horsetail Gulch

Pools

N

0   0.5   1
Miles

7,850 ft.

Begin at the west end of the parking lot next to the display about bighorn sheep. Turn south and hike on the cement path that goes beneath US 50, which connects the day use area with the campground on the south side of the highway. Leave the concrete path and begin hiking up the creek bed.

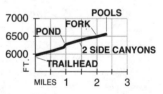

At the first junction, go to the right (west) along the main canyon. At 0.6 mile at the next canyon junction, stay to the left as the main canyon bends around to the east. At 0.7 mile you'll come to an interesting wetland dominated by horsetail reeds. Please hike out of the wetlands as much as possible here and at other points along the route to protect this unusual habitat.

At 0.9 mile is a little waterfall and pools above which there is a spring pipeline, which feeds the campground below. You may have to hike up and around to get by this point. At 1 mile you'll come to an old stock pond, the dam of which has been breached. This is the last evidence of humans in this

237

little valley until several miles farther where the canyon tops out on private land.

The creek is interesting. Where the valley widens it becomes a big, rocky, sandy wash, and where the valley narrows to bedrock, the stream flows for a little ways. At 1.4 miles two side canyons come in, from the west and from the east: the one on the east looks interesting to explore. At about 1.7 miles you finally gain a little cool shade and a live stream for a short distance. At 2 miles the canyon forks below some cliffs. Take the left fork and, although rocky and dry, at 2.3 miles you'll come to some pretty little pools in the streambed. These pools are as far as we got, but you can certainly go farther, then return as you came.

Options: Continue 2 miles past the pools in the main canyon to where a few forks come together. Each fork leads to jeep roads on private land within about 1 mile.

Another option is to take the main side canyon at mile 1.4 for a short distance.

Camping and services: None.

For more information: Bureau of Land Management, Royal Gorge Resource Area.

70 Grape Creek

Highlights:	Rugged canyon; wildlife; wilderness hiking.
Location:	Between Canon City and Westcliffe in the Grape Creek Wilderness Study Area.
Type of hike:	Bushwhack.
Total distance:	4.8 miles.
Difficulty:	Strenuous.
Elevation gain (or loss):	Minimal.
Best months:	May–June; September–October.
Maps:	USGS Curley Peak quad; San Isabel National Forest Map.

Special considerations: Rugged four-wheel-drive road prone to washouts. Check with the Bureau of Land Management on road conditions. Be prepared for stream wading. Even if you're day hiking, go prepared to spend a night out. File a "flight" plan for your hike and stick to it. This is mountain lion country: Avoid hiking at dawn and dusk or alone.

Finding the trailhead: The access is off of the Oak Creek Grade Road, about halfway between Canon City and Westcliffe. From Westcliffe head east on Colorado Highway 96 through Silver Cliff. At the east edge of Silver Cliff, turn south on Oak Creek Road (County Road 255). Go 13 miles and

Grape Creek

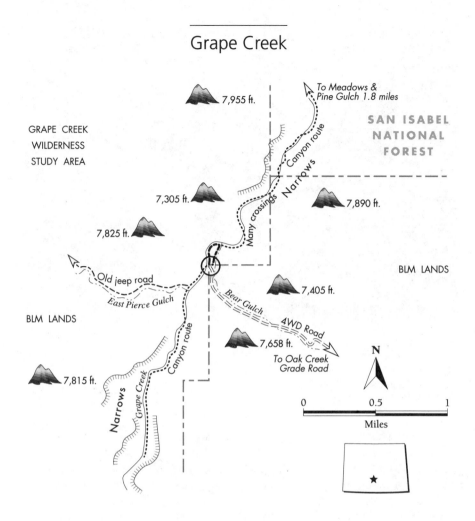

bear left (straight) onto CR 277 and left again in another mile, always staying on Oak Creek Grade Road (143 Road). At 15.3 miles turn left on BLM Grape Creek Access Road 6227.

From the south end of Canon City take Oak Creek Grade Road (143 Road) southwest up and through the Wet Mountains about 13 miles to Grape Creek Access Road, which is about 1.5 miles past the Oak Creek Campground. The first 1.5 miles is through private land, then you will enter national forest, state, and then BLM land. The road follows rugged Bear Gulch and is prone to washouts and can be very rough. Be prepared to park and walk part of the road, and to spend a night if necessary. It's 4.1 miles down to some limited parking sites just above Grape Creek. At the time we did this hike, the last 0.1 mile to better parking sites at the bottom was completely washed out.

Parking and trailhead facilities: Limited parking; no facilities.

Grape Creek.

Key points:
- 0.8   National forest and narrows
- 1.7   End of narrows
- 2.4   Canyon really opens up; back on BLM land

The hike: This hike is a rough wilderness adventure along the rugged canyon of Grape Creek, which drains from the Sangre de Cristo Mountains and the Wet Mountain Valley. Cattle graze the canyon bottom during part of the year, and although they've left their usual marks, they've grazed the banks of the stream like a lawn so that it's easy hiking through most of the meadow stretches of the canyon. This canyon has a combination of vegetation associated with both the middle-elevation mountains (ponderosa and Douglas-fir) and some of the low-elevation foothills (cactus, piñon-juniper) depending on the aspect of the canyon walls.

You can go either up- or downstream for several miles, but private land at each end prevents hiking through either to DeWeese Reservoir upstream or Temple Canyon Park and Canon City downstream.

We hiked 2 miles downstream for a day hike before turning around because of darkness. In either direction be prepared to ford the stream, because the canyon walls come right down to the creek in many places. Also, allow plenty of time for this hike—the going can be slow. As you hike through the narrows, look for old railroad rails, leftovers from the railroad that once ran through here. As hard as some of the canyon is to hike, imagine how anyone managed to get a railroad down here. Even more amazing is how flash floods and revegetation have nearly obliterated all evidence of the railroad.

Going downstream is initially a little more rugged as you reach a narrow 1-mile section of canyon after hiking almost 1 mile. If you continue on through the narrows, in 2.4 miles you'll come to where the canyon widens at the base of Tanner Peak. And at 4.2 miles is the side canyon of Pine Gulch. These are good destinations for a backpack and for exploring.

Options: Cross the creek just upstream of the trailhead and explore East Pierce Gulch on an old jeep road. If you head south, the canyon alternates between some easier stretches and some good narrows.

For a long hike, check with the BLM about access all the way downstream to Canon City. At some point they may attain an easement or ownership of a piece of private land to allow through hiking.

Camping and services: Best camping is downstream of the narrows or near the mouth of East Pierce Gulch. Camp away from the stream; no services.

For more information: Bureau of Land Management, Royal Gorge Resource Area.

71 Santa Fe Trail

Highlights: National Historic Trail; views; shortgrass prairie.
Location: Southwest of La Junta.
Type of hike: Out-and-back day hike or day hike with shuttle.
Total distance: 3.2 miles.
Difficulty: Easy.
Elevation gain (or loss): Minimal.
Best months: April–May; September–November.
Maps: Recreation Opportunity Guide from Comanche National Grassland; Comanche National Grassland Map.

Special considerations: Take water.

Finding the trailhead: From La Junta drive southwest on Colorado Highway 350 for 16 miles. (From Trinidad drive northeast for 53 miles on CO 350.) Turn right (northwest) at County Road 16.5, crossing the railroad tracks and then turn right (northeast) to the parking lot.

Parking and trailhead facilities: Parking, picnic area, and vault toilet provided.

Key points:
1.6   Sierra Vista Overlook

The hike: In 1913 a poem by Iona Cahill appeared in *Santa Fe Trail Magazine*. The first verse goes:

Santa Fe Trail

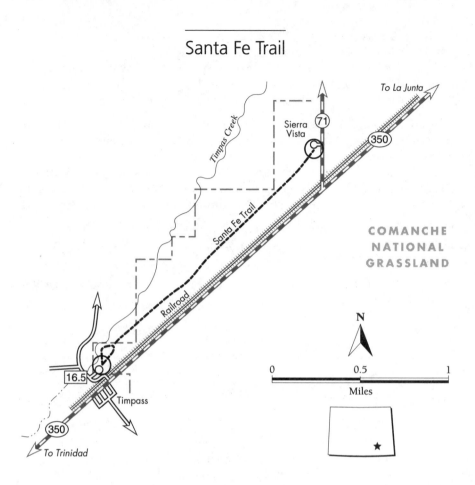

From Missouri's turbid stream
To the old post, Santa Fe,
In a long unbroken sea,
Runs a scarred and rutted way,
Ling'ring 'round which many a tale
Lives to mark the famous trail.

This hike takes you out a distance on the Colorado portion of the "famous trail," known as the Mountain Branch of the Santa Fe Trail. It came into Colorado at Bent's Fort and left the state by Raton Pass. You can walk the trail and feel what it was like to be out on the plains. Imagine what it must have been like to go on and on, your wagon train bending across the southeast corner of Colorado, down past the Spanish Peaks and into New Mexico, at last to reach Santa Fe.

Begin your hike on the Nature Trail, which is a 0.5-mile loop. Walk northwest to the stone trail and follow the Santa Fe Trail northeast. Stone posts mark the trail, which you'll walk to the Sierra Vista Overlook. As you walk, imagine the freight wagons rumbling over the trail; hear the sound of whips

View of the Spanish Peaks from the northeast as travelers on the Santa Fe Trail saw them. G. K. GILBERT PHOTO. COURTESY USGS.

and men shouting. This trail was primarily used for commercial purposes, freighting mostly, but some emigration did occur. At night the people would gather around campfires and talk, laugh, or sing.

The Sierra Vista Overlook, your destination on this hike, was an important high point for travelers on the trail. From here are views of the Spanish Peaks in the Culebra Range near La Veta Pass. These landmarks were a welcome sight to many, assuring them they were on the right track and nearing their destination.

Enjoy the view, then go back the way you came.

Options: You can hike a few other portions of the trail that cross public lands (check with the Comanche National Grassland). Unfortunately, much of the trail is on private land. You can also make a visit to Bent's Fort to the northeast for more background on the trail.

Camping and services: None.

For more information: Comanche National Grassland.

Vogel Canyon

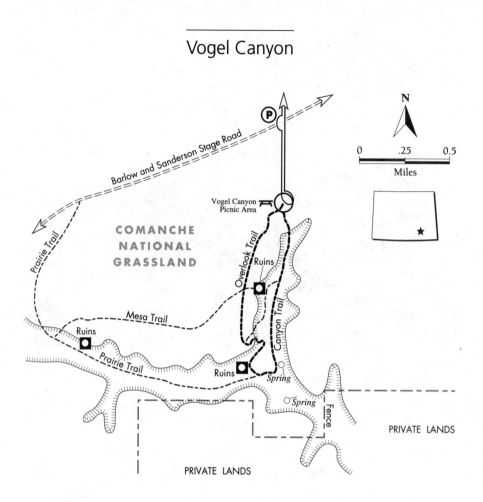

N

0   .25   0.5
Miles

P

Barlow and Sanderson Stage Road

Vogel Canyon
Picnic Area

COMANCHE
NATIONAL
GRASSLAND

Overlook Trail

Ruins

Canyon Trail

Prairie Trail

Mesa Trail

Ruins

Prairie Trail

Ruins

Spring

Spring

Fence

PRIVATE LANDS

PRIVATE LANDS

72 Vogel Canyon

Highlights: Canyon; springs; wildlife; history; rock art.
Location: South of La Junta.
Type of hike: Loop day hike.
Total distance: 2.75 miles.
Difficulty: Easy.
Elevation gain (or loss): Minimal.
Best months: April–May; September–November.
Maps: USGS La Junta SE quad; Comanche National Grassland flyer; Comanche National Grassland Map.

Special considerations: Take water.

Finding the trailhead: Drive south of La Junta on Colorado Highway 109 for 13 miles. At the sign for Vogel Canyon turn right (west) for 1 mile. Then turn left (south) and drive for 2 miles to the parking lot.

Parking and trailhead facilities: Parking, picnic area, vault toilet, horse hitching rails, and trailer parking are provided.

Key points:
1.0   Junction with Overlook Trail

The hike: This hike takes you across shortgrass prairie and through junipers to some nice views and to ruins of a stagecoach station and a homestead.

Begin your hike at the parking lot and walk south on the Canyon Trail into Vogel Canyon. On this trail you should find rock art, which was created by Native Americans some 300 to 800 years ago. You will pass a spring as the trail bends west, then come to a fork in the trail; left goes to the Prairie Trail. Go right on the Overlook Trail and soon you will see the ruins of the old Barlow & Sanderson Mail and Stage Line, which served customers here on a spur from the Santa Fe Trail in the 1870s.

Moving on, hike north, covering a couple switchbacks. In a short distance another fork will take you into the canyon again and to the ruins of the Westbrook homestead where people settled during the Depression in the 1930s. Take that trail, which returns to the Canyon Trail or continue north on the Overlook Trail, cross the Mesa Trail, and go north to the parking lot.

Options: You can have a longer hike by hiking the Prairie Trail off the south end of the Canyon Trail loop through the canyon, then north to the Barlow & Sanderson Stage Road, and following it northeast. Then walk south to the picnic area and parking.

Camping and services: None.

For more information: Comanche National Grassland.

73 Picket Wire Canyons

Highlights:	Naturally preserved dinosaur tracks; canyon; historical and archaeological sites.
Location:	South of La Junta in the canyon of the Purgatoire River.
Type of hike:	Out-and-back day hike.
Total distance:	10.6 miles.
Difficulty:	Strenuous.
Elevation gain (loss):	Minimal.
Maps:	USGS Riley Canyon, Beaty Canyon, and OV Mesa quads; Recreation Opportunity Guide provided by the USDA Forest Service; Comanche National Grassland Map.
Best months:	April–May; September–November.

Special considerations: Day use area only. Take lots of water.

Finding the trailhead: From La Junta, head south on Colorado Highway 109 for 13 miles, then turn right (west) on County Road 802 for 8 miles. Turn left (south) on CR 25 and continue for 6 miles. At Forest Road 500.A turn left (east) for 0.75 mile and go through a wire gate. This road demands a vehicle with high clearance. Continue for 2 miles until the road forks; take the left fork to the sign for parking. If you are unable to drive FR 500.A, park at the start of the road at the bulletin board and begin hiking there.

Parking and facilities at the trailhead: Parking and portable toilets are provided.

Key points:
    1.0   Purgatoire River
    3.7   Cemetery
    5.3   Dinosaur tracks

The hike: This hike goes through a riparian habitat in a canyon of Colorado's eastern plains to "the largest documented dinosaur track site in North America." The destination will be of interest to children; however, the environment is quite harsh and caution should be taken when young children are along. It is a good idea to hike in fall, winter, or spring and early in the day in summer. Bring a gallon of water for each person hiking in your party.

Begin by crossing through a gate and down a jeep road into a steep-sided canyon. This is the only really difficult part of this hike—the uphill climb on the way out. (At the bottom, continue in Withers Canyon.) At the mouth of the canyon is another old jeep road and a sign. Go right. It is easy walking along the canyon of the Purgatoire River from here to the dinosaur tracks with only a couple of short rises along the way. It can be very hot in the summer, however, with only occasional stands of cottonwoods providing shade.

Picket Wire Canyons

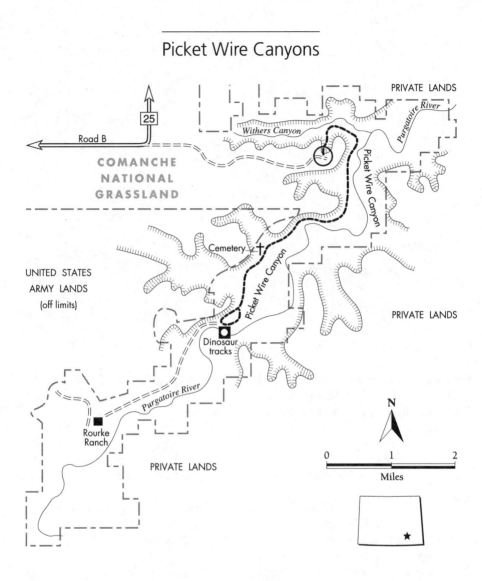

At 2.5 miles the trail climbs up and over some rock ledges where the river has undercut the cliff. About a mile past that point, at 3.7 miles, you will come to an old cemetery. Mexican pioneers first began permanent settlement in the valley; they built the Dolores Mission here and the cemetery you see on your right.

You are now in one of the widest spots in the canyon. The dinosaur tracks are southwest at the far end of this park where the river bends back to the west. Continue along until the jeep road forks to go down to the tracks 1.5 miles farther to the southwest.

The tracks are exposed where the river has cut into the sandstone, creating a rock ledge and ford of the river. Most of the tracks are on the south

Dinosaur print exposed by the Purgatoire River.

side across the river. The site extends for a quarter mile and includes 1,300 visible tracks of about 100 different trackways. Scientists have determined that 150 million years ago, allosaurs and brontosaurs traveled in herds here in what was then a shallow lake. Their footprints were recorded in the mud and sand.

The allosaurus (a theropod) was a ferocious meat-eating dinosaur that stood on three-toed feet with sharp talons. Its hands also had sharp claws up to 6 inches long.

The brontosaurus was a much gentler creature, being an herbivore and traveling in herds for protection from the meat eaters. Its nickname is "thunder lizard" because it weighed 33 tons and made the earth tremble as it walked. It stood on four feet that were like elephant's feet and it often walked on its toes. The brain of the brontosaurus (a sauropod) was about the size of a human's fist.

Enjoy looking at the dinosaur tracks and then go back the way you came.

Options: Continue another 3.4 miles to the Rourke Ranch then return for a total hike of about 17.5 miles.

Camping and services: None.

For more information: Comanche National Grassland.

74 Levsa Canyon

Highlights:	Piñon-juniper; views of Trinidad Reservoir; interpretive nature trail.
Location:	At Trinidad Lake State Park west of Trinidad.
Type of hike:	Loop day hike.
Total distance:	1 mile
Difficulty:	Easy.
Elevation gain:	Minimal.
Best months:	April–May; September–November.
Maps:	USGS Trinidad West quad; Trinidad Lake State Park Map.

Finding the trailhead: From the west edge of Trinidad go west on Colorado Highway 12 for 2 miles to Trinidad State Park. Continue past the dam road 0.7 mile to the main park entrance, and follow the signs for the campgrounds. The trailhead and limited parking are located next to the restrooms near the center of the campground.

Parking and trailhead facilities: Parking and restrooms are available.

The hike: This is a nice interpretive trail for families to learn about the piñon-juniper forest. Hike it from fall through winter and spring and on cool mornings and evenings in the summer. There is a sign and brochures for the interpretive trail at the trailhead west of the restrooms.

Start down the trail and in about 50 yards go left at the sign for Levsa Canyon and Reilly Canyon Trails. In another 100 yards turn right to start the interpretive loop. The trail winds through piñon-juniper forest with stations describing the various plant and shrub species, including piñon, juniper, rabbitbrush, Gambel's oak, and that famous cactus of southeastern Colorado, the cholla. About one-third of the way along this loop is the junction where the Reilly Canyon Trail takes off. For a short hike go left; for the longer hike go right.

The trail drops down to the west and offers views of the distant Culebra Range, Trinidad Reservoir, and some of the old mining communities to the south across the lake. There are rest areas at points along the trail. Look for deer along the loop, which ends at 1 mile.

Options: For a longer hike take the Reilly Canyon Trail along the north side of the reservoir to the Reilly Canyon Trailhead near Cokedale, a distance of 4 miles. You need to shuttle a car. The coke ovens at Cokedale add historical interest on this hike.

Camping and services: Camping is available at the campground where the trail begins.

For more information: Trinidad State Park.

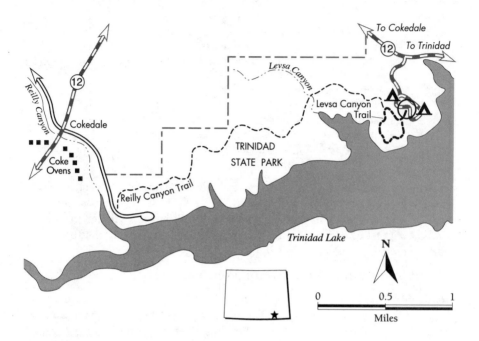

75 Fishers Peak Mesa

Highlights:	Views; interesting geology.
Location:	Southeast of Trinidad in the Raton Mesa area.
Type of hike:	Out-and-back day hike.
Total distance:	6.4 miles.
Difficulty:	Moderate.
Elevation gain:	1,300 feet.
Maps:	USGS Fishers Peak and Barela quads.
Best months:	June–October.

Special considerations: The state wildlife areas are closed from November 1 through April 1 each year and normally restricted to day use only. A daily fee is required for Sugarite Canyon State Park in New Mexico if you stop and use any facilities.

Finding the trailhead: From Trinidad, take Interstate 25 south to Raton, New Mexico. Turn off I-25 at Exit 452 and go left (east) on New Mexico Highway 72, following the signs to Sugarite Canyon State Park. After about 4 miles, bear left (north) onto NM 526. Continue for 6 miles, passing through Sugarite Canyon State Park to the Colorado state line, where the road changes to gravel and there is a sign for Lake Dorothy State Wildlife Area. Continue for 0.4 mile to the trailhead parking area located on the left (west) side of the road just after a bridge. The trail begins at the southeast corner of the parking area

Parking and trailhead facilities: Parking and outhouse are provided.

Key points:
- 0.4 Lake Dorothy Dam spillway and start of hiking trail
- 0.7 North end of Lake Dorothy
- 0.8 East Fork Schwachheim Creek crossing
- 1.9 Start of switchbacks and main climb
- 3.2 Top of mesa

The hike: This hike takes you to the southeast rim of Fishers Peak Mesa within the Lake Dorothy and James John State Wildlife Areas. It provides an introduction to the Raton Mesa region of high plateaus that straddle the Colorado–New Mexico border east of Raton Pass and extend southeast into New Mexico. The highest and most primitive of these plateaus is Fishers Peak Mesa, which terminates on the northwest in a spectacular butte called Fishers Peak, a prominent landmark overlooking the city of Trinidad. Most of the top of the mesa, which is several square miles in area, has been preserved through inclusion in the Lake Dorothy and James John State Wildlife Areas.

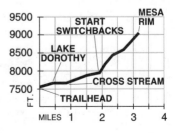

Fishers Peak near Trinidad in 1899. G. W. STOSE PHOTO. COURTESY USGS.

Public access, however, is available only from the southeast side of the mesa through the Lake Dorothy State Wildlife Area.

Begin your hike from the southeast corner of the parking area and follow the maintenance access road for Lake Dorothy south a short distance, then go along the edge of a meadow to the northwest toward Lake Dorothy. (The smaller trail, which continues south across the meadow, goes into Sugarite Canyon State Park.) Follow the access road 0.4 mile to the base of Lake Dorothy Dam. Just before the road drops down to cross the creek at the dam spillway is a large wildlife area sign and map. The trail to Fishers Peak Mesa begins near the sign and climbs to the top of the dam to the right (east) of the spillway.

From the top of the dam, hike along the east side of Lake Dorothy toward the intersection of two valleys formed by Schwachheim Creek on the west and the East Fork of Schwachheim Creek on the east. The trail follows the valley of the East Fork, then climbs northwest to the rim 0.5 mile beyond the mesa point dividing the two valleys. Note that the trail does not follow the entire length of the East Fork drainage as may be indicated on some of the state wildlife area signs and maps.

Just beyond the upper end of Lake Dorothy, at 0.8 mile, cross the East Fork of Schwachheim Creek—an easy jump except during the spring snowmelt. Beyond the creek the trail crosses a meadow and then turns north to follow the East Fork drainage. You can also reach this same point by following the dam access road to the west side of the dam, then taking a faint trail along the west side of Lake Dorothy to a crossing of Schwachheim Creek. However, this route is less distinct and disappears in places among

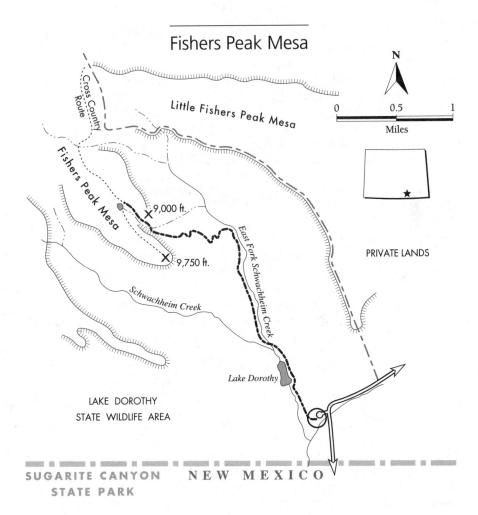

Fishers Peak Mesa

Cross Country Route

Little Fishers Peak Mesa

Fishers Peak Mesa

N

0   0.5   1
Miles

×9,000 ft.

×9,750 ft.

East Fork Schwachheim Creek

Schwachheim Creek

PRIVATE LANDS

Lake Dorothy

LAKE DOROTHY
STATE WILDLIFE AREA

SUGARITE CANYON   N E W   M E X I C O
STATE PARK

the willows. Most of the people who use the state wildlife area fish at Lake Dorothy or along the streams at the head of the lake; beyond this point you are likely to encounter few other hikers.

As you follow the valley of the East Fork and eventually climb to the mesa rim, note the transitions from oakbrush and scattered ponderosa pine to pine and aspen forest, then to pine, aspen, and Douglas-fir forest, and finally to the open meadows of the mesa top. These changes in vegetation reflect differences in slope, aspect, soils, and a gradual increase in elevation. Wildlife include elk, deer, wild turkeys, black bears, and mountain lions, as well as a number of bird species reflective of the variety of vegetation types. Like many state wildlife areas, this area has been set aside to preserve habitat and for public hunting. Hunting takes place primarily in the spring for wild turkeys, and in the fall for deer and elk. (We should respect these other uses and recognize that license fees paid by hunters and fishermen are responsible for the preservation of some of these special places.)

At about 1.9 miles, the trail climbs to the northwest toward the mesa rim. There are a number of alternating steep switchbacks and moderate sections. At one point, about halfway along the climb, the trail switches back to the south, and a short detour from the trail takes you to a point where you can look down the valley and toward the mesa rim above—a good resting spot. From here the trail continues to climb and eventually reaches a small drainage coming down from the mesa rim. This drainage provides a break in the cliffs through which you can gain access to the top of the mesa. A short way beyond the rim is a stock pond where the formal trail ends.

Once you reach the mesa rim, a whole different world of open meadows and far-reaching mesas unfolds in every direction. The mesa tops are formed of a resistant basalt caprock that overlies less resistant sandstones and shales. Basalt is a volcanic rock formed from lava flows. The source for some of the lavas was probably a volcanic vent or neck still visible as a small tower below the west side of the mesa along I-25 north of Raton Pass.

The general location and thickness of the basalt illustrate an inverted topography. What you see as prominent high plateaus were actually the valleys and low points of an ancient landscape into which the lava flowed and hardened. The softer rocks of hills that once stood above these ancient valleys have long since eroded, leaving these inverted remnants to spark our imaginations millions of years later.

From the rim you can return as you came.

Options: When we hiked this trail in early May, deep snow prevented us from following this last section along the drainage to the top. Instead we bushwhacked back around to the south where there was less snow and found a very steep route up through the rimrocks near the end of the mesa. Although we definitely do not recommend this route to anyone, it did afford us the opportunity of reaching the mesa point between the Schwachheim and East Fork drainages that overlooks Lake Dorothy. This point would make an easy cross-country side trip of 0.7 mile from the trail end and stock pond. Another, but longer, option is to head north from the pond approximately 1.5 miles and across the west end of Little Fishers Peak Mesa to the rim. This location offers a spectacular vantage overlooking the head of San Francisco Creek and the eastern plains of Colorado. It may also be possible to explore more of the mesa, including the high point to the northwest, by extending this hike into a backpack. Because the area is currently managed for hunting and day use recreation, you need to obtain special permission for a backpacking trip from the Colorado Division of Wildlife Pueblo office.

If you explore the mesa top by any of these or other cross-country routes, be sure and note the location of the notch in the rim through which your route descends. There are few landmarks with which to orient once on top, and fewer locations where you can safely descend to the valley.

Camping and services: Sugarite Canyon State Park (New Mexico).

For more information: Colorado Division of Wildlife, Southeast Region.

Appendix I: Hiking and Conservation Organizations

Colorado Environmental Coalition
1536 Wynkoop, #5C
Denver, CO 80202
303-534-7063

Colorado Mountain Club
710 Tenth Street, #200
Golden, CO 80401
303-279-3080

Colorado Outward Bound School (COBS)
945 Pennsylvania Street
Denver, CO 80203
303-837-0880

Colorado Wildlife Federation
445 Union Boulevard, Suite 302
Denver, CO 80228
303-987-0400

Earth First! Colorado
P.O. Box 1166
Boulder, CO 80306

Environmental Defense Fund
1405 Arapahoe
Boulder, CO 80302
303-440-4901

High Country Citizens Alliance
Box 1066
Crested Butte, CO 81224
970-349-7104

Jefferson County Open Space Division
700 Jefferson County Parkway, Suite 100
Golden, CO 80401
303-271-5925

National Audubon Society
Rocky Mountain Regional Office
4150 Darley Avenue, #5
Boulder, CO 80303
303-499-0219

National Audubon Society chapters are found in these Colorado cities, as well: Boulder, Colorado Springs, Denver, Durango, Evergreen, Fort Collins, Glenwood Springs, Grand Junction, Greeley, Paonia, Pueblo

The Nature Conservancy
Western Regional Office
2060 Broadway
Boulder, CO 80302
303-444-1060

Sierra Club
Rocky Mountain Chapter
777 Grant Street #606
Denver, CO 80203
303-861-8819

Sierra Club chapters are found in these cities, as well: Boulder, Colorado Springs, Denver, Dillon, Durango, Evergreen, Grand Junction, Greeley, Parker

Volunteers for Outdoor Colorado (VOC)
600 South Marion Parkway
Denver, CO 80209
303-715-1010

Wilderness Society
7475 Dakin
Denver, CO 80221
303-650-5818

Appendix II: Federal Land Management Agencies

Bureau of Land Management (BLM)
Colorado State Office
2850 Youngfield Street
Lakewood, CO 80215
303-239-3600
Website: www.co.blm.gov

Canon City District Office and Royal Gorge Resource Area
3170 East Main Street
Canon City, CO 81212
719-269-8500

Arkansas Headwaters Recreation Area
307 West Sackett
P.O. Box 126
Salida, CO 81201

San Luis Valley South Area
1921 State Street
Alamosa, CO 81101
719-589-4975

San Luis Valley West Area
13308 West HIghway 160
Del Norte, CO 81132
719-657-3321

San Luis Valley North Area
46525 Highway 114
P.O. Box 67
Saguache, CO 81149
719-655-2547

Craig District Office
455 Emerson Street
P.O. Box 248
Craig, CO 81625
970-826-5000

Kremmling Resource Area
1116 Park Avenue
Kremmling, CO 80459
970-724-3437

Little Snake Resource Area
455 Emerson Street
Craig, CO 81625
970-826-5087

White River Resource Area
73544 Highway 64
P.O. Box 928
Meeker, CO 81641

Grand Junction District Office and Resource Area
2815 H Road
Grand Junction, CO 81506
970-244-3000

Glenwood Springs Resouce Area
50629 Highways 6 & 24
Glenwood Springs, CO 81602
970-947-2800

Montrose District Office and Uncompahgre Basin Resource Area
2465 South Townsend
Montrose, CO 81401
970-240-5300

Anasazi Heritage Center
27501 Highway 184
Dolores, CO 81323
970-882-4811

Gunnison Resource Area
216 North Colorado
Gunnison, CO 81230
970-641-0471

San Juan Resource ARea
Federal Building
701 Camino Del Rio
Durango, CO 81301
970-247-4082

USDA Forest Service (USDAFS)
website: www.fs.fed.us

Rocky Mountain Region (Region 2)
Forests, Districts, and National Grasslands

Regional Office
740 Simms Street
P.O. Box 25127
Lakewood, CO 80225
303-275-5350

Arapaho (A) and Roosevelt (R) National Forests
Headquarters
240 West Prospect Road
Fort Collins, CO 80526
970-498-1100

Roosevelt Information Center
1311 South College, 2nd Floor
Fort Collins, CO 80526
970-498-2770

Boulder Ranger District
2995 Baseline Road Room 110
Boulder, CO 80303
303-444-6600

Pawnee National Grassland (R)
660 "O" Street
Greeley, CO 80631
970-353-5004

Grand Mesa (GM), Uncompahgre (U), and Gunnison (G) National Forests
Headquarters
2250 Highway 50
Delta, CO 81416
970-874-6600

Collbran Ranger District (GM)
218 East High Street, Box 330
Collbran, CO 81624
970-487-3534

Grand Junction Ranger District (GM/U)
764 Horizon Drive, Room 115
Grand Junction, CO 81506
970-242-8211

Norwood Ranger District (U)
1760 East Grand, Box 388
Norwood, CO 81401
970-327-4261

Ouray Ranger District (U)
2505 South Townsend
Montrose, CO 81401
970-249-3711

Cebolla/Taylor River Ranger District (G)
216 North Colorado
Gunnison, CO 81230
970-641-0471

Paonia Ranger District (G)
North Rio Grand Avenue, Box 1030
Paonia, CO 81428
970-527-4131

Pike (P) and San Isabel (SI) National Forests
Headquarters
1920 Valley Drive
Pueblo, CO 81008
719-545-8737

Comanche Ranger District and National Grassland (SI)
27162 Highway 287, Box 127
Springfield, CO 81073
719-523-6591

Routt National Forest
Headquarters
925 Weiss Drive
Steamboat Springs, CO 80487
970-879-1870

San Juan National Forest
Headquarters (Visitor Information)
701 Camino Del Rio, Room 301
Durango, CO 81301
970-247-4874

White River National Forest
Headquarters
Ninth and Grand, Box 948
Glenwood Springs, CO 81602
970-945-2521

National Park Service
Intermountain Regional Office
303-969-2000

Bent's Fort
National Historic Site
35110 Highway 194 East
La Junta, CO 81050
719-384-2596

Black Canyon of the Gunnison National Monument
2233 East Main
Montrose, CO 81401
970-249-7036

Colorado National Monument
Fruita, CO 81521-9530
970-858-3617

Curecanti National Recreation Area
102 Elk Creek
Gunnison, CO 81230
970-641-2337

Dinosaur National Monument
4545 Highway 40
Dinosaur, CO 81610-0210
970-374-3000

Florissant Fossil Beds National Monument
P.O. Box 185
Florissant, CO 80816-0185
719-748-3253

Great Sand Dunes National Monument
11500 Highway 150
Mosca, CO 81146-9798
719-378-2312

Hovenweep National Monument
McElmo Route
Cortez, CO 81321
970-529-4461

Mesa Verde National Park
Mesa Verde National Park, CO 81330-0008
970-529-4465

Rocky Mountain National Park
Estes Park, CO 80517-8397
970586-1206

Yucca House National Monument
c/o Mesa Verde National Park
Mesa Verde National Park, CO 81330
970529-4461

National Wildlife Refuges in Colorado
Alamosa–Monte Vista National Wildlife Refuge Complex
9383 El Rancho Lane
Alamosa, CO 81101
719-589-4021

Arapaho National Wildlife Refuge
Box 457
Walden, CO 80484
970723-8202

Browns Park National Wildlife Refuge
1318 Highway 381
Maybell, CO 81640
970365-3613

Appendix III: State and Local Land Management Agencies

Colorado Geological Survey
1313 Sherman Street, Room 715
Denver, CO 80203
303-866-2611

Department of Natural Resources
2401313 Sherman Street, Room 718, Denver, CO 80203
303-866-3311

Division of Parks and Recreation
1313 Sherman Street, Room 618
Denver, CO 80203
303-866-3437

State Historical Society
1300 Broadway
Denver, CO 80203
303-866-3682

Governor's Office
136 State Capitol Building
Denver, CO 80203
303-866-2471

Division of Wildlife
6060 Broadway
Denver, CO 80216
303-297-1192

State Climatologist
National Weather Service
10230 Smith Road
Denver, CO 80239
303-398-3964

Colorado Division of Parks and Outdoor Recreation
Wheelchair Accessible Parks
There are 33 state parks, all of which have different levels of accessibility for people with special needs.
   The parks that feature hiking as accessible or as accessible with assistance are:

Barr Lake State Park: 303-659-6005
Boyd Lake State Recreation Area: 970-669-1739
Chatfield State Recreation Area: 303-791-7275

Castlewood Canyon State Park: 303-688-7505
Cherry Creek State Recreation Area: 303-690-1166
Island Acres State Recreation Area: 970-464-0548
Pueblo State Recreation Area: 719-561-9320
Ridgway State Recreation Area: 970-626-5822
Stagecoach State Recreation Area: 970-736-2436
Vega State Recreation Area: 970-487-3407

Many of these also feature camping, fishing, picnic areas, and even hunting and fishing, and have visitor centers. All but three state parks (Mancos, Navajo, and Sweitzer Lake state recreation areas) have restrooms that are accessible or accessible with assistance.

Appendix IV: Volunteering in the Outdoors

Bureau of Land Management
Colorado State Office
2850 Youngfield Street
Lakewood, CO 80215
303-239-3600

Colorado Division of Parks and Outdoor Recreation
1313 Sherman Street, Room 618
Denver, CO 80203
303-866-3437

Colorado Division of Wildlife
6060 Broadway
Denver, CO 80216
303-291-7239

Colorado Mountain Club
710 Tenth Street, #200
Golden, CO 80401
303-279-3080

The Colorado Outdoor Education Center for the Handicapped
P.O. Box 697
Breckenridge, CO 80424
970-453-6422

Colorado Trail Foundation
548 Pine Song Trail
Golden, CO 80401

National Park Service VIP
(Volunteers in the Parks)
Rocky Mountain Regional Office
655 Parfet Street
P.O. Box 25287
Lakewood, CO 80225
303-236-8650

Sierra Club
Rocky Mountain Chapter
777 Grant Street, #606
Denver, CO 80203
303-861-8819

U.S. Forest Service
P.O. Box 25127
Lakewood, CO 80225-0127
303-275-5325

Volunteers for Outdoor Colorado
1410 Grant Street, Suite B-105
Denver, CO 80203
303-830-7792

Wilderness on Wheels Foundation
7125 West Jefferson Avenue, #155
Lakewood, CO 80235
303-988-2212

Any volunteering you can do in Colorado's outdoors will be appreciated by all of us. Thanks for your efforts.

Appendix V

For more information
American Camping Association
400 South Broadway
Denver, CO 80209
303-778-8774

The American Discovery Trail
William L. Stoehr
P.O. Box 3610
Evergreen, CO 80439-3425
303-670-3457
800-851-3442

American Hiking Society
P.O. Box 20160
Washington, D.C. 20041
703-255-9304

American Mountain Foundation
1520 Alamo Avenue
Colorado Springs, CO 80907
719-471-7736

Boulder Mountain Parks and Open Space
P.O. Box 471
2045 Thirteenth Street
Boulder, CO 80306

Colorado Association of Campgrounds, Cabins and Lodges
5101 Pennsylvania Avenue
Boulder, CO 80303
303-499-9343

Colorado Preservation, Inc.
P.O. Box 289
Aspen, CO 81612
970-920-5096

Colorado Springs Parks and Recreation Department
1401 Recreation Way
Colorado Springs, CO 80905
719-578-6640

Colorado State Trails Program
1313 Sherman Street, Room 618
Denver, CO 80203
303-866-3437

Fort Collins Parks and Recreation Department
281 North College
Fort Collins, CO 80524
970-221-6640

Friends of Dinosaur Ridge
P.O. Box 564
Morrison, CO 80465
303-420-0059

Friends of Florrisant Fossil Beds
P.O. Box 394
Florissant, CO 80816
719-632-4348

North Fork Trails Network
1508 Black Canyon Road
Crawford, CO 81415
970-921-3340

Pikes Peak Area Trails Coalition
P.O. Box 34
Colorado Springs, CO 80901
719-635-4825

Tenth Mountain Trail Association
1280 Ute Avenue
Aspen, CO 81611
970-925-4554

The Trail Group, Inc.
P.O. Box 50
Ouray, CO 81427
970-325-4543

(For more resources, pick up a copy of the *Colorado Trails Resource Guide: A Guide for All Trail Users*, edited by Alf Kober, published by Trail Mates™ of Colorado, Inc.)

Front Range Resources
The following resources offer various types of information to add to your enjoyment of Colorado's hiking trails. Though located in Front Range cities, they are valuable resources for people in all regions of Colorado—and to visiting hikers.

Colorado Historical Museum
1300 Broadway
Denver, CO 80203

Colorado School of Mines Geological Museum
Sixteenth and Maple Streets
Golden, CO 80401
303-273-3823

Denver Museum of Natural History
2001 Colorado Boulevard
Denver, CO 80205
303-322-7009

Denver Public Library
1357 Broadway
Denver, CO 80203
303-640-8800

Appendix VI: The Hiker's Checklist

Always make and check your own checklist!
If you've ever hiked into the backcountry and discovered that you've forgotten an essential, you know that it's a good idea to make a checklist and check the items off as you pack so that you won't forget the things you want and need. Here are some ideas:

Clothing
- ☐ Dependable rain parka
- ☐ Rain pants
- ☐ Windbreaker
- ☐ Thermal underwear
- ☐ Shorts
- ☐ Long pants or sweatpants
- ☐ Wood cap or balaclava
- ☐ Hat
- ☐ Wool shirt or sweater
- ☐ Jacket or parka
- ☐ Extra socks
- ☐ Underwear
- ☐ Lightweight shirts
- ☐ T-shirts
- ☐ Bandanna(s)
- ☐ Mittens or gloves
- ☐ Belt

Footwear
- ☐ Sturdy, comfortable boots
- ☐ Lightweight camp shoes

Bedding
- ☐ Sleeping Bag
- ☐ Foam pad or air mattress
- ☐ Ground sheet (plastic or nylon)
- ☐ Dependable tent

Hauling
- ☐ Backpack and/or day pack

Cooking
- ☐ 1-quart container (plastic)
- ☐ 1-gallon water container for camp use (collapsible)

- ☐ Backpack stove and extra fuel
- ☐ Funnel
- ☐ Aluminum foil
- ☐ Cooking pots
- ☐ Bowls/plates
- ☐ Utensils (spoons, forks, small spatula, knife)
- ☐ Pot scrubber
- ☐ Matches in waterproof container

Food and Drink

- ☐ Cereal
- ☐ Bread
- ☐ Crackers
- ☐ Cheese
- ☐ Trail mix
- ☐ Margarine
- ☐ Powdered soups
- ☐ Salt/pepper
- ☐ Main course meals
- ☐ Snacks
- ☐ Hot chocolate
- ☐ Tea
- ☐ Powdered milk
- ☐ Drink mixes

Photography

- ☐ Camera and film
- ☐ Filters
- ☐ Lens brush/paper

Miscellaneous

- ☐ Sunglasses
- ☐ Map and a compass
- ☐ Toilet paper
- ☐ Pocketknife
- ☐ Sunscreen
- ☐ Good insect repellent
- ☐ Lip balm
- ☐ Flashlight with good batteries and a spare bulb
- ☐ Candle(s)
- ☐ First-aid kit
- ☐ your FalconGuide

- ☐ Survival kit
- ☐ Small garden trowel or shovel
- ☐ Water filter or purification tablets
- ☐ Plastic bags (for trash)
- ☐ Soap
- ☐ Towel
- ☐ Toothbrush
- ☐ Fishing license
- ☐ Fishing rod, reel, lures, flies, etc.
- ☐ Binoculars
- ☐ Waterproof covering for pack
- ☐ Watch
- ☐ Sewing kit

Appendix VII: Finding Maps

Maps published by the United States Geological Survey (USGS), Trails Illustrated,, the Bureau of Land Management (BLM), and the National Forest Service are recommended as supplements to those in this guide. They are often available at sporting goods stores, bookstores, and visitor centers, among other places.

The USGS maps are detailed 7.5- and 15-minute quads and are the most detailed maps available. They are recommended for more difficult hikes, particularly if you are hiking in a little-used area or off-trail.

Trails Illustrated maps are based on USGS topographic maps modified by Trails Illustrated in conjunction with Forest Service and BLM personnel and other experts. These maps are printed on a 100 percent plastic material that is waterproof and tear resistant, which makes them easier to carry and use than USGS maps.

The Forest Service publishes maps for each of the 11 national forests and 2 national grasslands in Colorado. The Bureau of Land Management also publishes good maps that provide a general view of the area in which you'll be hiking and show most well-marked hiking trails. These maps are available at national forest and ranger districts, and BLM offices.

The National Park Service publishes maps—generally as part of a brochure—for each of the parks. Stop in at a ranger station on the way to a trailhead or call or write the regional office (see Appendix [TK], "Federal Land Management Agencies").

The Colorado Division of Parks and Outdoor Recreation offers brochures—and sometimes maps within them—on each of the state parks (see Appendix [TK], "State Offices and Land Management Agencies").

Many Front Range cities offer maps of their trail systems along with other information on their parks and recreation resources (see Appendix [TK], "Front Range Resources").

Trails Illustrated maps should be available at many outlets and may be purchased directly from the publisher. For a catalog write:

Trails Illustrated
P.O. Box 3610
Evergreen, CO 80439-3425

You may obtain a USGS map catalog and all topographic maps for the state over the counter or by mail-order from:

Western Distribution Branch
US Geological Survey
Box 25286, Federal Center, Building 41
Denver, CO 80225
303-202-4700

Afterword

We learned a few things as we created this book in the years 1995 to 1998. First of all, Colorado still offers the outdoor enthusiast many spectacular places–and many less spectacular places–to explore. The variety of Colorado's treasures still amazes us.

Second, there are many more people in Colorado, and there are many more outdoor recreationists in the Colorado backcountry than there were when we wrote *Hiking Colorado, Volume I*. You can still find solitude in Colorado, but you'll have to work harder at it. The fact is, when hiking many Colorado trails you're going to see more people, and that includes more people on mountain bikes and horseback.

The best thing hikers can do is cultivate a positive attitude toward other outdoorspeople, and focus on what we all have in common: a love of Colorado. When we meet other trail users, we go out of our way to be courteous. We try to step off the trail to let someone pass if we can; we offer a helping hand when one is needed; we try not to adopt self-righteous or elitist attitudes, believing everyone can enjoy the outdoors in their own ways; and when we hike with our dogs we keep them under control at all times. We have had a few conflicts on the trail, but very few for the miles we've covered.

Third, we've realized that while (happily) the mountains are being preserved with wilderness designation, there are riparian areas, wetlands, and places on the plains that still need protection. Trail users can get involved at a grassroots level to preserve some of Colorado's lesser-known wild places. See Appendix IV, "Volunteering in the Outdoors" and Appendix I, "Hiking and Conservation Organizations." A fairly easy place to start is to get involved in preserving open space around the area where you live. You can help on a trail project or two andhelp preserve some of the places we don't think of as often. There is still a lot to be done. You and your family can have fun doing some of it. We hope to see you out there in the next few years as we help out, too.

Caryn and Peter Boddie

Index

Page numbers in italic type refer to maps.
Page numbers in bold type refer to photos.

About the Authors

Peter Boddie is a hydrologist. Caryn Boddie is a writer and editor. They live with their family in Littleton, Colorado.

American Hiking Society

American Hiking Society is the only national nonprofit organization dedicated to establishing, protecting and maintaining foot trails in America.

Establishing...

American Hiking Society establishes hiking trails with the AHS National Trails Endowment, providing grants for grassroots organizations to purchase trail lands, construct and maintain trails, and preserve hiking trails' scenic values. The AHS affiliate club program, called the Congress of Hiking Organizations, brings trail clubs together to share information, collaborate on public policy, and advocate legislation and policies that protect hiking trails.

Protecting...

American Hiking Society protects hiking trails through highly focused public policy efforts in the nation's capital. AHS affects federal legislation, shapes public lands policy, collaborates with grassroots trail organizations, and partners with federal land managers to protect the hiking experience. Members become active with letter-writing campaigns and by attending the annual AHS Trails Lobby Week.

Maintaining...

American Hiking Society maintains hiking trails by sending volunteers to national parks, forests and recreation lands; organizing volunteer teams to help our affiliated hiking clubs; and publishing national volunteer directories. AHS members get involved, get dirty and get inspired by participating in AHS programs like National Trails Day, America's largest celebration of the outdoors; and Volunteer Vacations, our week-long work trips to beautiful, wild places.

American Hiking Society
1422 Fenwick Lane
Silver Spring, MD 20910
OR CALL: (888) 766 - HIKEx115
OR VISIT: www.ahs.simplenet.com

FALCON GUIDES ® Leading the Way™

FALCON GUIDES ® are available for where-to-go hiking, mountain biking, rock climbing, walking, scenic driving, fishing, rockhounding, paddling, birding, wildlife viewing, and camping. We also have FalconGuides on essential outdoor skills and subjects and field identification. The following titles are currently available, but this list grows every year. For a free catalog with a complete list of titles, call FALCON toll-free at 1-800-582-2665.

HIKING GUIDES

Hiking Alaska
Hiking Arizona
Hiking Arizona's Cactus Country
Hiking the Beartooths
Hiking Big Bend National Park
Hiking the Bob Marshall Country
Hiking California
Hiking California's Desert Parks
Hiking Carlsbad Caverns
   and Guadalupe Mtns. National Parks
Hiking Colorado
Hiking Colorado, Vol.II
Hiking Colorado's Summits
Hiking Colorado's Weminuche Wilderness
Hiking the Columbia River Gorge
Hiking Florida
Hiking Georgia
Hiking Glacier & Waterton Lakes National Parks
Hiking Grand Canyon National Park
Hiking Grand Staircase-Escalante/Glen Canyon
Hiking Grand Teton National Park
Hiking Great Basin National Park
Hiking Hot Springs in the Pacific Northwest
Hiking Idaho
Hiking Maine
Hiking Michigan
Hiking Minnesota
Hiking Montana
Hiking Mount Rainier National Park
Hiking Mount St. Helens
Hiking Nevada
Hiking New Hampshire

Hiking New Mexico
Hiking New York
Hiking North Carolina
Hiking the North Cascades
Hiking Northern Arizona
Hiking Olympic National Park
Hiking Oregon
Hiking Oregon's Eagle Cap Wilderness
Hiking Oregon's Mount Hood/Badger Creek
Hiking Oregon's Three Sisters Country
Hiking Pennsylvania
Hiking Shenandoah National Park
Hiking the Sierra Nevada
Hiking South Carolina
Hiking South Dakota's Black Hills Country
Hiking Southern New England
Hiking Tennessee
Hiking Texas
Hiking Utah
Hiking Utah's Summits
Hiking Vermont
Hiking Virginia
Hiking Washington
Hiking Wyoming
Hiking Wyoming's Cloud Peak Wilderness
Hiking Wyoming's Wind River Range
Hiking Yellowstone National Park
Hiking Zion & Bryce Canyon National Parks
The Trail Guide to Bob Marshall Country
Wild Country Companion
Wild Montana
Wild Utah

■ *To order any of these books, check with your local bookseller*
*or call FALCON ® at **1-800-582-2665**.*
Visit us on the world wide web at:
www.FalconOutdoors.com

FALCON®

Going Somewhere?

Insiders' Guides offer 60 current and upcoming titles to some of the country's most popular vacation destinations (including the ones listed below), and we're adding many more. Written by local authors and averaging 400 pages, our guides provide the information you need quickly and easily—whether searching for savory local cuisine, unique regional wares, amusements for the kids, a picturesque hiking spot, off-the-beaten-track attractions, new environs or a room with a view.

Explore America and experience the joy of travel with the Insiders' Guide® books.

Adirondacks
Atlanta, GA
Austin, TX
Baltimore
Bend & Central Oregon
Bermuda
Boca Raton & the Palm Beaches
Boise & Sun Valley
Boulder & the Rocky Mountain National Park
Branson & the Ozark Mountains
California's Wine Country
Cape Cod, Nantucket and Martha's Vineyard
Charleston, SC
Cincinnati
Civil War Sites in the Eastern Theater
Colorado's Mountains
Denver
The Florida Keys & Key West
Florida's Great Northwest
Golf in the Carolinas
Indianapolis
The Lake Superior Region
Las Vegas
Lexington, KY
Louisville, KY
Madison, WI
Maine's Mid-Coast
Maine's Southern Coast
Michigan's Traverse Bay Region
Mississippi

Montana's Glacier Country
Monterey Peninsula
Myrtle Beach
Nashville
New Hampshire
North Carolina's Central Coast & New Bern
North Carolina's Southern Coast & Wilmington
North Carolina's Mountains
North Carolina's Outer Banks
Phoenix
The Pocono Mountains
Portland
Relocation
Richmond
Salt Lake City
San Diego
Santa Barbara
Santa Fe
Sarasota & Bradenton
Savannah
Southwestern Utah
Tampa & St. Petersburg
Texas Coastal Bend
Tucson
Twin Cities
Virginia's Blue Ridge
Virginia's Chesapeake Bay
Washington, D.C.
Williamsburg
Yellowstone

Insiders' Guide® books retail between $14.95 and $17.95. To order, go to your local bookstore, call Falcon Publishing at 800-582-2665 or visit our website at www.insiders.com.

The Insiders' Guides are an imprint of Falcon Publishing, P.O. Box 1718, Helena, MT 59624
Fax 800-968-3550
www.FalconOutdoors.com

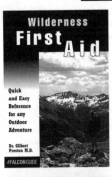

WILDERNESS FIRST AID

By Dr. Gilbert Preston M.D.

Enjoy the outdoors and face the inherent risks with confidence. By reading this easy-to-follow first-aid text, all outdoor enthusiasts can pack a little extra peace of mind on their next adventure. *Wilderness First Aid* offers expert medical advice for dealing with outdoor emergencies beyond the reach of 911. It easily fits in most backcountry first-aid kits.

LEAVE NO TRACE

By Will Harmon

The concept of "leave no trace" seems simple, but it actually gets fairly complicated. This handy quick-reference guidebook includes all the newest information on this growing and all-important subject. This book is written to help the outdoor enthusiast make the hundreds of decisions necessary to protect the natural landscape and still have an enjoyable wilderness experience. Part of the proceeds from the sale of this book go to continue leave-no-trace education efforts. The Official Manual of American Hiking Society.

BEAR AWARE

By Bill Schneider

Hiking in bear country can be very safe if hikers follow the guidelines summarized in this small, "packable" book. Extensively reviewed by bear experts, the book contains the latest information on the intriguing science of bear-human interactions. *Bear Aware* can not only make your hike safer, but it can help you avoid the fear of bears that can take the edge off your trip.

MOUNTAIN LION ALERT

By Steve Torres

Recent mountain lion attacks have received national attention. Although infrequent, lion attacks raise concern for public safety. *Mountain Lion Alert* contains helpful advice for mountain bikers, trail runners, horse riders, pet owners, and suburban landowners on how to reduce the chances of mountain lion-human conflicts.

Also Available

Wilderness Survival • Reading Weather • Backpacking Tips • Climbing Safely • Avalanche Aware • Desert Hiking Tips • Hiking with Dogs • Using GPS • Route Finding • Wild Country Companion

To order check with your local bookseller or

call FALCON® at **1-800-582-2665.**

www.FalconOutdoors.com